מגילת אסתר מסורת הרב

Megillat Esther Mesorat HaRav

קורן ירושלים

OU PRESS

Note on the Cover Design

The front cover depicts "King Ahasuerus hears of Mordecai in the book of records," from *The Bible Picture Book* (London: Thomas Nelson and Sons, c. 1880).

Adorning the back cover is the image of a small nightingale, one of the most musical of all songbirds. This artistic motif is an allusion to the Soloveitchik family name, which in Russian means "little nightingale." The Soloveitchik family are Levites, and legend has it that the origin of the name harks back to the family's sacred role as Levites in the Beit HaMikdash, gracing the service with song that accompanied the *korbanot*.

מגילת אסתר מסורת הרב

MEGILLAT ESTHER
MESORAT HARAV

WITH COMMENTARY ON MEGILLAT ESTHER
AND THE MA'ARIV EVENING SERVICE
BASED ON THE TEACHINGS
OF

Rabbi Joseph B. Soloveitchik

EDITED BY
Simon Posner, Eliyahu Krakowski and
Moshe Genack

•

OU PRESS
KOREN PUBLISHERS JERUSALEM

Megillat Esther Mesorat HaRav
First Edition, 2017

OU Press, an imprint of the Orthodox Union (hereafter "OU")
11 Broadway, New York, NY 10004
www.oupress.org

Koren Publishers Jerusalem Ltd.
POB 4044, Jerusalem 9104001, ISRAEL
POB 8531, New Milford, CT 06776, USA

www.korenpub.com

Printed in the United States of America

Hardcover, ISBN 978-965-301-184-7

MEMHR1

In Loving Memory of

Irving and Beatrice Stone

who dedicated their lives
to the advancement of Jewish education.
We are proud and honored to continue
in their legacy.

Dedicated by
Their Children, Grandchildren,
and Great-Grandchildren

Cleveland, Ohio

שמע בני מוסר אביך ואל תטוש תורת אמך
(משלי א, ח)

In Loving Memory of Our Parents

Alexander and Rose Shapiro

אלקנה בן משה יהודה לייב ופערל ז״ל

רייזל בת יעקב הלוי וצירל ז״ל

Samuel and Frances Schreiber

שמעון בן יוסף זאב ומרים ברכה ז״ל

פייגע בת יעקב שרגא ושרה ז״ל

Who taught and raised their family
to follow in the ways of Torah

Dedicated by

Irwin and Ruth Shapiro

In Loving Memory of Our Mother

Sara Anne Lehmann

שרה בת יצחק משולם פייש וחיה חנה איידל מושקוביץ ז״ל

Born SatuMare 1925, buried Jerusalem 2017

Escaping the horrors of Europe in 1941, our mother went on to become a pioneering international businesswoman, writer, painter and family matriarch. Beautiful, smart and fearless, Esther HaMalka was her role model. "ומי יודע אם לעת כזאת הגעת למלכות" was her credo. Our mother lived a life filled with *ḥesed* and imbued with *bitaḥon*.

In Loving Memory of Our Father

Manfred Raphael Lehmann

ר׳ מנשה רפאל בן החבר חיים ופייגא ז״ל

Born Stockholm 1922, buried Jerusalem 1997

An *Ish Eshkolot* who inspired us with his absolute faith in God and in *hashgaḥa peratit* in history. A true *Ohev* and *Yodea Sefer* whose depth of passion, breadth of interests and brilliant intellect were a continuous inspiration. יגעת ומצאת תאמין (*Megilla* 6b) was his guiding principle for our lives, always recognizing that our own struggles and efforts in pursuit of our lives' goals must be infused with *bitaḥon* in *HaKadosh Barukh Hu*. In all that he did, he dedicated himself to his family, Torah, and the people of Israel.

In Loving Memory of Our Brother

James Harald Lehmann

חיים מנחם בן מנשה רפאל ושרה ז״ל

Born New York 1950, buried Jerusalem 1982

Celebrated his Bar Mitzvah, reading Megillat Esther on Purim, 1963

A loving, joyful, gentle, brilliant soul, Jamie was the embodiment of *Torah im Derekh Eretz*. The legacy of our parents is enriched by the soul of their beloved son. He is missed more every day.

Dedicated by

Yitzchok and Barbie Lehmann Siegel and Family

In Loving Memory of Our Parents

Rabbi Yitzchok and Bluma Singer

הרב יצחק אהרן בן הרב ר׳ אליהו ז״ל

בלומא בת ר׳ ישראל אריה לייב ז״ל

Our Father was Rabbi of the Bialystoker
Synagogue and a renowned תלמיד חכם
Our Mother was a true אשת חיל

In Loving Memory of Our Uncles

Rabbi Dovid Singer and Rabbi Joseph Singer

הרב דוד בן הרב ר׳ אליהו ז״ל

הרב יוסף משה בן הרב ר׳ אליהו ז״ל

Both were scholars of great erudition

Dedicated by

Baruch and Susie Singer, Eli and Rivki Singer
Nussie and Ruchy Singer, Yossi and Suri Singer, Sruly Singer

In Tribute to

Rabbi Menachem Genack and Rabbi Simon Posner

In appreciation of all they do for OU Press,
the Orthodox Union, and *Klal Yisrael.*

Dedicated by

A Friend

In Loving Memory of Our Parents

Joseph and Gwendolyn Straus

יוסף שמואל בן בנימין ז״ל

גינענדל בת משה יעקב ז״ל

Dedicated by

Moshael and Zahava Straus

Daniel and Joyce Straus

ליהודים היתה אורה ושמחה וששון ויקר

(אסתר ח, טז)

In Honor of Our Children

Jeremy and Carli
Corey and Gemma
Jessie
Jolie

May you always have the *emunah* to see the hand of Hashem in your lives and to follow in His ways. May you and *Klal Yisrael* be blessed with light and gladness, joy and honor.

Dedicated by

Tim and Ria Levart

In Tribute to

Maury Litwack

for his outstanding service to the Jewish community in spearheading
the effort for government assistance to our schools.
In the footsteps of Esther and Mordekhai,
he has employed political action with selfless
dedication and consummate skill.

Dedicated by

Simcha and Pesh Katz

CONTENTS

PREFACE

Megillat Esther, a study in contrasts and a melange of seemingly random events, mirrors the inherent existential tension of the Jewish experience. The contours of the story are well known. The coarseness of Ahasuerus is contrasted to Esther's purity; Haman's irrational hatred of the Jews is juxtaposed to Mordekhai's selfless devotion to the community. The Jews are well integrated into an ethnically diverse Persian society; overnight they are singled out and selected for genocide. A lottery, the epitome of arbitrariness, seals the Jews' fate. The king orders the execution of his queen on the advice of his minister and hangs his prime minister at the urging of his queen. A mindless beauty contest that has all the trappings of buffoonery results in a simple Jewish girl being plucked from anonymity and ending up in the right place at the right time to save the Jewish people. The king's insomnia saves Mordekhai from the gallows in the nick of time and plants the seed in Ahasuerus' mind that Haman may not be as loyal as he would like the king to believe. As each layer of Megillat Esther unfolds, the list of seeming coincidences, improbable occurrences, and dramatic reversals grows. To any perceptive observer, the studied randomness highlights the unseen presence of the Almighty, the master choreographer controlling all that occurs.

Megillat Esther is the sole book of Tanakh in which God's name is not mentioned. This too can only be understood as an irony which confirms His pervasive, but hidden, presence. What on the surface seems to be merely a story of ambition, lust, and political intrigue, with its own dynamic, in fact has a deeper, unseen reality. God, though hidden from view, is ever-present and guiding all that transpires. Indeed, etymologically, the name Esther is related to the Hebrew word for "hidden" as in "*l'hastir.*" According to the Midrash (*Esther Rabba*, 3:10), whenever Megillat Esther mentions "*hamelekh*, the king," the explicit reference is to Ahasuerus, but the implicit reference is to the King of Kings who, unbeknownst to Ahasuerus, is moving the saga to its inevitable conclusion.

So much of Jewish history shares the same existential precariousness which underlies the Megilla's narrative, and can be comprehended ultimately only by acknowledging God's role in history. By any rational standard, when one views the span of Jewish history, the destruction of the two Temples, numerous exiles, and endless persecutions, the continued existence of the Jewish people is an anomaly. What is the nature of these events? Are they random occurrences subject only to the laws of history? If so, how does one explain the survival of the Jews and the vitality of the contemporary Jewish world? Ultimately, the historical record can be understood only by realizing that God, who may deliberately hide His presence, controls events and spreads His protective wings over us.

After all is said and done, what is the nature of Purim and the theme of Megillat Esther? Is the story a cause for unrestrained celebration or is it a cautionary tale which should command our sober attention? Consistent with the existential uncertainty that pervades the entire Megilla, the answer is both. The Rav, sensitive to the dialectic that often emerges from Halakha, expounded on the inherent duality of Megillat Esther and the holiday of Purim. In discussing the requirement of reading the Megilla twice, once on the evening of Purim and then again the following morning, the Gemara (*Megilla* 4a) quotes two proof texts. Rabbi Yehoshua ben Levi cites the verse from Psalms, "O my God, I call by day but You answer not, and at night and there is no surcease for me" (Ps. 22:3), while Rabbi Ḥelbo in the name of Ulla brings a different verse from Psalms, "So that my glory may sing praise to You, and not be silent; O Lord my God, I will give thanks to you forever" (Ps. 30:13). The Rav notes that these two verses are contradictory, yet each expresses a dimension of Megillat Esther. The verse cited by Rabbi Yehoshua ben Levi comes from Chapter 22 of Psalms, "My God, my God, why have You forsaken me?" and reflects the cry of total despair. Our Sages tell us that Esther recited this Psalm on her way into Ahasuerus' inner court, entreating the Almighty when all hope was lost. Diametrically opposed is the verse cited by Rabbi Ḥelbo, which expresses jubilation and an unceasing hymn of praise and thanks to the Almighty. The Rav further notes that the Gemara's dictum (*Megilla* 14a) that the reading of the Megilla is equivalent with the recitation of Hallel, is consistent with Rabbi Ḥelbo's view. The Rav explains that both verses are accurate characterizations of Megillat Esther. The Megilla is both a *tze'aka*, a cry of distress arising from insecurity and fear, and *shira*, a hymn of joy that marks Purim as no less an occasion for celebration than the other festivals on which Hallel is recited.

The Rav highlights several *minhagim* which confirm this nuanced view of Purim. Rav Amram Gaon recounts (*Seder Rav Amram Gaon*, Goldschmidt, p. 104) that the accepted practice in the *yeshiva* on Purim was for the *shaliaḥ tzibbur* to descend before the *Gaon* and the *Av Bet Din* and the leaders and the entire *yeshiva* to plead profusely and to recite *Taḥanun*. Rav Natronai Gaon was of the opinion that *Lamnatze'aḥ* should be recited on Purim. The *Shulḥan Arukh* (Rema, O.Ḥ. 695:2) states that one should eat *zer'onim*, seeds, on Purim as a remembrance of the *zer'onim*, a food eaten in exile, that Daniel ate in Babylonia. The Gemara, as well (*Megilla* 13a), notes that Esther ate *zer'onim* in Ahasuerus' palace, signaling her anxiety. All of these, posits the Rav, are clear indications of the elements of melancholy and distress which are themes in the Megilla that coexist with the dominant themes of joy and celebration.

The Rav also points to the commingling of Ta'anit Esther with Purim. The fast of Ta'anit Esther does not end until after the reading of the Megilla on Purim night. We would have expected that the fast would end, as all other fasts, with the conclusion of the day at *tzet hakokhavim*. Yet we continue to fast during reading of the Megilla; we fast while reciting the equivalent of Hallel, further emphasizing the uneasy coexistence of the disparate elements underlying the evening's observance.

There are no two days in the Jewish calendar more dissimilar than Purim, a day of frivolity and feasting, and Yom Kippur, a day of awe and fasting. Yet the Zohar comments (*Tikunei Zohar*, Tikun 21) that the Biblical name for Yom Kippur, *Yom Kippurim*, can be read *Yom k'Purim*, "a day like Purim." Having more in mind than a simple play on words, the Zohar is pointing to a common theme shared by both the sacred Yom Kippur and the joyous Purim. Both holidays revolve around a lottery. The central dramatic motif in the Purim narrative is Haman's lottery which decided the date of the Jews' extermination, a motif whose message is that fate is ultimately arbitrary. On Yom Kippur, the central ritual is the *Avoda*, the service in the Temple, and it is a lottery which determines the fate of two identical sacrificial goats, one to be offered to the Almighty on the altar and whose blood is sprinkled in the Holy of Holies, and the other to be ignominiously cast off a precipice in the desert. Although Purim and Yom Kippur are very different in tone, they express the same theme. What may seem haphazard, ruthless, a mere lottery, can be transformed

◂ into holiness

into holiness with the realization that the Almighty is behind the scenes directing all that transpires.

This relationship of Yom Kippur and Purim is highlighted in our High Holiday liturgy. The Tur and Avudraham point out a linguistic parallel between the *Yamim Noraim Amida* and Megillat Esther. Each of the three paragraphs of the third *berakha* of the *Amida* begins with the word "*u'vekhen*." This echoes Esther's statement, "*U'vekhen avo el hamelekh asher lo kadat*," expressing her willingness to risk her life by approaching Ahasuerus without first being summoned. Just as Esther felt fear and trembling before petitioning Ahasuerus, we too feel a sense of foreboding in approaching the Almighty on the *Yamim Noraim.*

There is another way in which Yom Kippur and Purim are similar. Both are days of *matan Torah*, the giving of the Torah. On Yom Kippur, the second tablets of the Ten Commandments were brought down by Moses from Mount Sinai. Purim also has the attributes of a day of *matan Torah*. The Megilla states (9:27), "קִיְּמוּ וְקִבְּלוּ הַיְּהוּדִים עֲלֵיהֶם וְעַל זַרְעָם, they established and accepted, for themselves and for their children," which the Gemara interprets as a reacceptance of the Torah akin to that of Mount Sinai (*Shabbat* 88a). Maimonides states (*Hilkhot Megilla* 2:18) that Megillat Esther, alone among the Books of the Prophets and Sacred Writings, will not be nullified when *Mashiaḥ* comes, but, just like the Five Books of Moses, will continue to exist forever. In fact, from the description of the Megilla as "words of peace and truth" (Es. 9:30), the Gemara derives (*Megilla* 16b) that the Megilla scroll requires *sirtut,* the straight ruled lines etched into the parchment, in the same manner as "the truth of Torah itself."

The equation of Purim and Yom Kippur confirmed by the halakhic identity of the Megilla with the *Sefer Torah*, further amplifies the common message that emanates from both days, that only Torah can give meaning and direction in the face of chaotic events, and that if one does not view the world through the prism of Torah, then all will appear arbitrary, nihilistic, and mere happenstance.

The Rav points to another statement in the Gemara that highlights Purim's dual nature. The Gemara comments (*Megilla* 19a) that Megillat Esther is referred to as both a letter (*iggeret)* and a book (*sefer*). A "*sefer*" is written on parchment and is designed to last; it is durable and connotes permanence. An "*iggeret*" is intended only to transmit a communication;

◂ it is ephemeral

it is ephemeral and meant to be discarded. Megillat Esther, notes the Rav, shares both of these qualities. On one level, it seems to be an interesting, but not very significant, narrative of a palace intrigue. It is an *iggeret,* a record of no lasting importance. On a deeper level, Megillat Esther is also a *sefer,* a profound book that expresses the fundamental principles of our faith, a book that testifies to our belief in Divine Providence even in the depth of the night of despair, when all hope seems lost.

It is singularly appropriate that the commentary of the Rav graces this edition of Megillat Esther, for the Rav, more than any other modern Jewish thinker, articulated and addressed the existential tensions which confront the Jew and characterize his struggle to find meaning in what appears to be an arbitrary universe. The Rav devoted his life to grappling with the most troubling questions confronting the Jew – the existential loneliness that besets the man of faith, the dialectical tension in which the man of halakha exists. The Rav addressed these and other similar issues in both his halakhic and philosophical works. For the Rav, the goal was not to find answers to the questions but to live within the tension and the dialectic, and the only way to accomplish this was through Torah. The ultimate response is that Torah gives meaning to an otherwise absurd existence.

OU Press is proud to present, together with Koren Publishers Jerusalem, *Megillat Esther Mesorat HaRav.* As with our other *Mesorat HaRav* publications, the Rav's commentary consists of excerpts from the Rav's published writings as well as from audio tapes of the Rav's lectures and *shiurim,* personal notes of *shiurim* taken by students of the *Rav,* and published *sefarim* written by students of the Rav. Also following the pattern of other of our *Mesorat HaRav* publications, we have included a section of *Reshimot,* more extensive presentations of the Rav's analysis of halakhic material than the discussions included in the commentary. Portions of the commentary which are taken from the Rav's published writings are followed by their respective sources. The other portions of the commentary, not followed by a source, are taken from the Rav's lectures, *shiurim,* and classes which he conducted over the years, many of which have been transcribed by his students and others and published. We extend thanks to Dr. Arnold Lustiger, editor of *Derashot HaRav,* and Rabbi David Schreiber editor of *Noraos HaRav,* for consenting to inclusion of material from their works in the commentary and the *Reshimot*. We acknowledge with thanks Rabbi Mikhel Shurkin, author of *Harerei Kedem*, whose work also served as a source for sections of the commentary and the *Reshimot*. Most of the commentary on *tefillat Ma'ariv* is from the *Koren Mesorat HaRav Siddur* which was edited by Dr. Arnold Lustiger, and we extend our appreciation to Dr. Lustiger.

Many dedicated individuals were involved in the preparation of this volume. My esteemed friend, Dr. Joel B. Wolowelsky, was the prime mover of the project over the course of several years, as he has been for so many other of the *Mesorat HaRav* projects, and provided the guidance and impetus to bring it to successful fruition. Rabbi Moshe Genack had the primary responsibility for assembling and editing the *Reshimot* and also assisted in the compilation of material for the commentary. Also involved in the preparation of the *Reshimot* were Rabbis Yosef Abraham, Shalom Baum, Daniel Besser, Ari Brandwein, Gad Buchbinder, Shaya First, Sholom Licht, Jeffrey Muehlgay, Yaakov Richter, Etan Schnall, Gil Student, Yaakov Taubes, and Ezra Zanger. Rabbi Eliyahu Krakowski, Associate Editor of OU Press, was in charge of the meticulous review and editing of the manuscript as it went through numerous drafts. Thanks as well to Debra Bree of OU Press for her assistance in preparation of the manuscript. Rabbi Simon Posner, Executive Editor of OU Press, was responsible for all aspects of the editing and production of this edition. I acknowledge as well Koren Publishers Jerusalem, our partners in this project, under the able leadership of Matthew Miller, for their outstanding work in editing, typesetting, and producing this edition.

Special thanks go to my colleague, Rabbi Steven Weil, Senior Managing Director of the OU. Rabbi Weil has consistently championed the dissemination of the Rav's works and the preservation of his legacy. Rabbi Weil has provided an extraordinary degree of encouragement and assistance to OU Press in its efforts to bring the Rav's writings to the public eye. The lay leadership of the OU has always fostered the efforts of OU Press, and I extend gratitude to Rabbi Julius Berman, Chairman of the OU Press Commission, and Moishe Bane, President of the Orthodox Union, for their support, as well.

This project could not have been realized without the generous support of our sponsors. We are grateful to the Weiss family and the other members of the extended Stone family for their generosity, and we thank, as well, the Katz, Lehmann Siegel, Levart, Shapiro, Singer, and Straus families for their assistance. All those who participated in this project can be justifiably proud of their contribution to *Klal Yisrael* which this volume represents.

Menachem Dov Genack
General Editor
OU Press

תפילת מעריב

TEFILLAT MA'ARIV

Ma'ariv for Purim Night

On Motza'ei Shabbat some have the custom to sing Psalm 144 and Psalm 67 before the Ma'ariv Service (page 140).

וְהוּא רַחוּם He is compassionate. *Ps. 78*
He forgives iniquity and does not destroy.
Repeatedly He suppresses His anger, not rousing His full wrath.
LORD, save! May the King, answer us on the day we call. *Ps. 20*

BLESSINGS OF THE SHEMA

The Leader says the following, bowing at "Bless," standing straight at "the LORD"; the congregation, followed by the Leader, responds, bowing at "Bless," standing straight at "the LORD":

Leader: **BLESS**
the LORD, the blessed One.

Congregation: Bless the LORD, the blessed One,
for ever and all time.

Leader: Bless the LORD, the blessed One,
for ever and all time.

---

blessed," that is, His explicit name. And although we do not explicitly utter that name, we do invoke it here.

We similarly invoke that name when we say Kaddish because the response "יְהֵא שְׁמֵהּ רַבָּא מְבָרַךְ, May His great name be blessed," is akin to the statement "בָּרוּךְ שֵׁם כְּבוֹד מַלְכוּתוֹ..., Blessed be the name of His glorious kingdom...," which is the required response upon hearing the Ineffable Name in the Temple (see Mishna, *Yoma* 3:7). As a result, the recitation of Kaddish also requires the presence of a *minyan*.

מעריב לליל פורים

On מוצאי שבת *some have the custom to sing* לְדָוִד, בָּרוּךְ יהוה צוּרִי *and* מִזְמוֹר שִׁיר לַמְנַצֵּחַ בִּנְגִינֹת *before* תפילת ערבית (*page 141*).

וְהוּא רַחוּם, יְכַפֵּר עָוֹן וְלֹא־יַשְׁחִית תהלים עח
וְהִרְבָּה לְהָשִׁיב אַפּוֹ, וְלֹא־יָעִיר כָּל־חֲמָתוֹ:
יהוה הוֹשִׁיעָה, הַמֶּלֶךְ יַעֲנֵנוּ בְיוֹם־קָרְאֵנוּ: תהלים כ

קריאת שמע וברכותיה

The שליח ציבור *says the following, bowing at* בָּרְכוּ*, standing straight at* ה'*; the* קהל*, followed by the* שליח ציבור*, responds, bowing at* בָּרוּךְ*, standing straight at* ה'*:*

ש״ץ: בָּרְכוּ

אֶת יהוה הַמְבֹרָךְ.

קהל: בָּרוּךְ יהוה הַמְבֹרָךְ לְעוֹלָם וָעֶד.

ש״ץ: בָּרוּךְ יהוה הַמְבֹרָךְ לְעוֹלָם וָעֶד.

בָּרְכוּ אֶת יהוה *Bless the Lord.* This phrase can be said only in the presence of a *minyan* (quorum of ten men) because it constitutes a *davar shebikedusha,* a responsive prayer which fulfills the imperative to publicly sanctify God. Interestingly, though, no explicit mention of *kedusha,* holiness, appears here.

A prayer qualifies as a *davar shebikedusha* when the explicit, ineffable name of God is invoked. Thus, when we are invited here to "Bless the Lord, the blessed One," we are called upon specifically to bless God's name "which is

בָּרוּךְ Blessed are You, LORD our God, King of the Universe,
who by His word brings on evenings,
by His wisdom opens the gates of heaven,
with understanding makes time change and the seasons rotate,
and by His will orders the stars in their constellations in the sky.
He creates day and night,
rolling away the light before the darkness,
and darkness before the light.
▸ He makes the day pass and brings on night,
distinguishing day from night:
the LORD of hosts is His name.
May the living and forever enduring God rule over us for all time.
Blessed are You, LORD, who brings on evenings.

אַהֲבַת עוֹלָם With everlasting love
have You loved Your people, the house of Israel.
You have taught us Torah and commandments,
decrees and laws of justice.

---

not be erased, while according to Rabbi Yose, it is not a divine name but a reference to the nation of Israel. Rabbi Yose translates ה׳ צְבָאוֹת as "the LORD of Israel." The other Sages disagree with Rabbi Yose because the divine name ה׳ cannot be part of a possessive phrase. According to them, ה׳ cannot be of anything. They understand the words ה׳ צְבָאוֹת as two divine names, meaning "ה׳, who is צְבָאוֹת." (*And From There You Shall Seek*)

חֻקִּים וּמִשְׁפָּטִים *Decrees and laws of justice.* Man, no matter what persuasion, faith or ideology, indignantly condemns the murderer and the act of murder. Yet, what about a situation so vividly illustrated by Dostoevsky in his novel *Crime and Punishment*? The book depicts a cruel, miserly old woman, a loan shark sucking the blood of those unfortunates caught in her web, a person who evicts the old and frail on a winter day in sub-zero temperatures. Portrayed in sharp contrast is a brilliant young student who cannot afford to continue his medical studies and who hopelessly watches as his sister is sold into white slavery and exiled. A loan of a few hundred rubles could have remedied his situation, yet the old woman refuses to advance him the money. In a moment of despair the student kills the miser. Do we have the right to condemn the student? Should we consider such a murder a crime? Yet, the Almighty has forbidden murder, whatever the motive.

בָּרוּךְ אַתָּה יהוה אֱלֹהֵינוּ מֶלֶךְ הָעוֹלָם
אֲשֶׁר בִּדְבָרוֹ מַעֲרִיב עֲרָבִים, בְּחָכְמָה פּוֹתֵחַ שְׁעָרִים
וּבִתְבוּנָה מְשַׁנֶּה עִתִּים וּמַחֲלִיף אֶת הַזְּמַנִּים
וּמְסַדֵּר אֶת הַכּוֹכָבִים בְּמִשְׁמְרוֹתֵיהֶם בָּרָקִיעַ כִּרְצוֹנוֹ.
בּוֹרֵא יוֹם וָלָיְלָה, גּוֹלֵל אוֹר מִפְּנֵי חֹשֶׁךְ וְחֹשֶׁךְ מִפְּנֵי אוֹר
◂ וּמַעֲבִיר יוֹם וּמֵבִיא לָיְלָה, וּמַבְדִּיל בֵּין יוֹם וּבֵין לָיְלָה
יהוה צְבָאוֹת שְׁמוֹ.
אֵל חַי וְקַיָּם תָּמִיד, יִמְלֹךְ עָלֵינוּ לְעוֹלָם וָעֶד.
בָּרוּךְ אַתָּה יהוה, הַמַּעֲרִיב עֲרָבִים.

אַהֲבַת עוֹלָם בֵּית יִשְׂרָאֵל עַמְּךָ אָהָבְתָּ
תּוֹרָה וּמִצְוֹת, חֻקִּים וּמִשְׁפָּטִים, אוֹתָנוּ לִמַּדְתָּ

בָּרוּךְ אַתָּה...אֲשֶׁר בִּדְבָרוֹ *Blessed are You… who by His word…* The blessings which form the prologue and epilogue to *Keriat Shema* constitute a commentary to the Shema itself. As such, the reading of the Shema and its blessings form one whole integrated entity. Each motif of Shema is isolated from the complex experience, elucidated and expressed in the form of a hymn or entreaty. The *berakhot* do not add any new elements that the Shema itself does not contain. Rather, they take an implicit motif and unfold its meaning and sense. What is merely implied in Shema is explicated and interpreted by the *berakhot*. When we examine carefully the content of the *berakhot* we discover that each one corresponds to one section of the Shema. The first *berakha* incorporates the motif of the first section of the Shema: the unity and kingship of God. The second *berakha* takes up the idea of revelation and the giving of the Law and thus develops the main theme of the second section of the Shema: the acceptance of divine authority and the commitment to the realization of the religious norm and the fulfillment of the commandments. And finally, the third *berakha*, which follows Shema, constitutes the liturgical correlate of the third section of the Shema, whose motto is the exodus from Egypt, redemption. (*Worship of the Heart*)

יהוה צְבָאוֹת שְׁמוֹ *The Lord of hosts is His name.* The Sages and Rabbi Yose debate whether the term **צְבָאוֹת**, once written, may be erased (*Shevuot* 35b). According to the Sages, **צְבָאוֹת** constitutes a divine name and therefore may

Therefore, Lord our God, when we lie down and when we rise up
we will speak of Your decrees, rejoicing in the words of Your Torah
and Your commandments for ever.
▸ For they are our life and the length of our days;
on them will we meditate day and night.
May You never take away Your love from us.
Blessed are You, Lord, who loves His people Israel.

The Shema must be said with intense concentration.
When not with a minyan, say:

God, faithful King!

The following verse should be said aloud, while covering the eyes with the right hand:

Listen, Israel: the Lord is our God, the Lord is One. *Deut. 6*

Quietly: Blessed be the name of His glorious kingdom for ever and all time.

---

prayer (Amida) is termed by the same halakha and Aggada as *avoda shebalev*, service of the heart; that is, worshiping God. Worship as service, or as acceptance of a yoke, occurs not through cultic ceremonials and formal service, but via an inner paradoxical movement of the soul. This movement includes both a flight to God and a withdrawal from Him. The full realization of the commandments of Shema and *tefilla* thus manifests itself in the great heterogeneous religious experience. Because this movement is subjective, the halakha taught us that in both cases, in reading the Shema and reciting *tefilla*, intention (*kavana*) is not a mere modality, expressing just the "how" of the mitzva-fulfillment as in other mitzvot, but rather is identical with the very substance and essence of the commandment. (*Worship of the Heart*)

אֶחָד *One.* When we affirm God's unity, we intend to state that in His dual role as Creator of the world and as Legislator of the moral norm, He is One. His word made heaven and earth spring into existence, and the same word founded the moral law, the Torah. The bird in its flight, the flower opening its leaves toward the sunlight, the tumbling pebbles and the sea waves transmitting energy all carry out a divine ethical command. Judaism found God both in the cosmos and in the conscience, in natural and in moral necessity, and uncovered oneness in both realms. (*Worship of the Heart*)

בָּרוּךְ שֵׁם כְּבוֹד מַלְכוּתוֹ *Blessed be the name of His glorious kingdom.* The Talmud (*Pesaḥim* 56a), explaining the presence of this hymnal refrain after the first

עַל כֵּן יהוה אֱלֹהֵינוּ בְּשָׁכְבֵנוּ וּבְקוּמֵנוּ נָשִׂיחַ בְּחֻקֶּיךָ
וְנִשְׂמַח בְּדִבְרֵי תוֹרָתֶךָ וּבְמִצְוֹתֶיךָ לְעוֹלָם וָעֶד
◂ כִּי הֵם חַיֵּינוּ וְאֹרֶךְ יָמֵינוּ, וּבָהֶם נֶהְגֶּה יוֹמָם וָלָיְלָה.
וְאַהֲבָתְךָ אַל תָּסִיר מִמֶּנּוּ לְעוֹלָמִים.
בָּרוּךְ אַתָּה יהוה, אוֹהֵב עַמּוֹ יִשְׂרָאֵל.

The שמע *must be said with intense concentration.*

When not with a מנין*, say:*

אֵל מֶלֶךְ נֶאֱמָן

The following verse should be said aloud, while covering the eyes with the right hand:

דברים ו שְׁמַע יִשְׂרָאֵל, יהוה אֱלֹהֵינוּ, יהוה ׀ אֶחָד:

Quietly בָּרוּךְ שֵׁם כְּבוֹד מַלְכוּתוֹ לְעוֹלָם וָעֶד.

We must surrender our intellectual pride and arrogance, and commit ourselves to the Almighty, even when we are unable to comprehend the *ḥukim*, those precepts whose moral necessity and practical utility are not obvious. Secular ethics have failed because the concept of *ḥok* is not acceptable to secular man. If the integrity of the moral law is to be preserved, then one must be ready to abstain from acts that seem to hold great promise, and conversely, to act in ways that may sometimes seem illogical and even painful.

וּבָהֶם נֶהְגֶּה יוֹמָם וָלָיְלָה *On them will we meditate day and night.* The study of Torah is not only an intellectual experience; it is an emotional experience as well. The word *higayon* (as opposed to *limmud*) involves this emotional aspect, signifying not merely learning, but dedication to learning. For this reason, in *Birkat HaTorah* at the beginning of Shaḥarit, we ask that God sweeten the words of Torah for us, so that we can emotionally bond with the Torah. Similarly, the same *berakha* starts with the words blessing God for commanding us *la'asok*, to engage in the words of the Torah – engagement must be an emotional experience.

THE SHEMA

The reading of Shema was designated by the halakha and Aggada as *kabbalat ol malkhut shamayim*, taking upon oneself the yoke of the kingdom of Heaven, the acknowledgment and acceptance of the absolute, universal and eternal authority of God. As we have noted, the recitation of the silent

וְאָהַבְתָּ Love the LORD your God with all your heart, with all your soul, and with all your might. These words which I command you today shall be on your heart. Teach them repeatedly to your children, speaking of them when you sit at home and when you travel on the way, when you lie down and when you rise. Bind them as a sign on your hand, and they shall be an emblem between your eyes. Write them on the doorposts of your house and gates. *Deut. 6*

וְהָיָה If you indeed heed My commandments with which I charge you today, to love the LORD your God and worship Him with all your heart and with all your soul, I will give rain in your land in its season, the early and late rain; and you shall gather in your grain, *Deut. 11*

---

destiny, full of import. In prayer, we experience the presence of God, we stand near and commune with Him. In reading the Shema, by contrast, we enter the presence of those persons who walked with Him, we stand in their shadow; we converse with men who, though they died a biological death, have been reincarnated time and again in our historical experience via divergent media and various forms of existence. The great drama of destiny, begun by the patriarchs, is reenacted again. (*Worship of the Heart*)

וּבְכָל *And with all.* The whole of man, body and spirit, nature and consciousness, must be engaged in the love of God, in the clear quest for Being. The word "all" (*kol*) conveys a central thought. In his search for Being, man discovers his completeness. He is moved and guided by intelligent planning; he rids himself of ethical indifference. There are no more neutral areas in his existence from which the halakhic ethical norm is barred. Through this commitment man finds the oneness of Being in which he shares. (*Worship of the Heart*)

וּלְעָבְדוֹ בְּכָל לְבַבְכֶם *And worship Him with all your heart.* According to Maimonides, prayer, service of the heart, is a biblical obligation. Although the act of prayer involves an objective act, that is, the recital of words, the external act is only a representation of the full state of mind. This aspect delivers the inner activity from its amorphous, ephemeral state and achieves objectification in concrete action. One turns toward God with the heart and not merely with the lips, with thoughts and not only with words. Prayer constitutes a basic method of religious representation, a physical portraiture of miscible, mingled experiences. (*Worship of the Heart*)

וְאָהַבְתָּ אֵת יהוה אֱלֹהֶיךָ, בְּכָל־לְבָבְךָ וּבְכָל־נַפְשְׁךָ וּבְכָל־מְאֹדֶךָ: דברים ו
וְהָיוּ הַדְּבָרִים הָאֵלֶּה, אֲשֶׁר אָנֹכִי מְצַוְּךָ הַיּוֹם, עַל־לְבָבֶךָ: וְשִׁנַּנְתָּם
לְבָנֶיךָ וְדִבַּרְתָּ בָּם, בְּשִׁבְתְּךָ בְּבֵיתֶךָ וּבְלֶכְתְּךָ בַדֶּרֶךְ, וּבְשָׁכְבְּךָ
וּבְקוּמֶךָ: וּקְשַׁרְתָּם לְאוֹת עַל־יָדֶךָ וְהָיוּ לְטֹטָפֹת בֵּין עֵינֶיךָ:
וּכְתַבְתָּם עַל־מְזֻזוֹת בֵּיתֶךָ וּבִשְׁעָרֶיךָ:

וְהָיָה אִם־שָׁמֹעַ תִּשְׁמְעוּ אֶל־מִצְוֹתַי אֲשֶׁר אָנֹכִי מְצַוֶּה אֶתְכֶם דברים יא
הַיּוֹם, לְאַהֲבָה אֶת־יהוה אֱלֹהֵיכֶם וּלְעָבְדוֹ, בְּכָל־לְבַבְכֶם וּבְכָל־
נַפְשְׁכֶם: וְנָתַתִּי מְטַר־אַרְצְכֶם בְּעִתּוֹ, יוֹרֶה וּמַלְקוֹשׁ, וְאָסַפְתָּ דְגָנֶךָ

---

verse of Shema, draws on a tradition according to which the practice of reciting the Shema in that way, inserting the refrain, goes back to Jacob and his sons at their last encounter:

> Jacob wished to reveal to his sons the end of days, but the holy spirit withdrew from him. He said: "Perhaps, Heaven forbid, there is a defect in my bed, like Abraham from whom Ishmael was engendered, and my father Isaac, from whom Esau was engendered." His sons said to him: "Hear O Israel, the Lord our God, the Lord is One. Just as there is only One in your heart, so there is only One in our hearts." Then did our father Jacob recite, "Blessed be the name of His glorious kingdom for ever and ever."

The creed of Shema is not merely a theoretical truth, a philosophical pronouncement, a religious dogma, a norm, however central and endowed with meaning. It is rather the shibboleth of our historical uniqueness, a living doctrine which bears witness to our charismatic quality and which keeps us together as one, spanning almost the whole course of ages, uniting us with our patriarchs, drawing them into our temporal ontic circle, thus lending to our own existence the tenor of "timelessness." The reading of Shema is a solemn and vigorous response to Jacob's challenge of old, which rings through the distances of time. It is indeed the acceptance of a great task, the declaration addressed to the remote past that joins the march of generations committed to one idea.

In a word, the reading of Shema is a dialogue between the continual restaging of the historic meeting of Jacob and his sons, pregnant with paradoxical

wine and oil. I will give grass in your field for your cattle, and you shall eat and be satisfied. Be careful lest your heart be tempted and you go astray and worship other gods, bowing down to them. Then the LORD's anger will flare against you and He will close the heavens so that there will be no rain. The land will not yield its crops, and you will perish swiftly from the good land that the LORD is giving you. Therefore, set these, My words, on your heart and soul. Bind them as a sign on your hand, and they shall be an emblem between your eyes. Teach them to your children, speaking of them when you sit at home and when you travel on the way, when you lie down and when you rise. Write them on the doorposts of your house and gates, so that you and your children may live long in the land that the LORD swore to your ancestors to give them, for as long as the heavens are above the earth.

וַיֹּאמֶר The LORD spoke to Moses, saying: Speak to the Israelites *Num. 15*
and tell them to make tassels on the corners of their garments for all generations. They shall attach to the tassel at each corner a thread of blue. This shall be your tassel, and you shall see it and remember all of the LORD's commandments and keep them, not straying after your heart and after your eyes, following your own sinful desires. Thus you will be reminded to keep all My

---

throne." They associated blue with distance and inapproachability. The blue sky is very distant; the blue sea is wide and endless. And, of course, the throne of God is beyond the universe. Whatever we cannot reach, whatever is outside of our control, whatever suggests mystery to us, is considered by our Sages as *tekhelet*.

Man sometimes meets with mystery, with something numinous and awesome, something beyond the bounds of the rational and intelligible. Everything becomes distant and strange, remote as the sky and distant from our minds. But we have been trained to accept both. If the experience is understandable, then our intellect interprets the experience. If the experience is not understandable, unintelligible, we interpret it through an act of faith.

וְתִירֹשְׁךָ וְיִצְהָרֶךָ: וְנָתַתִּי עֵשֶׂב בְּשָׂדְךָ לִבְהֶמְתֶּךָ, וְאָכַלְתָּ וְשָׂבָעְתָּ:
הִשָּׁמְרוּ לָכֶם פֶּן־יִפְתֶּה לְבַבְכֶם, וְסַרְתֶּם וַעֲבַדְתֶּם אֱלֹהִים אֲחֵרִים
וְהִשְׁתַּחֲוִיתֶם לָהֶם: וְחָרָה אַף־יהוה בָּכֶם, וְעָצַר אֶת־הַשָּׁמַיִם
וְלֹא־יִהְיֶה מָטָר, וְהָאֲדָמָה לֹא תִתֵּן אֶת־יְבוּלָהּ, וַאֲבַדְתֶּם מְהֵרָה
מֵעַל הָאָרֶץ הַטֹּבָה אֲשֶׁר יהוה נֹתֵן לָכֶם: וְשַׂמְתֶּם אֶת־דְּבָרַי
אֵלֶּה עַל־לְבַבְכֶם וְעַל־נַפְשְׁכֶם, וּקְשַׁרְתֶּם אֹתָם לְאוֹת עַל־יֶדְכֶם,
וְהָיוּ לְטוֹטָפֹת בֵּין עֵינֵיכֶם: וְלִמַּדְתֶּם אֹתָם אֶת־בְּנֵיכֶם לְדַבֵּר בָּם,
בְּשִׁבְתְּךָ בְּבֵיתֶךָ וּבְלֶכְתְּךָ בַדֶּרֶךְ, וּבְשָׁכְבְּךָ וּבְקוּמֶךָ: וּכְתַבְתָּם
עַל־מְזוּזוֹת בֵּיתֶךָ וּבִשְׁעָרֶיךָ: לְמַעַן יִרְבּוּ יְמֵיכֶם וִימֵי בְנֵיכֶם עַל
הָאֲדָמָה אֲשֶׁר נִשְׁבַּע יהוה לַאֲבֹתֵיכֶם לָתֵת לָהֶם, כִּימֵי הַשָּׁמַיִם
עַל־הָאָרֶץ:

וַיֹּאמֶר יהוה אֶל־מֹשֶׁה לֵּאמֹר: דַּבֵּר אֶל־בְּנֵי יִשְׂרָאֵל וְאָמַרְתָּ במדבר טו
אֲלֵהֶם, וְעָשׂוּ לָהֶם צִיצִת עַל־כַּנְפֵי בִגְדֵיהֶם לְדֹרֹתָם, וְנָתְנוּ עַל־
צִיצִת הַכָּנָף פְּתִיל תְּכֵלֶת: וְהָיָה לָכֶם לְצִיצִת, וּרְאִיתֶם אֹתוֹ
וּזְכַרְתֶּם אֶת־כָּל־מִצְוֹת יהוה וַעֲשִׂיתֶם אֹתָם, וְלֹא תָתֻרוּ אַחֲרֵי
לְבַבְכֶם וְאַחֲרֵי עֵינֵיכֶם, אֲשֶׁר־אַתֶּם זֹנִים אַחֲרֵיהֶם: לְמַעַן תִּזְכְּרוּ

פְּתִיל תְּכֵלֶת *A thread of blue. Tekhelet* and *lavan*, blue and white, represent two approaches of man to himself and to the world outside. In classical Hebrew, *lavan* signifies the color white, but it also signifies clarity, distinctiveness and openness. It denotes rationality, simplicity and truthfulness, something which is obvious to everybody as an elementary truth. A Jew is expected to focus his glance on the white and attempt to understand the world. The Torah did not want people to live in obscurity. It encourages man to explore all the phenomena of nature, to use his mind and make discoveries, to be scientifically oriented and technologically minded.

Tekhelet is just the opposite. Our Sages said (*Sota* 17a): "*Tekhelet* resembles the sea, and the sea resembles the sky, and the sky resembles the celestial

commandments, and be holy to your God. I am the Lord your God, who brought you out of the land of Egypt to be your God. I am the Lord your God.

True –

The Leader repeats:

‣ The Lord your God is true –

וֶאֱמוּנָה – and faithful is all this,
and firmly established for us
that He is the Lord our God,
and there is none besides Him,
and that we, Israel, are His people.
He is our King, who redeems us from the hand of kings
and delivers us from the grasp of all tyrants.
He is our God,
who on our behalf repays our foes
and brings just retribution on our mortal enemies;
who performs great deeds beyond understanding
and wonders beyond number;
who kept us alive, not letting our foot slip; *Ps. 66*
who led us on the high places of our enemies,
raising our pride above all our foes;

---

finite order; this is the notion of *tzimtzum*. God contracted to make room for the world. But man is still overwhelmed by the cosmos and he thus insists on another act of sacrifice: he invites God to join him in his historic destiny, to become his leader, friend, and guide, but also his prisoner. It is in a sense impudent on man's part to restrict God's Presence to an even smaller area by including Him in a comparatively limited historical process, thereby making His "sacrifice" even greater. Yet God indeed engages in this act of regression, from infinite to finite; He willingly descends from the unalterable cosmic drama to the fleeting historical process.

וַעֲשִׂיתֶם אֶת־כָּל־מִצְוֹתָי, וִהְיִיתֶם קְדֹשִׁים לֵאלֹהֵיכֶם: אֲנִי יְהוָה אֱלֹהֵיכֶם, אֲשֶׁר הוֹצֵאתִי אֶתְכֶם מֵאֶרֶץ מִצְרַיִם, לִהְיוֹת לָכֶם לֵאלֹהִים, אֲנִי יְהוָה אֱלֹהֵיכֶם:

אֱמֶת

The שליח ציבור *repeats:*

◂ יהוה אֱלֹהֵיכֶם אֱמֶת

וֶאֱמוּנָה כָּל זֹאת וְקַיָּם עָלֵינוּ
כִּי הוּא יהוה אֱלֹהֵינוּ וְאֵין זוּלָתוֹ
וַאֲנַחְנוּ יִשְׂרָאֵל עַמּוֹ.
הַפּוֹדֵנוּ מִיַּד מְלָכִים
מַלְכֵּנוּ הַגּוֹאֲלֵנוּ מִכַּף כָּל הֶעָרִיצִים.
הָאֵל הַנִּפְרָע לָנוּ מִצָּרֵינוּ
וְהַמְשַׁלֵּם גְּמוּל לְכָל אוֹיְבֵי נַפְשֵׁנוּ.
הָעוֹשֶׂה גְדוֹלוֹת עַד אֵין חֵקֶר, וְנִפְלָאוֹת עַד אֵין מִסְפָּר
הַשָּׂם נַפְשֵׁנוּ בַּחַיִּים, וְלֹא־נָתַן לַמּוֹט רַגְלֵנוּ: תהלים סו
הַמַּדְרִיכֵנוּ עַל בָּמוֹת אוֹיְבֵינוּ
וַיָּרֶם קַרְנֵנוּ עַל כָּל שׂוֹנְאֵינוּ.

אֲשֶׁר הוֹצֵאתִי אֶתְכֶם מֵאֶרֶץ מִצְרַיִם *Who brought you out of the land of Egypt.* God is not portrayed here as the Creator, because the cosmic experience is too formal and abstract. God does not wish to appear as a tyrant to whom man must submit. The vastness of the cosmos frightens man, and he cannot transport himself to the outer fringes of the universe to meet Him. The mystics have termed the act of creation as a sacrifice. Since He is infinite and unique, for Him to tolerate another creature is an expression of grace – and sacrifice. God, therefore, moves from all-exclusiveness to all-inclusiveness, where the world shares His existence and God imprisons Himself, as it were, in the

who did miracles for us
and brought vengeance against Pharaoh;
who performed signs and wonders
in the land of Ham's children;
who smote in His wrath all the firstborn of Egypt,
and brought out His people Israel from their midst
into everlasting freedom;
who led His children through the divided Reed Sea,
plunging their pursuers and enemies into the depths.
When His children saw His might,
they gave praise and thanks to His name,
▸ and willingly accepted His Sovereignty.
Moses and the children of Israel
then sang a song to You with great joy,
and they all exclaimed:

מִי־כָמֹכָה "Who is like You, LORD, among the mighty? *Ex. 15*
Who is like You, majestic in holiness,
awesome in praises, doing wonders?"

▸ Your children beheld Your majesty
as You parted the sea before Moses.
"This is my God!" they responded,
and then said:

"The LORD shall reign for ever and ever." *Ex. 15*

▸ And it is said, "For the LORD has redeemed Jacob *Jer. 31*
and rescued him from a power stronger than his own."
Blessed are You, LORD, who redeemed Israel.

---

mandments which begin, "I am the Lord your God who brought you out of the land of Egypt" (Ex. 20:2). Accordingly, the obligation to remember the exodus is not an independent obligation; rather, it is a particular manner of fulfilling the more general obligation of accepting the yoke of Heaven's kingship, fulfilled by reciting the Shema. (*Shiurim LeZekher Abba Mari*)

הָעוֹשֶׂה לָּנוּ נִסִּים וּנְקָמָה בְּפַרְעֹה
אוֹתוֹת וּמוֹפְתִים בְּאַדְמַת בְּנֵי חָם.
הַמַּכֶּה בְעֶבְרָתוֹ כָּל בְּכוֹרֵי מִצְרָיִם
וַיּוֹצֵא אֶת עַמּוֹ יִשְׂרָאֵל מִתּוֹכָם לְחֵרוּת עוֹלָם.
הַמַּעֲבִיר בָּנָיו בֵּין גִּזְרֵי יַם סוּף
אֶת רוֹדְפֵיהֶם וְאֶת שׂוֹנְאֵיהֶם בִּתְהוֹמוֹת טִבַּע
וְרָאוּ בָנָיו גְּבוּרָתוֹ, שִׁבְּחוּ וְהוֹדוּ לִשְׁמוֹ
◂ וּמַלְכוּתוֹ בְּרָצוֹן קִבְּלוּ עֲלֵיהֶם.
מֹשֶׁה וּבְנֵי יִשְׂרָאֵל, לְךָ עָנוּ שִׁירָה בְּשִׂמְחָה רַבָּה
וְאָמְרוּ כֻלָּם

מִי־כָמֹכָה בָּאֵלִם יהוה שמות טו
מִי כָּמֹכָה נֶאְדָּר בַּקֹּדֶשׁ
נוֹרָא תְהִלֹּת עֹשֵׂה פֶלֶא:

◂ מַלְכוּתְךָ רָאוּ בָנֶיךָ, בּוֹקֵעַ יָם לִפְנֵי מֹשֶׁה
זֶה אֵלִי עָנוּ, וְאָמְרוּ
יהוה יִמְלֹךְ לְעֹלָם וָעֶד: שמות טו
◂ וְנֶאֱמַר
כִּי־פָדָה יהוה אֶת־יַעֲקֹב, וּגְאָלוֹ מִיַּד חָזָק מִמֶּנּוּ: ירמיהו לא
בָּרוּךְ אַתָּה יהוה, גָּאַל יִשְׂרָאֵל.

The obligation to remember the exodus is subsumed under the obligation to accept the yoke of Heaven's kingship. The Gemara (*Rosh HaShana* 32a) explains that the words "I am the Lord your God" in Leviticus 23:22 are synonymous with the idea of kingship and accepting the yoke of Heaven's kingship. This phrasing is also used here in the third paragraph of the Shema (from Num. 15:41). The juxtaposition of God's kingship and the Egyptian exodus implies that the remembrance of the exodus is an inherent part of accepting the yoke of Heaven's kingship. This concept is also apparent in the Ten Com-

הַשְׁכִּיבֵנוּ Help us lie down, O Lord our God, in peace,
and rise up, O our King, to life.
Spread over us Your canopy of peace.
Direct us with Your good counsel,
and save us for the sake of Your name.
Shield us and remove from us every enemy,
plague, sword, famine and sorrow.
Remove the adversary from before and behind us.
Shelter us in the shadow of Your wings,
for You, God, are our Guardian and Deliverer;
You, God, are a gracious and compassionate King.
▸ Guard our going out and our coming in,
for life and peace, from now and for ever.
Blessed are You, Lord, who guards His people Israel for ever.

In Israel the service continues with Half Kaddish on page 20.

בָּרוּךְ Blessed be the Lord for ever. Amen and Amen. *Ps. 89*
Blessed from Zion be the Lord *Ps. 135*
who dwells in Jerusalem. Halleluya!
Blessed be the Lord, God of Israel, *Ps. 72*
who alone does wondrous things.
Blessed be His glorious name for ever,
and may the whole earth be filled with His glory. Amen and Amen.
May the glory of the Lord endure for ever; *Ps. 104*
may the Lord rejoice in His works.
May the name of the Lord be blessed now and for all time. *Ps. 113*
For the sake of His great name *I Sam. 12*
the Lord will not abandon His people,
for the Lord vowed to make you a people of His own.

God to shelter us the way a mother shelters a child. For this reason, it was our patriarch Jacob who instituted the Ma'ariv prayer (see *Berakhot* 26b) as he was praying for his survival in his confrontation with both Laban and Esau.

הַשְׁכִּיבֵנוּ יהוה אֱלֹהֵינוּ לְשָׁלוֹם, וְהַעֲמִידֵנוּ מַלְכֵּנוּ לְחַיִּים
וּפְרֹשׂ עָלֵינוּ סֻכַּת שְׁלוֹמֶךָ, וְתַקְּנֵנוּ בְּעֵצָה טוֹבָה מִלְּפָנֶיךָ
וְהוֹשִׁיעֵנוּ לְמַעַן שְׁמֶךָ.
וְהָגֵן בַּעֲדֵנוּ, וְהָסֵר מֵעָלֵינוּ אוֹיֵב, דֶּבֶר וְחֶרֶב וְרָעָב וְיָגוֹן
וְהָסֵר שָׂטָן מִלְּפָנֵינוּ וּמֵאַחֲרֵינוּ, וּבְצֵל כְּנָפֶיךָ תַּסְתִּירֵנוּ
כִּי אֵל שׁוֹמְרֵנוּ וּמַצִּילֵנוּ אָתָּה
כִּי אֵל מֶלֶךְ חַנּוּן וְרַחוּם אָתָּה.
◄ וּשְׁמֹר צֵאתֵנוּ וּבוֹאֵנוּ לְחַיִּים וּלְשָׁלוֹם מֵעַתָּה וְעַד עוֹלָם.
בָּרוּךְ אַתָּה יהוה, שׁוֹמֵר עַמּוֹ יִשְׂרָאֵל לָעַד.

In ארץ ישראל *the service continues with* חצי קדיש *on page 21.*

בָּרוּךְ יהוה לְעוֹלָם, אָמֵן וְאָמֵן: תהלים פט
בָּרוּךְ יהוה מִצִּיּוֹן, שֹׁכֵן יְרוּשָׁלָםִ, הַלְלוּיָהּ: תהלים קלה
בָּרוּךְ יהוה אֱלֹהִים אֱלֹהֵי יִשְׂרָאֵל, עֹשֵׂה נִפְלָאוֹת לְבַדּוֹ: תהלים עב
וּבָרוּךְ שֵׁם כְּבוֹדוֹ לְעוֹלָם
וְיִמָּלֵא כְבוֹדוֹ אֶת־כָּל־הָאָרֶץ, אָמֵן וְאָמֵן:
יְהִי כְבוֹד יהוה לְעוֹלָם, יִשְׂמַח יהוה בְּמַעֲשָׂיו: תהלים קד
יְהִי שֵׁם יהוה מְבֹרָךְ מֵעַתָּה וְעַד־עוֹלָם: תהלים קיג
כִּי לֹא־יִטֹּשׁ יהוה אֶת־עַמּוֹ בַּעֲבוּר שְׁמוֹ הַגָּדוֹל שמואל א, יב
כִּי הוֹאִיל יהוה לַעֲשׂוֹת אֶתְכֶם לוֹ לְעָם:

הַשְׁכִּיבֵנוּ *Help us lie down.* In this blessing, man asks God to personally care for him as he surrenders his soul and retires. Amidst the confusion and insecurity associated with the nighttime, man wants to be sheltered by God. To alleviate the fear of the night, trust in God is insufficient for us; we yearn for

When all the people saw [God's wonders] they fell on their faces *1 Kings 18*
and said: "The LORD, He is God; the LORD, He is God."
Then the LORD shall be King over all the earth; *Zech. 14*
on that day the LORD shall be One and His name One.
May Your love, LORD, be upon us, as we have put our hope in You. *Ps. 33*
הוֹשִׁיעֵנוּ Save us, LORD our God, gather us *Ps. 106*
and deliver us from the nations,
to thank Your holy name, and glory in Your praise.
All the nations You made shall come and bow before You, LORD, *Ps. 86*
and pay honor to Your name,
for You are great and You perform wonders:
You alone are God.
We, Your people, the flock of Your pasture, will praise You for ever. *Ps. 79*
For all generations we will relate Your praise.

בָּרוּךְ Blessed is the LORD by day, blessed is the LORD by night.
Blessed is the LORD when we lie down;
blessed is the LORD when we rise.
For in Your hand are the souls of the living and the dead,
[as it is written:] "In His hand is every living soul, *Job 12*
and the breath of all mankind."
Into Your hand I entrust my spirit: *Ps. 31*
You redeemed me, LORD, God of truth.
Our God in heaven, bring unity to Your name,
establish Your kingdom constantly
and reign over us for ever and all time.

יִרְאוּ May our eyes see, our hearts rejoice,
and our souls be glad in Your true salvation,
when Zion is told, "Your God reigns."
The LORD is King, the LORD was King,
the LORD will be King for ever and all time.

וַיַּרְא כׇּל־הָעָם וַיִּפְּלוּ עַל־פְּנֵיהֶם מלכים א, יח
וַיֹּאמְרוּ, יהוה הוּא הָאֱלֹהִים, יהוה הוּא הָאֱלֹהִים:
וְהָיָה יהוה לְמֶלֶךְ עַל־כׇּל־הָאָרֶץ זכריה יד
בַּיּוֹם הַהוּא יִהְיֶה יהוה אֶחָד וּשְׁמוֹ אֶחָד:
יְהִי־חַסְדְּךָ יהוה עָלֵינוּ, כַּאֲשֶׁר יִחַלְנוּ לָךְ: תהלים לג
הוֹשִׁיעֵנוּ יהוה אֱלֹהֵינוּ, וְקַבְּצֵנוּ מִן־הַגּוֹיִם תהלים קו
לְהוֹדוֹת לְשֵׁם קׇדְשֶׁךָ, לְהִשְׁתַּבֵּחַ בִּתְהִלָּתֶךָ:
כׇּל־גּוֹיִם אֲשֶׁר עָשִׂיתָ, יָבוֹאוּ וְיִשְׁתַּחֲווּ לְפָנֶיךָ, אֲדֹנָי תהלים פו
וִיכַבְּדוּ לִשְׁמֶךָ:
כִּי־גָדוֹל אַתָּה וְעֹשֵׂה נִפְלָאוֹת, אַתָּה אֱלֹהִים לְבַדֶּךָ:
וַאֲנַחְנוּ עַמְּךָ וְצֹאן מַרְעִיתֶךָ, נוֹדֶה לְּךָ לְעוֹלָם תהלים עט
לְדוֹר וָדֹר נְסַפֵּר תְּהִלָּתֶךָ:

בָּרוּךְ יהוה בַּיּוֹם, בָּרוּךְ יהוה בַּלָּיְלָה
בָּרוּךְ יהוה בְּשׇׁכְבֵנוּ, בָּרוּךְ יהוה בְּקוּמֵנוּ.
כִּי בְיָדְךָ נַפְשׁוֹת הַחַיִּים וְהַמֵּתִים.
אֲשֶׁר בְּיָדוֹ נֶפֶשׁ כׇּל־חָי, וְרוּחַ כׇּל־בְּשַׂר־אִישׁ: איוב יב
בְּיָדְךָ אַפְקִיד רוּחִי, פָּדִיתָה אוֹתִי יהוה אֵל אֱמֶת: תהלים לא
אֱלֹהֵינוּ שֶׁבַּשָּׁמַיִם, יַחֵד שִׁמְךָ וְקַיֵּם מַלְכוּתְךָ תָּמִיד
וּמְלֹךְ עָלֵינוּ לְעוֹלָם וָעֶד.

יִרְאוּ עֵינֵינוּ וְיִשְׂמַח לִבֵּנוּ
וְתָגֵל נַפְשֵׁנוּ בִּישׁוּעָתְךָ בֶּאֱמֶת
בֶּאֱמֹר לְצִיּוֹן מָלַךְ אֱלֹהָיִךְ.
יהוה מֶלֶךְ, יהוה מָלָךְ, יהוה יִמְלֹךְ לְעֹלָם וָעֶד.

▸ For sovereignty is Yours,
and to all eternity You will reign in glory,
for we have no king but You.
Blessed are You, LORD,
the King who in His constant glory will reign over us
and all His creation for ever and all time.

HALF KADDISH

Leader: יִתְגַּדַּל Magnified and sanctified
may His great name be,
in the world He created by His will.
May He establish His kingdom
in your lifetime and in your days,
and in the lifetime of all the house of Israel,
swiftly and soon –
and say: Amen.

All: May His great name be blessed for ever and all time.

Leader: Blessed and praised, glorified and exalted,
raised and honored, uplifted and lauded
be the name of the Holy One,
blessed be He,
beyond any blessing,
song, praise and consolation
uttered in the world –
and say: Amen.

• כִּי הַמַּלְכוּת שֶׁלְּךָ הִיא, וּלְעוֹלְמֵי עַד תִּמְלֹךְ בְּכָבוֹד
כִּי אֵין לָנוּ מֶלֶךְ אֶלָּא אָתָּה.
בָּרוּךְ אַתָּה יהוה
הַמֶּלֶךְ בִּכְבוֹדוֹ תָּמִיד, יִמְלֹךְ עָלֵינוּ לְעוֹלָם וָעֶד
וְעַל כָּל מַעֲשָׂיו.

חצי קדיש

ש״ץ: יִתְגַּדַּל וְיִתְקַדַּשׁ שְׁמֵהּ רַבָּא (קהל: אָמֵן)
בְּעָלְמָא דִּי בְרָא כִרְעוּתֵהּ
וְיַמְלִיךְ מַלְכוּתֵהּ
בְּחַיֵּיכוֹן וּבְיוֹמֵיכוֹן וּבְחַיֵּי דְכָל בֵּית יִשְׂרָאֵל
בַּעֲגָלָא וּבִזְמַן קָרִיב
וְאִמְרוּ אָמֵן. (קהל: אָמֵן)

קהל וש״ץ: יְהֵא שְׁמֵהּ רַבָּא מְבָרַךְ לְעָלַם וּלְעָלְמֵי עָלְמַיָּא.

ש״ץ: יִתְבָּרַךְ וְיִשְׁתַּבַּח וְיִתְפָּאַר וְיִתְרוֹמַם וְיִתְנַשֵּׂא
וְיִתְהַדָּר וְיִתְעַלֶּה וְיִתְהַלָּל
שְׁמֵהּ דְּקֻדְשָׁא בְּרִיךְ הוּא (קהל: בְּרִיךְ הוּא)
לְעֵלָּא מִן כָּל בִּרְכָתָא וְשִׁירָתָא, תֻּשְׁבְּחָתָא וְנֶחֱמָתָא
דַּאֲמִירָן בְּעָלְמָא
וְאִמְרוּ אָמֵן. (קהל: אָמֵן)

THE AMIDA

The following prayer, until "in former years" on page 46, is said silently, standing with feet together. Take three steps forward and at the points indicated by ▾, bend the knees at the first word, bow at the second, and stand straight before saying God's name.

O LORD, open my lips, *Ps. 51*
so that my mouth may declare Your praise.

PATRIARCHS

▾בָּרוּךְ Blessed are You, LORD our God and God of our fathers,
God of Abraham, God of Isaac and God of Jacob;
the great, mighty and awesome God, God Most High,
who bestows acts of loving-kindness and creates all,
who remembers the loving-kindness of the fathers
and will bring a Redeemer to their children's children
for the sake of His name, in love.
King, Helper, Savior, Shield:
▾Blessed are You, LORD, Shield of Abraham.

---

involved in that great transcendental universe; it is overwhelmed by its power, flooded by its light, and completely drawn into this marvelous state, in which man joins God. Intrinsically, the state of prayer is a mystical experience not confined to a single area of our personality. (*Worship of the Heart*)

וְקֹנֵה הַכֹּל *And [who] creates all.* This phrase can also mean "and [who] owns all." The Master of the Universe owns the world through His having created it, just as an artisan who produces a vessel acquires ownership of its incremental value. The world was created *ex nihilo*; God created the raw material and formed it into the world as we know it. There can thus be no contender for ownership rights.

וְזוֹכֵר חַסְדֵי אָבוֹת *Who remembers the loving-kindness of the fathers.* The everlasting continuity of the Jewish people guarantees the individual's worth and value in the eyes of God. If sanctity is not part of one's personality *per se*, it nevertheless takes hold by virtue of his identification with those generations that struggled for the existence of the nation. On his own, the person who prays may be without worth; but in the context of the generations, he reflects the image of Abraham, the father of all generations. (*Worship of the Heart*)

עמידה

The following prayer, until קַדְמֹנִיּוֹת *on page 47, is said silently, standing with feet together. Take three steps forward and at the points indicated by* ', *bend the knees at the first word, bow at the second, and stand straight before saying God's name.*

תהלים נא

אֲדֹנָי, שְׂפָתַי תִּפְתָּח, וּפִי יַגִּיד תְּהִלָּתֶךָ:

אבות

'בָּרוּךְ אַתָּה יהוה, אֱלֹהֵינוּ וֵאלֹהֵי אֲבוֹתֵינוּ
אֱלֹהֵי אַבְרָהָם, אֱלֹהֵי יִצְחָק, וֵאלֹהֵי יַעֲקֹב
הָאֵל הַגָּדוֹל הַגִּבּוֹר וְהַנּוֹרָא, אֵל עֶלְיוֹן
גּוֹמֵל חֲסָדִים טוֹבִים, וְקוֹנֵה הַכֹּל
וְזוֹכֵר חַסְדֵי אָבוֹת
וּמֵבִיא גוֹאֵל לִבְנֵי בְנֵיהֶם לְמַעַן שְׁמוֹ בְּאַהֲבָה.
מֶלֶךְ עוֹזֵר וּמוֹשִׁיעַ וּמָגֵן.
'בָּרוּךְ אַתָּה יהוה, מָגֵן אַבְרָהָם.

בָּרוּךְ אַתָּה *Blessed are You. Avoda shebalev* asserts itself in the great experience of Divine Presence, the awareness of God, of His proximity and closeness to us. In service of the heart, the finite being encounters his infinite, invisible God, stands before Him and addresses himself to Him. The praying soul is sensitive to the unseen Presence, responsive to its word. *Tefilla* is considered a dialogue, a conversation, a colloquy between God and man, between Infinity and finitude, Being and nothingness. Man does not talk about God as a third person, as someone who is not there. He employs the "Thou," the grammatical form which brings together two unique individualities, which draws the inaccessible Thou into the bounded I, and the mysterious I into the strange Thou. The Thou in prayer drives finitude to its very boundary. What is more, it lets finitude transcend itself and join infinity. In short, in prayer man establishes contact with God – the miracle of revelation repeats itself.

Prayer is like a rising river during the spring thaw, refusing to follow the direction of the bounded riverbed, inundating its environs with elemental, primordial and uncontrollable force. The whole human personality becomes

DIVINE MIGHT

אַתָּה גִּבּוֹר You are eternally mighty, Lord.
You give life to the dead
and have great power to save.
He makes the wind blow and the rain fall.
He sustains the living with loving-kindness,
and with great compassion revives the dead.
He supports the fallen, heals the sick, sets captives free,
and keeps His faith with those who sleep in the dust.
Who is like You, Master of might,
and to whom can You be compared,
O King who brings death and gives life,
and makes salvation grow?
Faithful are You to revive the dead.
Blessed are You, Lord, who revives the dead.

HOLINESS

אַתָּה קָדוֹשׁ You are holy and Your name is holy,
and holy ones praise You daily, Selah!
Blessed are You, Lord, the holy God.

---

has risen and set in the abyss of the silent grave. The dead person, too, needs deliverance, and God will resurrect the dead. The *ḥesed* that God performs with the dead is the most miraculous and majestic ethical act. This blessing of Divine Might ends with repeated reference to the motif of resurrection of the dead. Some spark of this conception is embodied in the halakha about the obligation to bury a *met mitzva* (an unattended corpse) which overrides many other commandments; also in the idea of *ḥesed shel emet*, the *ḥesed* of truth, because it is offered to one who is helpless. (*Worship of the Heart*)

אַתָּה קָדוֹשׁ *You are holy.* The understanding of God as awesome, closely linked to His being holy, likewise conveys absolute separation. God is not accessible to the human search, but is rather separated and isolated from it. But if He appears as the awesome God, how can prayer subsist? The praying individual stands and whispers: "You are holy and Your name is holy." Prayer in this

גבורות

אַתָּה גִּבּוֹר לְעוֹלָם, אֲדֹנָי
מְחַיֵּה מֵתִים אַתָּה, רַב לְהוֹשִׁיעַ
מַשִּׁיב הָרוּחַ וּמוֹרִיד הַגֶּשֶׁם
מְכַלְכֵּל חַיִּים בְּחֶסֶד, מְחַיֵּה מֵתִים בְּרַחֲמִים רַבִּים
סוֹמֵךְ נוֹפְלִים, וְרוֹפֵא חוֹלִים, וּמַתִּיר אֲסוּרִים
וּמְקַיֵּם אֱמוּנָתוֹ לִישֵׁנֵי עָפָר.
מִי כָמוֹךָ, בַּעַל גְּבוּרוֹת, וּמִי דּוֹמֶה לָּךְ
מֶלֶךְ, מֵמִית וּמְחַיֶּה וּמַצְמִיחַ יְשׁוּעָה.
וְנֶאֱמָן אַתָּה לְהַחֲיוֹת מֵתִים.
בָּרוּךְ אַתָּה יהוה, מְחַיֵּה הַמֵּתִים.

קדושת השם

אַתָּה קָדוֹשׁ וְשִׁמְךָ קָדוֹשׁ
וּקְדוֹשִׁים בְּכָל יוֹם יְהַלְלוּךָ סֶּלָה.
בָּרוּךְ אַתָּה יהוה, הָאֵל הַקָּדוֹשׁ.

רַב לְהוֹשִׁיעַ *Great power to save.* Man perceives God not only as abundant in kindness but also as omnipotent. No action lies beyond His capacity, and man is completely dependent on His assistance, His blessing and His supervision. This benediction emphasizes, however, that God's might is not only in the cosmic sense, but in the ethical sense as well. Because He is omnipotent and mighty, He is also the great Savior, who saves those who cannot be delivered and redeemed on their own. (*Worship of the Heart*)

מְחַיֵּה הַמֵּתִים *Who revives the dead.* Interesting is the Jewish conception that the greatest of all benefits, the singular ethical act, is resurrection of the dead. God involves Himself with the dead, whose existence has already ceased, who is not only unable to act and attain anything, but who is also stripped of the capacity to demand and complain, to plead and entreat, whose being

KNOWLEDGE

אַתָּה חוֹנֵן You grace humanity with knowledge
and teach mortals understanding.

On Motza'ei Shabbat add:

אַתָּה חוֹנַנְתָּנוּ You have graced us with the knowledge of Your Torah, and taught us to perform the statutes of Your will. You have distinguished, LORD our God, between sacred and profane, light and darkness, Israel and the nations, and between the seventh day and the six days of work. Our Father, our King, may the days approaching us bring peace; may we be free from all sin, cleansed from all iniquity, holding fast to our reverence of You. And

---

Grace us with the knowledge, understanding
and discernment that come from You.
Blessed are You, LORD,
who graciously grants knowledge.

אַתָּה חוֹנַנְתָּנוּ *You have graced us.* On Motza'ei Shabbat and Motza'ei Yom Tov, one commences with אַתָּה חוֹנֵן לְאָדָם דַּעַת and then says אַתָּה חוֹנַנְתָּנוּ לְמַדַּע תּוֹרָתֶךָ. *Ata Ḥonen* refers to a universal situation and stresses the fact that the human being alone was endowed by his Maker with a mysterious power: intelligence and the ability to observe, to judge, to interpret, to infer, to comprehend, to anticipate, and to plan for the future. We then state that there is a second endowment which is not universal but private, particularistic. This is the endowment of the Jew with an understanding of the Torah and the norms of mitzvot. Man differs from the beasts only because of his intellectual endowment. We state at the conclusion of Shabbat or Yom Tov, however, that, superimposed upon the universal dimension in which every human being shares, there is a special endowment to the Jew, a *havdala bein Yisrael la'amim,* a separation between Israel and the nations, that expresses itself in both a practical and theoretical gesture, in observance of the mitzvot and in Torah study.

בֵּין אוֹר לְחֹשֶׁךְ *Between… light and darkness.* The separation between light and darkness is perceptible and clear to everyone; even animals and birds feel the contrast between light and dark. The separation between sacred and profane is entirely different. The eye no longer sees the border between them; the senses cannot feel what is holy and what is mundane. One cannot notice it

דעת

אַתָּה חוֹנֵן לְאָדָם דַּעַת, וּמְלַמֵּד לֶאֱנוֹשׁ בִּינָה.

On מוצאי שבת *add:*

אַתָּה חוֹנַנְתָּנוּ לְמַדַּע תּוֹרָתֶךָ, וַתְּלַמְּדֵנוּ לַעֲשׂוֹת חֻקֵּי רְצוֹנֶךָ, וַתַּבְדֵּל יהוה אֱלֹהֵינוּ בֵּין קֹדֶשׁ לְחֹל, בֵּין אוֹר לְחֹשֶׁךְ, בֵּין יִשְׂרָאֵל לָעַמִּים, בֵּין יוֹם הַשְּׁבִיעִי לְשֵׁשֶׁת יְמֵי הַמַּעֲשֶׂה. אָבִינוּ מַלְכֵּנוּ, הָחֵל עָלֵינוּ הַיָּמִים הַבָּאִים לִקְרָאתֵנוּ לְשָׁלוֹם, חֲשׂוּכִים מִכָּל חֵטְא וּמְנֻקִּים מִכָּל עָוֹן וּמְדֻבָּקִים בְּיִרְאָתֶךָ. וְ

חָנֵּנוּ מֵאִתְּךָ דֵּעָה בִּינָה וְהַשְׂכֵּל.
בָּרוּךְ אַתָּה יהוה, חוֹנֵן הַדָּעַת.

---

context is an enormous riddle. How can a finite being attempt dialogue with the Infinite? Nonetheless, he continues: "And holy ones praise You daily." It is indeed possible for the praying person to stand before God, to cleave to Him. (*Worship of the Heart*)

אַתָּה חוֹנֵן לְאָדָם דַּעַת *You grace humanity with knowledge.* This is the only *berakha* which commences with an affirmative statement. It is the reverse of all other *berakhot* where we start with the petitionary sentence and conclude with an affirmative statement. *Ata Ḥonen* expresses the fact that human intelligence is a source of man's greatest pride and bliss, a source of his greatness and uniqueness. Without intelligence, man would be a brute in the field and progress would be impossible, for only through intellectual powers can man distinguish himself as an independent and powerful being who can free himself from his environment. And at the same time, human intelligence is also the source of man's misery and suffering. Because of his intellect, man realizes his own tragic destiny and the distressful and sorrowful state of being in which he finds himself. So before we are ready to present God with our petitions, we state the cause: we pray because we realize that we are lacking. We are thankful to God for the intellectual talents and powers He has bestowed upon us. In spite of the fact that knowledge and intelligence are responsible for our misery and sorrow, we want as much knowledge and intelligence as God sees fit to bestow upon us. We are ready to accept the burden and carry it. However, at the same time, we must come before Him to pray for our salvation, for our survival, for our peace of mind, for our happiness, for our success.

REPENTANCE

הֲשִׁיבֵנוּ Bring us back, our Father, to Your Torah.
Draw us near, our King, to Your service.
Lead us back to You in perfect repentance.
Blessed are You, LORD,
who desires repentance.

FORGIVENESS

Strike the left side of the chest at °.

סְלַח לָנוּ Forgive us, our Father, for we have °sinned.
Pardon us, our King, for we have °transgressed;
for You pardon and forgive.
Blessed are You, LORD,
the gracious One who repeatedly forgives.

REDEMPTION

רְאֵה Look on our affliction,
plead our cause,
and redeem us soon for Your name's sake,
for You are a powerful Redeemer.
Blessed are You, LORD,
the Redeemer of Israel.

מְחַל לָנוּ מַלְכֵּנוּ *Pardon us, our King.* One who suffers an indignity can choose to pardon the offender. Through this gesture, the scorned individual indicates that the indignity is no longer painful to him, and that the original act is forgotten. In this *berakha,* the request for a pardon addresses the alienation between man and God which results from sin. If, for example, one were to discover that his child had robbed him, the injury would not be limited to the monetary loss caused by the robbery itself; it would also result in a true feeling of betrayal at the child's action. By pardoning us, God indicates that the betrayal is no longer painful and has been forgotten.

רְאֵה בְעָנְיֵנוּ *Look on our affliction.* The term "our affliction" refers to silent suffering which is not accompanied by prayer. We ask God here to respond even when we lack a conscious understanding of how tragic our situation really is,

תשובה

הֲשִׁיבֵנוּ אָבִינוּ לְתוֹרָתֶךָ, וְקָרְבֵנוּ מַלְכֵּנוּ לַעֲבוֹדָתֶךָ
וְהַחֲזִירֵנוּ בִּתְשׁוּבָה שְׁלֵמָה לְפָנֶיךָ.
בָּרוּךְ אַתָּה יהוה, הָרוֹצֶה בִּתְשׁוּבָה.

סליחה

Strike the left side of the chest at °.

סְלַח לָנוּ אָבִינוּ כִּי °חָטָאנוּ
מְחַל לָנוּ מַלְכֵּנוּ כִּי °פָשָׁעְנוּ
כִּי מוֹחֵל וְסוֹלֵחַ אָתָּה.
בָּרוּךְ אַתָּה יהוה, חַנּוּן הַמַּרְבֶּה לִסְלֹחַ.

גאולה

רְאֵה בְעָנְיֵנוּ, וְרִיבָה רִיבֵנוּ
וּגְאָלֵנוּ מְהֵרָה לְמַעַן שְׁמֶךָ
כִּי גּוֹאֵל חָזָק אָתָּה.
בָּרוּךְ אַתָּה יהוה, גּוֹאֵל יִשְׂרָאֵל.

---

through superficial observation; for this, one needs a far view, a broad concept, and an especially deep intuition. The boundary between the sanctified and the ordinary is, after all, abstract; but one who is attentive can feel it. Deep in the Jewish soul, no matter how sunken in sin it is, there is something holy and mysterious which cannot be erased or eliminated, and upon which there lies the seal of individuality and originality. But in order to perceive this separation, one must be capable of peering into the depths of the soul. In Egypt, the Almighty had to distinguish between Israel and the nations at a time when there was hardly any contrast between Jew and Egyptian. Only God, the knower of thoughts, He who distinguishes inner things, saw the difference. "God saw the children of Israel and God knew" (Ex. 2:25). He saw sanctity in the abyss of the Jewish soul, even though it was full of profanity and sin, and therefore He saved His people.

HEALING

רְפָאֵנוּ Heal us, LORD, and we shall be healed.
Save us and we shall be saved,
for You are our praise.
Bring complete recovery for all our ailments,

The following prayer for a sick person may be said here:
May it be Your will, O LORD my God and God of my ancestors, that You speedily send a complete recovery from heaven, a healing of both soul and body, to the patient (*name*), son/daughter of (*mother's name*) among the other afflicted of Israel.

---

for You, God, King, are a faithful and compassionate Healer.
Blessed are You, LORD,
Healer of the sick of His people Israel.

PROSPERITY

בָּרֵךְ Bless this year for us, LORD our God,
and all its types of produce for good.
Grant dew and rain as a blessing
on the face of the earth, and from its goodness satisfy us,
blessing our year as the best of years.
Blessed are You, LORD,
who blesses the years.

טַל וּמָטָר לִבְרָכָה *Dew and rain as a blessing.* Judaism places great emphasis on detail. An ardent prayer, flowing from the depths of one's heart, saturated with zeal and fervor, is invalidated if the incorrect phrase is recited in the proper season. However, while *tefilla* is an example of Judaism's attention to detail, it is still an impassioned dialogue. Of course, the inner experience plays an important role in our worldview. But even when our hearts overflow with great passionate love, thought and action must be disciplined.

רפואה

רְפָאֵנוּ יהוה וְנֵרָפֵא
הוֹשִׁיעֵנוּ וְנִוָּשֵׁעָה, כִּי תְהִלָּתֵנוּ אָתָּה
וְהַעֲלֵה רְפוּאָה שְׁלֵמָה לְכָל מַכּוֹתֵינוּ

The following prayer for a sick person may be said here:

יְהִי רָצוֹן מִלְּפָנֶיךָ יהוה אֱלֹהַי וֵאלֹהֵי אֲבוֹתַי, שֶׁתִּשְׁלַח מְהֵרָה רְפוּאָה שְׁלֵמָה
מִן הַשָּׁמַיִם רְפוּאַת הַנֶּפֶשׁ וּרְפוּאַת הַגּוּף לַחוֹלֶה/לַחוֹלָה *name of patient*
בֶּן/בַּת *mother's name* בְּתוֹךְ שְׁאָר חוֹלֵי יִשְׂרָאֵל.

כִּי אֵל מֶלֶךְ רוֹפֵא נֶאֱמָן וְרַחֲמָן אָתָּה.
בָּרוּךְ אַתָּה יהוה, רוֹפֵא חוֹלֵי עַמּוֹ יִשְׂרָאֵל.

ברכת השנים

בָּרֵךְ עָלֵינוּ יהוה אֱלֹהֵינוּ אֶת הַשָּׁנָה הַזֹּאת
וְאֶת כָּל מִינֵי תְבוּאָתָהּ, לְטוֹבָה
וְתֵן טַל וּמָטָר לִבְרָכָה
עַל פְּנֵי הָאֲדָמָה, וְשַׂבְּעֵנוּ מִטּוּבָהּ
וּבָרֵךְ שְׁנָתֵנוּ כַּשָּׁנִים הַטּוֹבוֹת.
בָּרוּךְ אַתָּה יהוה, מְבָרֵךְ הַשָּׁנִים.

---

even if we cannot articulate or perhaps even recognize our own suffering. The experience of Abraham at Mount Moriah is an example of this. The Mishna (*Ta'anit* 2:4) invokes the idea of God responding to Abraham at Mount Moriah. Yet nowhere in the biblical narrative is there an indication that Abraham made any request of God during the *Akeda*. But God witnessed Abraham's silent, subconscious suffering, including pain of which even Abraham himself was unaware, and He answered him in his time of need.

INGATHERING OF EXILES

תְּקַע Sound the great shofar for our freedom,
raise high the banner to gather our exiles,
and gather us together from the four quarters of the earth.
Blessed are You, LORD,
who gathers the dispersed of His people Israel.

JUSTICE

הָשִׁיבָה Restore our judges as at first,
and our counselors as at the beginning,
and remove from us sorrow and sighing.
May You alone, LORD,
reign over us
with loving-kindness and compassion,
and vindicate us in justice.
Blessed are You, LORD,
the King who loves righteousness and justice.

AGAINST INFORMERS

וְלַמַּלְשִׁינִים For the slanderers let there be no hope,
and may all wickedness perish in an instant.
May all Your people's enemies swiftly be cut down.
May You swiftly uproot, crush, cast down
and humble the arrogant swiftly in our days.
Blessed are You, LORD,
who destroys enemies and humbles the arrogant.

---

that the Temple be rebuilt and that Messianic rule be implemented. However, as soon as we mention the ingathering of the exiles, we cannot go on to make the next requests until praying for the establishment of a system of perfect justice in order to defeat those who oppose it and highlight the triumph of those who are righteous in justice. Only after we make these requests can we ask that the Temple be rebuilt and the Messiah arrive.

וְלַמַּלְשִׁינִים *For the slanderers.* After the destruction of the Temple, many apostates made peace with the foreign oppressor and conspired against our people,

קבוץ גלויות

תְּקַע בְּשׁוֹפָר גָּדוֹל לְחֵרוּתֵנוּ, וְשָׂא נֵס לְקַבֵּץ גָּלֻיּוֹתֵינוּ

וְקַבְּצֵנוּ יַחַד מֵאַרְבַּע כַּנְפוֹת הָאָרֶץ.

בָּרוּךְ אַתָּה יהוה, מְקַבֵּץ נִדְחֵי עַמּוֹ יִשְׂרָאֵל.

השבת המשפט

הָשִׁיבָה שׁוֹפְטֵינוּ כְּבָרִאשׁוֹנָה, וְיוֹעֲצֵינוּ כְּבַתְּחִלָּה

וְהָסֵר מִמֶּנּוּ יָגוֹן וַאֲנָחָה

וּמְלֹךְ עָלֵינוּ אַתָּה יהוה לְבַדְּךָ בְּחֶסֶד וּבְרַחֲמִים

וְצַדְּקֵנוּ בַּמִּשְׁפָּט.

בָּרוּךְ אַתָּה יהוה, מֶלֶךְ אוֹהֵב צְדָקָה וּמִשְׁפָּט.

ברכת המינים

וְלַמַּלְשִׁינִים אַל תְּהִי תִקְוָה

וְכָל הָרִשְׁעָה כְּרֶגַע תֹּאבֵד

וְכָל אוֹיְבֵי עַמְּךָ מְהֵרָה יִכָּרֵתוּ

וְהַזֵּדִים מְהֵרָה תְעַקֵּר וּתְשַׁבֵּר וּתְמַגֵּר וְתַכְנִיעַ בִּמְהֵרָה בְיָמֵינוּ.

בָּרוּךְ אַתָּה יהוה, שׁוֹבֵר אוֹיְבִים וּמַכְנִיעַ זֵדִים.

מְקַבֵּץ נִדְחֵי עַמּוֹ יִשְׂרָאֵל *Who gathers the dispersed of His people Israel.* The Jews who are subjugated in exile are "the dispersed," cast off, physically oppressed. The dispersed are characterized by loneliness, isolation from the larger community, and even a danger of complete assimilation. However, God promised in the Torah (Deut. 30:4) that if a single Jew will be in distant exile, He will gather him from there. God refuses to abandon any Jew.

הָשִׁיבָה שׁוֹפְטֵינוּ *Restore our judges.* After initially laying out our individual needs, such as forgiveness, health and sustenance, the Amida addresses itself to Israel's communal redemption. Following the request for the ingathering of the exiles in the blessing of "תְּקַע בְּשׁוֹפָר גָּדוֹל, Sound the great shofar," it would have been logical to transition immediately to the blessings requesting

THE RIGHTEOUS

עַל הַצַּדִּיקִים To the righteous, the pious,
the elders of Your people the house of Israel,
the remnant of their scholars,
the righteous converts, and to us,
may Your compassion be aroused,
LORD our God.
Grant a good reward to all
who sincerely trust in Your name.
Set our lot with them,
so that we may never be ashamed,
for in You we trust.
Blessed are You, LORD,
who is the support and trust of the righteous.

---

of the tradition, need at least one individual who can connect the generations, who witnessed the lofty events of the distant past. We need to draw courage from tradition in the form of a living personality, serving as a bridge between fathers and sons. The trembling, wrinkled handshake with its rhythm of generations, the fatherly or motherly glance in which dwells the mystery of the past, the strains of a shaky voice in which eternity is preserved, these can tip the balance in favor of holiness against the profane.

סוֹפְרֵיהֶם *Their scholars.* In Talmudic literature, the word *sofer,* which literally means "scribe," carries the connotation of a scholar of the Oral Law. Biblical law is referred to as the words of Torah, while rabbinic decrees based on the Oral Law are often called the words of *sofrim,* scribes. The true scribes are those who instill the law within us, those who impart the Torah not on parchment, but rather on people's souls. The ability to do this is the signature of every great person in Jewish history. After the passing of Moses, a voice from heaven uttered the words: "וַיָּמָת מֹשֶׁה סַפְרָא רַבָּה דְיִשְׂרָאֵל, Moses died, the great scribe of Israel" (*Sota* 13b). The description of "great scribe" means that he wrote upon the hearts of his people, not just on scrolls. He etched the Torah into the very soul of the nation, into their hearts, with each generation passing the message to the next, each later generation being the "book" for the earlier one.

על הצדיקים

עַל הַצַּדִּיקִים וְעַל הַחֲסִידִים
וְעַל זִקְנֵי עַמְּךָ בֵּית יִשְׂרָאֵל
וְעַל פְּלֵיטַת סוֹפְרֵיהֶם
וְעַל גֵּרֵי הַצֶּדֶק, וְעָלֵינוּ
יֶהֱמוּ רַחֲמֶיךָ יהוה אֱלֹהֵינוּ
וְתֵן שָׂכָר טוֹב לְכָל הַבּוֹטְחִים בְּשִׁמְךָ בֶּאֱמֶת
וְשִׂים חֶלְקֵנוּ עִמָּהֶם
וּלְעוֹלָם לֹא נֵבוֹשׁ כִּי בְךָ בָּטָחְנוּ.
בָּרוּךְ אַתָּה יהוה, מִשְׁעָן וּמִבְטָח לַצַּדִּיקִים.

---

both spiritually and physically. A request with weighty consequences was therefore proclaimed by Rabban Gamliel (*Berakhot* 28b): "Is there anyone who can formulate a benediction [within the Amida] regarding the heretics?" The blessing could not be written by anyone who harbored hatred. The person chosen, Shmuel HaKatan, was entirely enveloped in the attribute of mercy. Only such a person could request of his Father in heaven the erasure of evil and the destruction of the heretics. Only Shmuel HaKatan, whose motto was: "If your enemy falls, do not rejoice" (Ethics of the Fathers 4:24) who was modest and unassuming, who never had the desire to settle accounts, who never complained about insults, was suitable to fulfill this task. If Rabban Gamliel had introduced this blessing himself, his enemies would have impugned his motives.

וְעַל פְּלֵיטַת סוֹפְרֵיהֶם *[To] the remnant of their scholars.* Why does the *berakha* here emphasize the remnant of a past generation? Why could it not have read simply, "And to the scholars"? The answer is that it does not matter how many scholars or leaders there are unless they can be linked to the great chain of tradition, unless they include a remnant of sages from our lofty past. Tradition includes not only theoretical innovations, abstract concepts, halakhic formulas and logical principles. It also involves feelings and reactions, reflecting an experiential continuity. In each and every era, we, the receivers

REBUILDING JERUSALEM

וְלִירוּשָׁלַיִם To Jerusalem, Your city, may You return in compassion,
and may You dwell in it as You promised.
May You rebuild it rapidly in our days
as an everlasting structure,
and install within it soon the throne of David.
Blessed are You, LORD,
who builds Jerusalem.

KINGDOM OF DAVID

אֶת צֶמַח May the offshoot of Your servant David soon flower,
and may his pride be raised high by Your salvation,
for we wait for Your salvation all day.
Blessed are You, LORD,
who makes the glory of salvation flourish.

RESPONSE TO PRAYER

שְׁמַע קוֹלֵנוּ Listen to our voice, LORD our God.
Spare us and have compassion on us,
and in compassion and favor accept our prayer,
for You, God, listen to prayers and pleas.
Do not turn us away, O our King,
empty-handed from Your presence,
for You listen with compassion
to the prayer of Your people Israel.
Blessed are You, LORD,
who listens to prayer.

Europe rather than immigrate to America. God in His compassion did not accept my prayer.

שׁוֹמֵעַ תְּפִלָּה *Who listens to prayer.* We have the assurance that God indeed hears our prayers, but not necessarily that He accedes to our specific requests. It is our persistent hope that our requests may be fulfilled, but it is not our primary motivation for prayer. In praying, we do not seek a response to a particular request as much as we desire a fellowship with God.

בניין ירושלים

וְלִירוּשָׁלַיִם עִירְךָ בְּרַחֲמִים תָּשׁוּב
וְתִשְׁכֹּן בְּתוֹכָהּ כַּאֲשֶׁר דִּבַּרְתָּ
וּבְנֵה אוֹתָהּ בְּקָרוֹב בְּיָמֵינוּ בִּנְיַן עוֹלָם
וְכִסֵּא דָוִד מְהֵרָה לְתוֹכָהּ תָּכִין.
בָּרוּךְ אַתָּה יהוה, בּוֹנֵה יְרוּשָׁלָיִם.

משיח בן דוד

אֶת צֶמַח דָּוִד עַבְדְּךָ מְהֵרָה תַצְמִיחַ
וְקַרְנוֹ תָּרוּם בִּישׁוּעָתֶךָ
כִּי לִישׁוּעָתְךָ קִוִּינוּ כָּל הַיּוֹם.
בָּרוּךְ אַתָּה יהוה, מַצְמִיחַ קֶרֶן יְשׁוּעָה.

שומע תפלה

שְׁמַע קוֹלֵנוּ יהוה אֱלֹהֵינוּ
חוּס וְרַחֵם עָלֵינוּ
וְקַבֵּל בְּרַחֲמִים וּבְרָצוֹן אֶת תְּפִלָּתֵנוּ
כִּי אֵל שׁוֹמֵעַ תְּפִלּוֹת וְתַחֲנוּנִים אָתָּה
וּמִלְּפָנֶיךָ מַלְכֵּנוּ רֵיקָם אַל תְּשִׁיבֵנוּ
כִּי אַתָּה שׁוֹמֵעַ תְּפִלַּת עַמְּךָ יִשְׂרָאֵל בְּרַחֲמִים.
בָּרוּךְ אַתָּה יהוה, שׁוֹמֵעַ תְּפִלָּה.

וְקַבֵּל בְּרַחֲמִים וּבְרָצוֹן אֶת תְּפִלָּתֵנוּ *And in compassion and favor accept our prayer.* Often a person can pray for something that is not ultimately in his best interest. We therefore ask that He accept only those requests that are for our ultimate good (that is, to accept only those prayers that are consistent with God's "compassion and favor"), and reject those that are not. In 1932, I fervently prayed for circumstances that would have allowed me to stay in

TEMPLE SERVICE

רְצֵה Find favor, LORD our God,
in Your people Israel and their prayer.
Restore the service to Your most holy House,
and accept in love and favor
the fire-offerings of Israel and their prayer.
May the service of Your people Israel always find favor with You.
And may our eyes witness
Your return to Zion in compassion.
Blessed are You, LORD,
who restores His Presence to Zion.

THANKSGIVING

Bow at the first nine words.

מוֹדִים We give thanks to You,
for You are the LORD our God and God of our ancestors
for ever and all time.
You are the Rock of our lives,
Shield of our salvation from generation to generation.

---

anyone who leaves the Temple is obligated to bow down. As we conclude the sacrificial service of *Retzeh*, we must bow at *Modim*. Similarly, Rabbi Yehuda HaLevi (*Kuzari* 3:19) highlights that at this juncture in the Amida, we are praying for the *Shekhina* to return to Jerusalem. We must, therefore, bow at *Modim* as if we were standing in the presence of the restored *Shekhina*.

מוֹדִים אֲנַחְנוּ לָךְ *We give thanks to You.* After the satisfaction of his request for the acceptance of his sacrifice, man thanks God for its fulfillment. He adopts the optimistic position that God has hearkened to his prayer. As God has accepted his great sacrifice surely his prayer shall emerge into the light. He is grateful for the past, and also for the future. He engages in thanksgiving and prayer, although the future is still wrapped in its mysterious secrecy. In this blessing, the experience of trust reaches its climax and the vision becomes reality, the desire becomes fact, the prayer becomes complete certitude; this trust is founded primarily on the absolute morality of divine activity. As He is

עבודה

רְצֵה יהוה אֱלֹהֵינוּ בְּעַמְּךָ יִשְׂרָאֵל, וּבִתְפִלָּתָם
וְהָשֵׁב אֶת הָעֲבוֹדָה לִדְבִיר בֵּיתֶךָ
וְאִשֵּׁי יִשְׂרָאֵל וּתְפִלָּתָם בְּאַהֲבָה תְקַבֵּל בְּרָצוֹן
וּתְהִי לְרָצוֹן תָּמִיד עֲבוֹדַת יִשְׂרָאֵל עַמֶּךָ.
וְתֶחֱזֶינָה עֵינֵינוּ בְּשׁוּבְךָ לְצִיּוֹן בְּרַחֲמִים.
בָּרוּךְ אַתָּה יהוה, הַמַּחֲזִיר שְׁכִינָתוֹ לְצִיּוֹן.

הודאה

Bow at the first five words.

מוֹדִים אֲנַחְנוּ לָךְ
שָׁאַתָּה הוּא יהוה אֱלֹהֵינוּ וֵאלֹהֵי אֲבוֹתֵינוּ לְעוֹלָם וָעֶד.
צוּר חַיֵּינוּ, מָגֵן יִשְׁעֵנוּ
אַתָּה הוּא לְדוֹר וָדוֹר.

וְאִשֵּׁי יִשְׂרָאֵל וּתְפִלָּתָם בְּאַהֲבָה תְקַבֵּל בְּרָצוֹן *And accept in love and favor the fire-offerings of Israel and their prayer.* According to one interpretation in Tosafot (*Menaḥot* 110a, s.v. *uMikha'el*), the phrase "the fire-offerings of Israel" is connected to the phrase "and their prayer." The reference is not to a physical fire-offering but to a transcendent offering. The sacrifice is the soul, the individual personal being of man, a sacrifice which continues to exist to this day, even after the cessation of the offerings in the Temple. Prayer is synonymous with sacrifice in this sense, as man offers his entire self before God. (*Worship of the Heart*)

מוֹדִים *We give thanks.* With the *berakha* of רְצֵה, "Find favor," there is a transition in the Amida from personal requests to sacrificial rites. As the Jew recites *Retzeh* and beseeches God to accept his sacrifices, he is no longer praying in his local synagogue in Warsaw, Vilna or New York. He is suddenly transported to Jerusalem, and his prayer is transformed into an offering in the *Beit HaMikdash.* The Vilna Gaon (*Aderet Eliyahu, Ki Tavo*) teaches that

We will thank You and declare Your praise for our lives,
which are entrusted into Your hand;
for our souls, which are placed in Your charge;
for Your miracles which are with us every day;
and for Your wonders and favors at all times,
evening, morning and midday.
You are good –
for Your compassion never fails.
You are compassionate –
for Your loving-kindnesses never cease.
We have always placed our hope in You.

עַל הַנִּסִּים [We thank You also] for the miracles,
the redemption, the mighty deeds, the salvations,
and the victories in battle which You performed for our ancestors
in those days at this time.
In the days of Mordekhai and Esther,
in Shushan the capital, the wicked Haman rose up against them
and sought to destroy, slay and exterminate all the Jews, *Esther 3*
young and old, children and women, on one day,

God's redemption generates a need to prospectively thank Him for the result we are confident will come about.

בִּימֵי מָרְדְּכַי וְאֶסְתֵּר *In the days of Mordekhai and Esther.* In the *Al HaNissim* prayer of Purim, there is nothing mentioned of Mordekhai and Esther's role in the unfolding of the dramatic events about which the Megilla tells us. We know from the Megilla that Mordekhai took the initiative and Esther was ready to sacrifice herself. But in *Al HaNissim,* the names of Mordekhai and Esther are mentioned only as an indication of the period during which the events transpired. In this respect, the liturgy is creating a resemblance between Purim and another event in which human action is not mentioned – the exodus from Egypt, *Yetziat Mitzrayim.* On Pesaḥ night, we read the Haggada, but we emphasize that Moses played no role. We read, "And the Lord brought us forth out of Egypt – not through an angel… not through a messenger, but the Holy One, blessed be He, alone and in His glory."

נוֹדֶה לְּךָ וּנְסַפֵּר תְּהִלָּתֶךָ
עַל חַיֵּינוּ הַמְּסוּרִים בְּיָדֶךָ
וְעַל נִשְׁמוֹתֵינוּ הַפְּקוּדוֹת לָךְ
וְעַל נִסֶּיךָ שֶׁבְּכָל יוֹם עִמָּנוּ
וְעַל נִפְלְאוֹתֶיךָ וְטוֹבוֹתֶיךָ שֶׁבְּכָל עֵת
עֶרֶב וָבֹקֶר וְצָהֳרָיִם.
הַטּוֹב, כִּי לֹא כָלוּ רַחֲמֶיךָ
וְהַמְרַחֵם, כִּי לֹא תַמּוּ חֲסָדֶיךָ
מֵעוֹלָם קִוִּינוּ לָךְ.

עַל הַנִּסִּים וְעַל הַפֻּרְקָן וְעַל הַגְּבוּרוֹת
וְעַל הַתְּשׁוּעוֹת וְעַל הַמִּלְחָמוֹת שֶׁעָשִׂיתָ לַאֲבוֹתֵינוּ
בַּיָּמִים הָהֵם בַּזְּמַן הַזֶּה.
בִּימֵי מָרְדְּכַי וְאֶסְתֵּר בְּשׁוּשַׁן הַבִּירָה
כְּשֶׁעָמַד עֲלֵיהֶם הָמָן הָרָשָׁע
בִּקֵּשׁ לְהַשְׁמִיד לַהֲרֹג וּלְאַבֵּד אֶת־כָּל־הַיְּהוּדִים אסתר ג
מִנַּעַר וְעַד־זָקֵן טַף וְנָשִׁים בְּיוֹם אֶחָד

infinitely merciful, His goodness is unconditional and unlimited, why should He not come to the aid of an abashed, downtrodden person who reaches out to Him? (*Worship of the Heart*)

וְעַל הַמִּלְחָמוֹת *And the victories in battle [lit. the wars]*. Why do we thank God for our wars? Would we not be better off without them? Some have an alternative text which reads וְעַל הַתְּשׁוּעוֹת עַל הַמִּלְחָמוֹת, without the *vav*. This would thank God for His effecting our salvation of the wars. *Beit HaLevi* (*Parashat Beshallaḥ*, s.v. *az yashir*) explains that when we thank God for saving us, we must also thank Him for the crisis that necessitated the salvation, because the entire process glorifies God's name. Even during the wars, our belief in

the thirteenth day of the twelfth month, which is the month of Adar,
and to plunder their possessions. Then You in Your great
compassion thwarted his counsel, frustrated his plans,
and caused his scheme to recoil on his own head,
so that they hanged him and his sons on the gallows.

וְעַל כֻּלָּם For all these things may Your name be blessed and
exalted, our King, continually, for ever and all time.
Let all that lives thank You, Selah! and praise Your name in truth,
God, our Savior and Help, Selah!
▾Blessed are You, LORD, whose name is "the Good"
and to whom thanks are due.

PEACE

שָׁלוֹם רָב Grant great peace to Your people Israel for ever,
for You are the sovereign LORD of all peace;
and may it be good in Your eyes
to bless Your people Israel
at every time, at every hour, with Your peace.
Blessed are You, LORD, who blesses His people Israel with peace.

---

nature, then the initiative belongs to man. Man engages in the struggle for spiritual survival. For this reason, the Hasmoneans took the initiative, and we remember their efforts when we commemorate their victory on Ḥanukka. (*Days of Deliverance*)

שָׁלוֹם רָב עַל יִשְׂרָאֵל עַמְּךָ תָּשִׂים *Grant great peace to Your people Israel.* After all the transformations and oscillations during the Amida – from feelings of love and mercy to the sense of dread and helplessness, after the descent from the heights of yearning and aspiration to the depths of confusion and terror, after self-negation and self-recovery, after the sacrifice and then the return to mundane reality – we come back once again to a calm and delightful experience, full of joy and confidence. God appears as a safe haven, a secure abode. The worshiper lies down in green pastures (Ps. 23:2), close to Him as a son to his father. His torn and troubled soul finds happiness and serenity. His fear and anxiety are forgotten; the awesome mystery is gone. In their place

בִּשְׁלוֹשָׁה עָשָׂר לְחֹדֶשׁ שְׁנֵים־עָשָׂר, הוּא־חֹדֶשׁ אֲדָר
וּשְׁלָלָם לָבוֹז: וְאַתָּה בְּרַחֲמֶיךָ הָרַבִּים הֵפַרְתָּ אֶת עֲצָתוֹ
וְקִלְקַלְתָּ אֶת מַחֲשַׁבְתּוֹ, וַהֲשֵׁבוֹתָ לּוֹ גְּמוּלוֹ בְּרֹאשׁוֹ,
וְתָלוּ אוֹתוֹ וְאֶת בָּנָיו עַל הָעֵץ.

וְעַל כֻּלָּם יִתְבָּרַךְ וְיִתְרוֹמַם שִׁמְךָ מַלְכֵּנוּ תָּמִיד לְעוֹלָם וָעֶד.
וְכֹל הַחַיִּים יוֹדוּךָ סֶּלָה, וִיהַלְלוּ אֶת שִׁמְךָ בֶּאֱמֶת
הָאֵל יְשׁוּעָתֵנוּ וְעֶזְרָתֵנוּ סֶלָה.
·בָּרוּךְ אַתָּה יהוה, הַטּוֹב שִׁמְךָ וּלְךָ נָאֶה לְהוֹדוֹת.

ברכת שלום

שָׁלוֹם רָב עַל יִשְׂרָאֵל עַמְּךָ תָּשִׂים לְעוֹלָם
כִּי אַתָּה הוּא מֶלֶךְ אָדוֹן לְכָל הַשָּׁלוֹם.
וְטוֹב בְּעֵינֶיךָ לְבָרֵךְ אֶת עַמְּךָ יִשְׂרָאֵל
בְּכָל עֵת וּבְכָל שָׁעָה בִּשְׁלוֹמֶךָ.
בָּרוּךְ אַתָּה יהוה, הַמְבָרֵךְ אֶת עַמּוֹ יִשְׂרָאֵל בַּשָּׁלוֹם.

When there is a physical menace or the threat of physical destruction, God uses the human hand as an instrument of His will. He recruits man. He uses human energy, human resources, to implement the plan that He has devised. But Judaism has said that in this case, the man who is the messenger of God should not be credited with the salvation. No matter how much the human being accomplishes as far as political and material achievements are concerned, he cannot attribute them to himself. He must not claim credit, because the worst sin is to say: "My power and the might of my hand has gotten me this wealth" (Deut. 8:17). That is idolatry.

On Purim we celebrate a physical victory. In the liturgy we make no mention of Mordekhai and Esther's deeds because, if the achievements are in the realm of military conquest and of a material nature, victory should be attributed to the Almighty. On Ḥanukka, the story was different. Antiochus was interested in destroying the Jews spiritually. When the menace is of a spiritual

Some say the following verse:
May the words of my mouth and the meditation of my heart Ps. 19
find favor before You, LORD, my Rock and Redeemer.

אֱלֹהַי My God, Berakhot 17a
guard my tongue from evil and my lips from deceitful speech.
To those who curse me, let my soul be silent;
may my soul be to all like the dust.
Open my heart to Your Torah
and let my soul pursue Your commandments.
As for all who plan evil against me,
swiftly thwart their counsel and frustrate their plans.
Act for the sake of Your name; act for the sake of Your right hand;
act for the sake of Your holiness; act for the sake of Your Torah.
That Your beloved ones may be delivered, Ps. 60
save with Your right hand and answer me.
May the words of my mouth Ps. 19
and the meditation of my heart find favor before You,
LORD, my Rock and Redeemer.

Bow, take three steps back, then bow, first left, then right, then center, while saying:
May He who makes peace in His high places,
make peace for us and all Israel – and say: Amen.

וְלִמְקַלְלַי נַפְשִׁי תִדֹּם *To those who curse me, let my soul be silent.* A Jew entreats God thrice daily at the conclusion of his silent prayer: "To those who curse me, let my soul be silent; may my soul be to all like the dust." The Jew is a proud being who is aware of his mission and responsibilities. He does not enjoy abuse and ridicule. However, he knows that one who is spiritually different cannot escape humiliating situations, for his existential experience is incommensurate with the feelings and sentiments of others. Realizing one's destiny demands the ability to suffer disapproval and anguish at the hands of the crowd. (*Abraham's Journey*)

עוֹשֶׂה שָׁלוֹם בִּמְרוֹמָיו הוּא יַעֲשֶׂה שָׁלוֹם עָלֵינוּ *May He Who makes peace in His high places, make peace for us.* The Talmud (*Derekh Eretz Zuta, Perek HaShalom*) explains the verse upon which this phrase is based (Job 25:2) to mean that God

Some say the following verse:

תהלים יט יִהְיוּ לְרָצוֹן אִמְרֵי־פִי וְהֶגְיוֹן לִבִּי לְפָנֶיךָ, יהוה צוּרִי וְגוֹאֲלִי:

ברכות יז. אֱלֹהַי

נְצֹר לְשׁוֹנִי מֵרָע וּשְׂפָתַי מִדַּבֵּר מִרְמָה

וְלִמְקַלְלַי נַפְשִׁי תִדֹּם, וְנַפְשִׁי כֶּעָפָר לַכֹּל תִּהְיֶה.

פְּתַח לִבִּי בְּתוֹרָתֶךָ, וּבְמִצְוֹתֶיךָ תִּרְדֹּף נַפְשִׁי.

וְכָל הַחוֹשְׁבִים עָלַי רָעָה

מְהֵרָה הָפֵר עֲצָתָם וְקַלְקֵל מַחֲשַׁבְתָּם.

עֲשֵׂה לְמַעַן שְׁמֶךָ, עֲשֵׂה לְמַעַן יְמִינֶךָ

עֲשֵׂה לְמַעַן קְדֻשָּׁתֶךָ, עֲשֵׂה לְמַעַן תּוֹרָתֶךָ.

תהלים ס לְמַעַן יֵחָלְצוּן יְדִידֶיךָ, הוֹשִׁיעָה יְמִינְךָ וַעֲנֵנִי:

תהלים יט יִהְיוּ לְרָצוֹן אִמְרֵי־פִי וְהֶגְיוֹן לִבִּי לְפָנֶיךָ, יהוה צוּרִי וְגוֹאֲלִי:

Bow, take three steps back, then bow, first left, then right, then center, while saying:

עֹשֶׂה שָׁלוֹם בִּמְרוֹמָיו

הוּא יַעֲשֶׂה שָׁלוֹם עָלֵינוּ וְעַל כָּל יִשְׂרָאֵל, וְאִמְרוּ אָמֵן.

---

reigns happiness, and the desire for communion with the Source of all existence. Man does not flee from God; rather, he runs toward Him, embraces Him, nestles close to the Divine Presence. All is surrounded by peace and quiet. The blessings and bounty of the Infinite One descend on all creation. (*Worship of the Heart*)

יִהְיוּ לְרָצוֹן אִמְרֵי־פִי *May the words of my mouth… find favor.* The opening request of the Amida, "O Lord, open my lips," suggests that we need God's help to formulate prayer. From a mood of hope and confidence in the ultimate redemption, articulated in the last blessing of the Shema, we immediately start the Amida on a note of apprehension. Jews have always operated within the dialectic, combining opposites. At the end of the Amida, we once again regain our mood of optimism, stating: "May the words of my mouth and the meditation of my heart find favor before You, Lord, my Rock and Redeemer," confident that our prayer is indeed acceptable.

יְהִי רָצוֹן May it be Your will, LORD our God and God of our ancestors,
that the Temple be rebuilt speedily in our days, and grant us a share in Your Torah.
And there we will serve You with reverence,
as in the days of old and as in former years.
Then the offering of Judah and Jerusalem *Mal. 3*
will be pleasing to the LORD as in the days of old and as in former years.

FULL KADDISH

Leader: יִתְגַּדַּל Magnified and sanctified may His great name be,
in the world He created by His will.
May He establish His kingdom
in your lifetime and in your days,
and in the lifetime of all the house of Israel,
swiftly and soon –
and say: Amen.

All: May His great name be blessed for ever and all time.

Leader: Blessed and praised,
glorified and exalted,
raised and honored,
uplifted and lauded be
the name of the Holy One,
blessed be He, beyond any blessing,
song, praise and consolation
uttered in the world –
and say: Amen. ◂

---

there is no dichotomy; all opposites are reconciled, all contradictions are resolved. In Him, thesis and antithesis merge into one; in Him, there is only harmony and peace. After concluding the Amida and stepping backwards, we pray that the great eschatological era will soon arrive so that mankind too may achieve this harmony.

יְהִי רָצוֹן מִלְּפָנֶיךָ יהוה אֱלֹהֵינוּ וֵאלֹהֵי אֲבוֹתֵינוּ
שֶׁיִּבָּנֶה בֵּית הַמִּקְדָּשׁ בִּמְהֵרָה בְיָמֵינוּ, וְתֵן חֶלְקֵנוּ בְּתוֹרָתֶךָ
וְשָׁם נַעֲבָדְךָ בְּיִרְאָה כִּימֵי עוֹלָם וּכְשָׁנִים קַדְמֹנִיּוֹת.
וְעָרְבָה לַיהוה מִנְחַת יְהוּדָה וִירוּשָׁלָםִ כִּימֵי עוֹלָם וּכְשָׁנִים קַדְמֹנִיּוֹת: מלאכי ג

קדיש שלם

ש״ץ: יִתְגַּדַּל וְיִתְקַדַּשׁ שְׁמֵהּ רַבָּא (קהל: אָמֵן)
בְּעָלְמָא דִּי בְרָא כִרְעוּתֵהּ
וְיַמְלִיךְ מַלְכוּתֵהּ
בְּחַיֵּיכוֹן וּבְיוֹמֵיכוֹן וּבְחַיֵּי דְכָל בֵּית יִשְׂרָאֵל
בַּעֲגָלָא וּבִזְמַן קָרִיב, וְאִמְרוּ אָמֵן. (קהל: אָמֵן)

קהל וש״ץ: יְהֵא שְׁמֵהּ רַבָּא מְבָרַךְ לְעָלַם וּלְעָלְמֵי עָלְמַיָּא.

ש״ץ: יִתְבָּרַךְ וְיִשְׁתַּבַּח וְיִתְפָּאַר וְיִתְרוֹמַם וְיִתְנַשֵּׂא
וְיִתְהַדָּר וְיִתְעַלֶּה וְיִתְהַלָּל
שְׁמֵהּ דְּקֻדְשָׁא בְּרִיךְ הוּא (קהל: בְּרִיךְ הוּא)
לְעֵלָּא מִן כָּל בִּרְכָתָא וְשִׁירָתָא, תֻּשְׁבְּחָתָא וְנֶחֱמָתָא
דַּאֲמִירָן בְּעָלְמָא, וְאִמְרוּ אָמֵן. (קהל: אָמֵן) ◂

makes peace between the angels Gabriel and Michael. Each angel represents one of God's attributes. The angel Michael represents *ḥesed,* loving-kindness, and hence forgiveness and compassion. The angel Gabriel represents the opposite attribute: *din,* justice, and hence strictness, punishment and sometimes retribution. Despite the endless divide separating these two representatives of mutually exclusive traits, God is able to make peace between them. In God,

May the prayers and pleas of all Israel
be accepted by their Father in heaven –
and say: Amen.

May there be great peace from heaven,
and life for us and all Israel –
and say: Amen.

Bow, take three steps back, as if taking leave of the Divine Presence, then bow, first left, then right, then center, while saying:

May He who makes peace in His high places,
make peace for us and all Israel –
and say: Amen.

---

that relate to Jewish destiny and the ultimate redemption. An enigmatic verse in Isaiah (21:12) can be similarly explained: "אָמַר שֹׁמֵר אָתָה בֹקֶר וְגַם לָיְלָה אִם תִּבְעָיוּן בְּעָיוּ, The watchman said, 'The morning comes, and also the night. If you will inquire, inquire.'" The meaning of the phrase in Isaiah: "אִם־תִּבְעָיוּן בְּעָיוּ, If you will inquire, inquire," is that the dawn of our salvation will break – even though we are in the midst of a dark, bitter night of exile – if our vision is not limited to the present and immediate circumstances, but rather encompasses the boundless opportunities of redemption in the future. If our view is not riveted in current historical circumstances, but rather glimpses our future destiny, salvation is at hand.

תִּתְקַבַּל צְלוֹתְהוֹן וּבָעוּתְהוֹן דְּכָל יִשְׂרָאֵל
קֳדָם אֲבוּהוֹן דִּי בִשְׁמַיָּא
וְאִמְרוּ אָמֵן. (קהל: אָמֵן)

יְהֵא שְׁלָמָא רַבָּא מִן שְׁמַיָּא
וְחַיִּים, עָלֵינוּ וְעַל כָּל יִשְׂרָאֵל
וְאִמְרוּ אָמֵן. (קהל: אָמֵן)

Bow, take three steps back, as if taking leave of the Divine Presence, then bow, first left, then right, then center, while saying:

עֹשֶׂה שָׁלוֹם בִּמְרוֹמָיו
הוּא יַעֲשֶׂה שָׁלוֹם עָלֵינוּ וְעַל כָּל יִשְׂרָאֵל
וְאִמְרוּ אָמֵן. (קהל: אָמֵן)

צְלוֹתְהוֹן וּבָעוּתְהוֹן *Prayers and pleas.* In his blessing to Joseph, Jacob refers to land that he had taken from the Amorites "בְּחַרְבִּי וּבְקַשְׁתִּי, with my sword and with my bow" (Gen. 48:22). Since there is no record of Jacob ever having done battle with the Amorites, the *Targum* translates these two words metaphorically as "בִּצְלוֹתִי וּבְבָעוּתִי, with my prayer and with my plea." The distinction between the sword and the bow is that the sword is used for close combat, while the bow and arrow are utilized from a distance. Correspondingly, צְלוֹתְהוֹן prayers, are our requests for immediate personal needs, such as wisdom, health and sustenance, while בָּעוּתְהוֹן, pleas, are the supplications

מגילת אסתר

MEGILLAT ESTHER

The story of Esther tells us in the most lively, realistic fashion, with a tinge of refined yet biting sarcasm, about paradoxical, absurd events, which are both tragic and comical at the same time. It is a strange story, both sad and funny, about a king, neither wicked nor cruel per se, who signed, upon the spur of the moment, a decree to exterminate a people he did not know, without even inquiring as to their identity, and a short time later forgot the whole incident and became very indignant over Haman's foul conspiracy. It is a story about a commonwealth where many races lived, many languages were spoken, many rituals practiced, a pluralistic society, culturally and religiously, which suddenly decided to commit genocide for one reason only: the people who were to be exterminated were abiding by religious statutes and laws that differed from those of other people. It is a puzzling story about millions and millions of people, about countless liberal-minded, decent individuals who indifferently accepted the satanic, bloodthirsty, murderous royal edict, without even asking themselves, Can we tolerate that? Can we stand by and witness the extermination of a people? It is a story about a conspiracy of silence agreed to by the entire citizenry of the great Persian empire. A short time before, the entire population was invited to the seven-day feast on the grounds of the royal palace. The invitations were extended to everybody, Jew and gentile alike, to all races and faiths, "for all the men of the imperial city, Shushan, from the greatest to the lowliest" (1:5). The invited guests fraternized, drank toasts, shook hands, and hugged each other. A little later, the ruthless, inhuman edict was issued and sent hastily with the couriers to all parts of the commonwealth "that they wipe out, kill and destroy all the Jews, young and old, children and women alike, all in one day" (3:13). The king and Haman celebrated by feasting on wine! How is it possible? The answer to this riddle can be found in our philosophy of man as a dual, dichotomous being, burdened with an inner contradiction.

On the one hand, Judaism looks upon man with a sympathetic, appreciative eye – indeed with admiration. He is the king of all creatures. Judaism has time and again expressed faith in man and belief in human uniqueness, in man's royal status, in his contemplative, meditative power. After all, he is the only rational being in the universe. In a word: he is a great figure.

That this thesis is correct, that Judaism is optimistic about man and his nature, can be attested by our stand on human freedom. Judaism has declared without any reservations that the human being enjoys unrestricted moral freedom. God does not interfere with man's liberty to plot his own existential course. Apparently, man is deserving of freedom. It has not been granted to any other creature.

On the other hand, Judaism has also treated man with extreme caution, alas suspicion. The Judaic skepticism concerning man is due to our historical experience and memory – that man, though endowed with divine rationality, may turn at a moment's notice into either a non-rational or an irrational being. That is why Judaism took all the extravagance of man in stride. It has never been stunned, amazed, or aghast watching the latter suddenly run amok. In the opinion of Judaism, there is no element of surprise in man's abrupt changes and transformations; his unpredictability is a part of his humanity, and I would say that his unpredictability is quite predictable. (Days of Deliverance)

SERVICE FOR PURIM

Before the reading of the Megilla, the congregation stands and the Reader says the following three blessings:

בָּרוּךְ Blessed are You, Lord our God, King of the Universe,
who has made us holy through His commandments,
and has commanded us about reading the Megilla.

בָּרוּךְ Blessed are You, Lord our God, King of the Universe,
who performed miracles for our ancestors in those days at this time.

בָּרוּךְ Blessed are You, Lord our God, King of the Universe,
who has given us life, sustained us, and brought us to this time.

---

lighting, and "*asher ge'alanu*" for the four cups of the Seder. The fact that no such blessing was enacted for sitting in the *sukka* demonstrates that in this case, *pirsumei nisa* is not a component of the mitzva.

שֶׁהֶחֱיָנוּ וְקִיְּמָנוּ וְהִגִּיעָנוּ לַזְּמַן הַזֶּה *who has given us life, sustained us, and brought us to this time.* There is a dispute between Maimonides and Ri about whether one recites the *berakha* of *sheheḥeyanu* during the daytime reading of the Megilla. Maimonides (*Hilkhot Megilla* 1:3) writes that since *sheheḥeyanu* has already been recited at night, we do not say it again during the day. Ri (Tosafot, *Megilla* 4a) argues that since the primary requirement for publicizing the miracle is during the day (and the obligation to eat the Purim *seuda* is during the day as well), one is obligated to recite *sheheḥeyanu* at night and again during the daytime reading.

We can offer another explanation for the repetition of *sheheḥeyanu* during the day based on the Gemara's explanation as to why we do not recite Hallel on Purim (*Megilla* 14a). Rav Naḥman taught that the reading of the Megilla itself is like the recitation of Hallel. According to Rav Naḥman, there is a special fulfillment to the daytime reading of the Megilla which does not exist at night. Since Hallel is generally only recited during the day, the daytime reading of the Megilla contains an additional aspect of Hallel and *tefilla*, and it is for that new aspect of the mitzva that we recite *sheheḥeyanu*.

סדר קריאת המגילה בפורים

Before the reading of the מגילה*, the* קהל *stands and the* קורא *says the following three blessings:*

בָּרוּךְ אַתָּה יהוה אֱלֹהֵינוּ מֶלֶךְ הָעוֹלָם
אֲשֶׁר קִדְּשָׁנוּ בְּמִצְוֹתָיו וְצִוָּנוּ עַל מִקְרָא מְגִלָּה.

בָּרוּךְ אַתָּה יהוה אֱלֹהֵינוּ מֶלֶךְ הָעוֹלָם
שֶׁעָשָׂה נִסִּים לַאֲבוֹתֵינוּ בַּיָּמִים הָהֵם בַּזְּמַן הַזֶּה.

בָּרוּךְ אַתָּה יהוה אֱלֹהֵינוּ מֶלֶךְ הָעוֹלָם
שֶׁהֶחֱיָנוּ וְקִיְּמָנוּ וְהִגִּיעָנוּ לַזְּמַן הַזֶּה.

שֶׁעָשָׂה נִסִּים לַאֲבוֹתֵינוּ בַּיָּמִים הָהֵם בַּזְּמַן הַזֶּה *who performed miracles for our ancestors in those days at this time.* Although women are generally exempt from positive time-bound commandments, they are nonetheless obligated to read the Megilla, light Ḥanukka candles, and drink the four cups at the Seder. The Talmud relates that the source for these three commandments is that "they too were part of the miracle" that transpired on each of these three holidays (*af hen hayu be'oto ha'nes*). *Tosafot* (*Pesaḥim* 108b s.v. *hayu*) ask why women are not thereby obligated in the mitzva to sit in the *sukka,* as its obligation stems from the *sukkot* in which all of the Jews dwelled upon leaving Egypt. As such, why should women not be included in the mitzva by virtue of the principle of *af hen hayu be'oto ha'nes*?

Perhaps it can be argued that the obligation of women because of their part in the miracle that transpired applies only to the mitzvot whose essence is that of *pirsumei nisa,* publicizing the miracle. With regard to reading the Megilla, lighting Ḥanukka lights, and drinking the four cups at the Seder, the commemoration of the miracle is not merely the reason for the mitzva, it is an intrinsic part of the obligation. Sitting in the *sukka,* however, although commemorative of the miracle that transpired, is not an obligation of *pirsumei nisa. Ḥazal* enacted a specific blessing for all mitzvot whose essence is that of *pirsumei nisa,* namely that of "*she'asa nisim*" for Megilla reading and Ḥanukka

It is customary for the congregation to say aloud the passages marked by arrows, followed by the Reader.

1 1 It happened in the days of Ahasuerus; Ahasuerus who ruled a hundred and
2 twenty-seven provinces – from India to Ethiopia. At that time, when King
3 Ahasuerus sat upon his royal throne in the imperial city of Shushan, in the
third year of his rule, he made a feast for all his ministers and courtiers, the
military men of Persia and Medea, the noblemen and the ministers of the
4 provinces, all coming before him. And there, for many days together, one
hundred and eighty days in all, he displayed all the wealth of his noble reign,
and the glory of his dazzling greatness.

5 When that time had passed, the king held a feast for all the men of the
imperial city, Shushan, from the greatest to the lowliest, in the courtyard
6 of the king's palace garden. There were swathes of fine white fabric there, of
precious cotton and sky blue wool, all corded with strands of the finest linen
and scarlet, and draped over silver bars and columns of marble; and there
were couches of gold and silver, arranged on a terrace paved with alabaster

---

He was involved in solidifying his empire, and he judged every event in terms of how it would affect his rule over his kingdom. Had Ahasuerus been sure of himself, he would have acted differently. (*Days of Deliverance*)

עָשָׂה מִשְׁתֶּה לְכָל שָׂרָיו וַעֲבָדָיו *he made a feast for all his ministers and courtiers.* The Jew is involved in events which at the outset seemed to have no relevance to him. When the curtain rises on Act I of the drama, we see on the stage a half-drunk mob feasting, indulging, and passing judgment on the beauty of the women. As events progress we see a proud queen refusing to obey the order issued by her lord and master and the punishment which was meted out to her. *Prima facie,* these events are of no relevance to the hundreds of thousands of Jews who lived in the Persian empire. However, as we continue reading we discover the significance of these events and their relatedness to our people. The conclusion is obvious. There are no neutral events in human history which the Jew may dismiss as irrelevant. The Jew is totally involved in all events and in all major struggles. Even now, the future welfare of the Jew is dependent upon the outcome of the titanic struggle between East and West. Even the final redemption of our people will be precipitated by the apocalyptic battle between Gog and Magog. Providence involves the Jew in great events. Willy nilly, the Jew plays his part on the universal historical stage.

It is customary for the congregation to say aloud the passages marked by arrows, followed by the Reader.

א א וַיְהִי בִּימֵי אֲחַשְׁוֵרוֹשׁ הוּא אֲחַשְׁוֵרוֹשׁ הַמֹּלֵךְ מֵהֹדּוּ וְעַד־כּוּשׁ שֶׁבַע
ב וְעֶשְׂרִים וּמֵאָה מְדִינָה: בַּיָּמִים הָהֵם כְּשֶׁבֶת ׀ הַמֶּלֶךְ אֲחַשְׁוֵרוֹשׁ עַל
ג כִּסֵּא מַלְכוּתוֹ אֲשֶׁר בְּשׁוּשַׁן הַבִּירָה: בִּשְׁנַת שָׁלוֹשׁ לְמָלְכוֹ עָשָׂה
מִשְׁתֶּה לְכָל־שָׂרָיו וַעֲבָדָיו חֵיל ׀ פָּרַס וּמָדַי הַפַּרְתְּמִים וְשָׂרֵי הַמְּדִינוֹת
ד לְפָנָיו: בְּהַרְאֹתוֹ אֶת־עֹשֶׁר כְּבוֹד מַלְכוּתוֹ וְאֶת־יְקָר תִּפְאֶרֶת גְּדוּלָּתוֹ
ה יָמִים רַבִּים שְׁמוֹנִים וּמְאַת יוֹם: וּבִמְלוֹאת ׀ הַיָּמִים הָאֵלֶּה עָשָׂה
הַמֶּלֶךְ לְכָל־הָעָם הַנִּמְצְאִים בְּשׁוּשַׁן הַבִּירָה לְמִגָּדוֹל וְעַד־קָטָן
ו מִשְׁתֶּה שִׁבְעַת יָמִים בַּחֲצַר גִּנַּת בִּיתַן הַמֶּלֶךְ: חוּר ׀ כַּרְפַּס וּתְכֵלֶת
אָחוּז בְּחַבְלֵי־בוּץ וְאַרְגָּמָן עַל־גְּלִילֵי כֶסֶף וְעַמּוּדֵי שֵׁשׁ מִטּוֹת ׀

וַיְהִי בִּימֵי אֲחַשְׁוֵרוֹשׁ *It happened in the days of Ahasuerus.* The Bible here is not concerned with a coincidence in time. The Bible is interested in a more relevant question: what precipitated such an event? Why did it happen? Who is responsible for the absurd tragedy that almost destroyed an entire community? The answer is: "Now it came to pass in the days of Ahasuerus." All these events happened – and could have happened – *only* in the days of Ahasuerus. Only in his time, under his reign, owing to his paradoxical mentality was such a tragicomical experience possible. "It happened in the days of Ahasuerus" should be interpreted in the following manner: it happened *because* Ahasuerus ruled in those days.

I believe that the phrase הוּא אֲחַשְׁוֵרוֹשׁ, literally, "this is Ahasuerus," confirms our interpretation of the verse, that only in the days of Ahasuerus could such events occur. They could not have taken place during the rule of someone else. "This is Ahasuerus"; he is known to all of us. Only his erratic, strange character brought all this about. In fact, the Bible points out two causes of the events: first, as we have said, the neurotic personality of Ahasuerus. Second, Ahasuerus was involved in establishing his empire from India to Ethiopia. The term הַמֹּלֵךְ can be translated as a participle, "who was ruling," which has the connotation of attempting to rule, of subjugating, of organizing the government, of being fearful of failure. The fact that Ahasuerus was not yet firmly entrenched is responsible for many of the strange events.

7 and marble, with mother of pearl and black onyx. And the guests were served
their drink in vessels of gold – vessels unlike any other – royal wine, abundant
8 as the king's largesse. And the drinking was strictly without duress; for so
the king had instructed all the overseers of his home: to honor the wishes
of each and every man.

9 Meanwhile, Vashti the queen made a feast of her own; a women's feast, in
10 King Ahasuerus' royal palace. And on the seventh day of the feasts, when the
king had grown merry with wine, he instructed Mehuman, Bizta, Ḥarvona,
Bigta and Avagta, Zeitar and Karkas – the seven eunuchs who attended the

---

attains the finale is called "*atzeret*," a day of restraint, of complete dedication to God. "On the seventh day shall be an *atzeret* to the Lord your God" (Deut. 16:8). The great ideal of standing before God is achieved on the seventh day. (*Days of Deliverance*)

כְּטוֹב לֵב הַמֶּלֶךְ בַּיָּיִן *when the king had grown merry with wine.* Emotional life is, of course, stimulated by imbibing alcoholic beverages. However, the stimulation may drag man down into the gutter. It may also – if the drinking is moderate – raise man emotionally. Wine sometimes arouses noble emotions in man by making him more sensitive and responsive. The Torah taught the Jew how to feast with responsibility.

The Torah is setting out to teach man how to act. There are two alternatives: either to act like Ahasuerus or to act the way one would in the presence of God. When one drinks wine in the latter case, the nervous system is stimulated, the sensitivity enhanced, emotions aroused but disciplined. There is a longing for something beautiful and fascinating. Man is under emotional pressure; he wants to release tension. He sings a song to the Almighty: "We do not sanctify [the Sabbath] except over wine" (*Pesaḥim* 107a). What does a Jew do on Passover night when he fills his fourth cup? Does he engage in idle, coarse talk? No. He recites the Hallel. At this juncture, we are reminded of the Jewish concept of the meal: the *seuda*. It is a very strange institution. The *seuda* combines two contradictory elements: on the one hand, eating, drinking, gratifying an animal, instinctual drive, a profane, primitive function; and on the other hand, the offering of a sacrifice, for the table is the altar and taking a meal is a sacerdotal act, a service. How is it possible to combine these two mutually exclusive states of mind into one experience?

ז זָהָ֣ב וָכֶ֗סֶף עַ֛ל רִֽצְפַ֥ת בַּהַט־וָשֵׁ֖שׁ וְדַ֥ר וְסֹחָֽרֶת׃ וְהַשְׁקוֹת֙ בִּכְלֵ֣י זָהָ֔ב
ח וְכֵלִ֖ים מִכֵּלִ֣ים שׁוֹנִ֑ים וְיֵ֥ין מַלְכ֛וּת רָ֖ב כְּיַ֥ד הַמֶּֽלֶךְ׃ וְהַשְּׁתִיָּ֥ה כַדָּ֖ת
אֵ֣ין אֹנֵ֑ס כִּי־כֵ֣ן ׀ יִסַּ֣ד הַמֶּ֗לֶךְ עַ֚ל כָּל־רַ֣ב בֵּית֔וֹ לַעֲשׂ֖וֹת כִּרְצ֥וֹן אִישׁ־
ט וָאִֽישׁ׃ גַּ֚ם וַשְׁתִּ֣י הַמַּלְכָּ֔ה עָשְׂתָ֖ה מִשְׁתֵּ֣ה נָשִׁ֑ים בֵּ֚ית
י הַמַּלְכ֔וּת אֲשֶׁ֖ר לַמֶּ֥לֶךְ אֲחַשְׁוֵרֽוֹשׁ׃ בַּיּוֹם֙ הַשְּׁבִיעִ֔י כְּט֥וֹב לֵב־הַמֶּ֖לֶךְ
בַּיָּ֑יִן אָמַ֡ר לִ֠מְהוּמָן בִּזְּתָ֨א חַרְבוֹנָ֜א בִּגְתָ֤א וַאֲבַגְתָא֙ זֵתַ֣ר וְכַרְכַּ֔ס

וְכֵלִים מִכֵּלִים שׁוֹנִים *vessels unlike any other.* The Book of Esther tells us much about Ahasuerus' decorations because they were not simply decorations. The "vessels unlike any other" were the sacred vessels of the *Beit HaMikdash*. They belonged to Belshazzar and, apparently, Ahasuerus inherited them from him. The sacred vessels were a precious treasure even for these pagan kings who greatly appreciated them. What was attractive about them that they brought them from Jerusalem to Persia, to Shushan or to any other city, that they should engage the fantasy of Ahasuerus, Belshazzar, and Nebuchadnezzar? Why were they interested in having the vessels in their possession? Something in the Jew intrigues the Gentile. They did not just reject the Torah; they were intrigued by it, and wondered about it. Apparently, Ahasuerus, Belshazzar, and all the pagan kings who destroyed the *Beit HaMikdash* kept on asking their Jewish servants this same question: "What attracts you to rebuild the *Beit HaMikdash*? Something attracts you because you want to go back to Jerusalem and rebuild it. But why?" They simply did not, and do not, understand. (*The Lord Is Righteous in All His Ways*)

בַּיּוֹם הַשְּׁבִיעִי *And on the seventh day of the feasts.* The "seventh day" was introduced in order to emphasize the contrast between the role assigned to the seventh day in our worldview and that which the Persians attributed to the same. On the seventh day, the feasting reaches its pinnacle – the joy is great; the merriment and the gaiety are overwhelming. But what does it mean? For the Persians, it means loss of human dignity, the abolition of all standards of decency. In a word: when the heart of man is merry with wine, he turns into an undignified, coarse voluptuary; his refinement is gone by the seventh day. For the Jew, when the feasting reaches its apex, he finds himself in the presence of God. The seventh (or the eighth) day on which the celebration

11 king, Ahasuerus – to bring Vashti the queen before the king in her royal
crown, to show the peoples and the ministers her charms, for she was beauti-
12 ful indeed. But the queen, Vashti, refused to come at the word the king had
conveyed through the eunuchs. And fury engulfed the king, and his rage
blazed up within him.

---

order the eunuchs to bring Vashti into the arena would alienate the entire aristocracy. Such vulgarity would have been too much of a display for a volatile king such as Ahasuerus, and high society would have condemned it. His downfall would have been certain. However, when the nobles and rulers of the states departed Shushan, and Ahasuerus found himself among his own, he felt that doing something utterly obnoxious and horrible, something tactless, bordering on the pornographic, would win the sympathy of the wild masses. In particular, it would meet with the approval of the mob, because it would expose to humiliation the aristocratic queen whom the people hated. On the seventh day, Ahasuerus felt free to act the way his coarse character told him to act. He cast off all the restrictive measures of decency and modesty. He was among his own. (*Days of Deliverance*)

וַתְּמָאֵן הַמַּלְכָּה וַשְׁתִּי לָבוֹא בִּדְבַר הַמֶּלֶךְ אֲשֶׁר בְּיַד הַסָּרִיסִים *But the queen, Vashti, refused to come at the word the king had conveyed through the eunuchs.* Of course, at the very moment a person is drunk and loses the capacity of self-restraint, the real I comes to the fore. What did this real I demonstrate? Vulgarity and moral filth. In his state of intoxication, Ahasuerus forgot, first, that Vashti was a princess. He did not personally request her presence. He sent his seven chamberlains. Vashti did not resent the request *per se,* but the way it was addressed to her: The queen "refused to come at the word the king had conveyed through the eunuchs." She refused because the king issued an order and delivered it via his underlings. Vashti was a princess, and the king had offended her dignity. But he also forgot that every human, not only a princess, has dignity. Ahasuerus did not grasp the meaning of human dignity in general and the dignity of the woman in particular. Judaism displays enormous sensitivity vis-à-vis the woman, particularly when she is put on exhibit as a sex object whose task is to gratify man's brutish drives. Many Jewish laws pertaining to separation serve one objective, namely, to convince man that woman is of equal worth. Quite often I have the impression that the Torah considered woman of a higher existential caliber than man. (*Days of Deliverance*)

יא שִׁבְעַת הַסָּרִיסִים הַמְשָׁרְתִים אֶת־פְּנֵי הַמֶּלֶךְ אֲחַשְׁוֵרוֹשׁ: לְהָבִיא
אֶת־וַשְׁתִּי הַמַּלְכָּה לִפְנֵי הַמֶּלֶךְ בְּכֶתֶר מַלְכוּת לְהַרְאוֹת הָעַמִּים
יב וְהַשָּׂרִים אֶת־יָפְיָהּ כִּי־טוֹבַת מַרְאֶה הִיא: וַתְּמָאֵן הַמַּלְכָּה וַשְׁתִּי
לָבוֹא בִּדְבַר הַמֶּלֶךְ אֲשֶׁר בְּיַד הַסָּרִיסִים וַיִּקְצֹף הַמֶּלֶךְ מְאֹד וַחֲמָתוֹ

In fact, this combination is typically Jewish. Our Sages taught: "If three have eaten at one table and spoken over it no words of Torah, it is as if they had eaten of sacrifices to the dead" (*Avot* 3:3). The meal in Judaism is not merely an occasion for eating. The meal is transformed into a symposium; it precipitates Torah debate. Moreover, the meal in Judaism has another purpose. Unlike the animal, a person almost never eats alone. He invites others. The Jew invites the poor man: "the stranger and the fatherless, and the widow who are within your gates" (Deut. 14:29). The meal is thus transformed into an act of charity, of *ḥesed,* of lovingkindness. Hence, Judaism elevates the meal and turns it into a Torah experience and a *ḥesed* experience. (*Days of Deliverance*)

לְהָבִיא אֶת וַשְׁתִּי הַמַּלְכָּה לִפְנֵי הַמֶּלֶךְ בְּכֶתֶר מַלְכוּת *to bring Vashti the queen before the king in her royal crown.* Vashti, the queen, was not called before the nobles and princes during the long celebration of one hundred and eighty days, but during the second one-week feast to which all residents of Shushan were invited. Why did Ahasuerus not try to put Vashti on display before the aristocracy? Ahasuerus was a parvenu. According to our tradition, he worked in the stables of the Babylonian king Nebuchadnezzar. Consequently, he lacked tact; he was ill-mannered and uncouth. He hated the nobility, but he had to play host to them since they were responsible for his and the empire's security. He felt out of place while feasting with them. Their cultivated speech, their fine table manners, their trained postures irritated him. However, during the week of feasting with the mob of Shushan, the old Ahasuerus, the stable boy, reawakened. Such a voluptuous, vulgar mood may precipitate any kind of action. The inner controls in a human being become numb, and the animal in man comes to the surface. Why did Ahasuerus issue the instruction concerning Vashti only on the seventh day of the second feast? The answer is plain. In the company of the distinguished aristocrats, Ahasuerus tried to behave respectfully with some semblance of dignity. No matter how drunk he was, he understood that to

13 Now the king addressed the wise men, who knew how to read the times –
for it was the king's practice to consult with those who knew the statutes
14 and the law. And the men of his closest circle, those who came freely into
the king's presence and occupied the first position in the realm, were seven
ministers of Persia and Media named Karshena, Shetar, Admata, Tarshish,
15 Meres, Marsena and Memukhan. "What," he asked, "would the law have us
do with Vashti the queen, for refusing to obey the king's word, conveyed to
her by the eunuchs?"

16 And Memukhan replied, before the king and the ministers: "It is not only
the king that Vashti the queen has wronged, but all the ministers and all the
17 peoples in all King Ahasuerus' provinces. For this tale of the queen will go
out to all the women, casting their husbands into their contempt, as they say,
'King Ahasuerus commanded Queen Vashti to be brought before him – but
18 she did not come!' Yes, this very day, all the ministers' wives of Persia and
Medea who heard what the queen did will tell all the king's ministers, and
there will be no end to the contempt and the fury.

19 "If, then, it so please the king, let a royal declaration be sent out from him,
and be written among the laws of Persia and Medea, that it never be revoked –
that Vashti shall come no more before King Ahasuerus; and the king shall
give her rule over to some other woman; to one who is better than she.
20 And the king's decree shall be heeded and obeyed in all his empire, great
as it is: that all women must honor their husbands, from the greatest to the
lowliest."

21 The suggestion pleased the king and the ministers, and the king did just as

---

this most ridiculous order, which undermined his prestige in the eyes of the people. They lost faith in him as a responsible leader. They looked upon him with contempt. Why was it necessary that he lose his credibility?

The answer was given by our Rabbis: "Rava said: Were it not for the first letters, not one survivor would have been left among the Jewish people" (*Megilla* 12b). Rashi (*ad loc.*) adds, "For the people would have hastened to kill them at the command of the king in the second letters and would not have waited until the appointed day." If the order about the rights of the male had not been sent by Ahasuerus, all the Jews would have been exterminated. Neither Esther nor Mordekhai could have saved them. The whole miracle of

יג בְּעֵרָה בוֹ׃ וַיֹּאמֶר הַמֶּלֶךְ לַחֲכָמִים יֹדְעֵי הָעִתִּים כִּי־כֵן
יד דְּבַר הַמֶּלֶךְ לִפְנֵי כָּל־יֹדְעֵי דָּת וָדִין׃ וְהַקָּרֹב אֵלָיו כַּרְשְׁנָא שֵׁתָר
אַדְמָתָא תַרְשִׁישׁ מֶרֶס מַרְסְנָא מְמוּכָן שִׁבְעַת שָׂרֵי ׀ פָּרַס וּמָדַי רֹאֵי
טו פְּנֵי הַמֶּלֶךְ הַיֹּשְׁבִים רִאשֹׁנָה בַּמַּלְכוּת׃ כְּדָת מַה־לַּעֲשׂוֹת בַּמַּלְכָּה
וַשְׁתִּי עַל ׀ אֲשֶׁר לֹא־עָשְׂתָה אֶת־מַאֲמַר הַמֶּלֶךְ אֲחַשְׁוֵרוֹשׁ בְּיַד
טז הַסָּרִיסִים׃ וַיֹּאמֶר מומכן לִפְנֵי הַמֶּלֶךְ וְהַשָּׂרִים לֹא עַל־ מְמוּכָן
הַמֶּלֶךְ לְבַדּוֹ עָוְתָה וַשְׁתִּי הַמַּלְכָּה כִּי עַל־כָּל־הַשָּׂרִים וְעַל־כָּל־הָעַמִּים
יז אֲשֶׁר בְּכָל־מְדִינוֹת הַמֶּלֶךְ אֲחַשְׁוֵרוֹשׁ׃ כִּי־יֵצֵא דְבַר־הַמַּלְכָּה עַל־
כָּל־הַנָּשִׁים לְהַבְזוֹת בַּעְלֵיהֶן בְּעֵינֵיהֶן בְּאָמְרָם הַמֶּלֶךְ אֲחַשְׁוֵרוֹשׁ
יח אָמַר לְהָבִיא אֶת־וַשְׁתִּי הַמַּלְכָּה לְפָנָיו וְלֹא־בָאָה׃ וְהַיּוֹם הַזֶּה
תֹּאמַרְנָה ׀ שָׂרוֹת פָּרַס־וּמָדַי אֲשֶׁר שָׁמְעוּ אֶת־דְּבַר הַמַּלְכָּה לְכֹל
יט שָׂרֵי הַמֶּלֶךְ וּכְדַי בִּזָּיוֹן וָקָצֶף׃ אִם־עַל־הַמֶּלֶךְ טוֹב יֵצֵא דְבַר־מַלְכוּת
מִלְּפָנָיו וְיִכָּתֵב בְּדָתֵי פָרַס־וּמָדַי וְלֹא יַעֲבוֹר אֲשֶׁר לֹא־תָבוֹא וַשְׁתִּי
לִפְנֵי הַמֶּלֶךְ אֲחַשְׁוֵרוֹשׁ וּמַלְכוּתָהּ יִתֵּן הַמֶּלֶךְ לִרְעוּתָהּ הַטּוֹבָה מִמֶּנָּה׃
כ וְנִשְׁמַע פִּתְגָם הַמֶּלֶךְ אֲשֶׁר־יַעֲשֶׂה בְּכָל־מַלְכוּתוֹ כִּי רַבָּה הִיא וְכָל־
כא הַנָּשִׁים יִתְּנוּ יְקָר לְבַעְלֵיהֶן לְמִגָּדוֹל וְעַד־קָטָן׃ וַיִּיטַב הַדָּבָר בְּעֵינֵי

וְכָל הַנָּשִׁים יִתְּנוּ יְקָר לְבַעְלֵיהֶן לְמִגָּדוֹל וְעַד קָטָן *that all women must honor their husbands, from the greatest to the lowliest.* One question troubles the mind: why was it necessary to tell us about this incident? All the Megilla had to do was mention that Ahasuerus married Esther after killing Vashti for her refusal to comply with his orders. The royal edict that Ahasuerus sent to all provinces of the far-flung Persian empire was absurd: that women should give honor to their husbands, and that the man bear rule in his own house. Only an idiot could have issued orders pertaining to a matter that could not be determined by legislation. In this matter, all depends on the character of the husband and the wife. No legislation is capable of regulating the intimate relationship of husband and wife. Yet, Providence willed Ahasuerus to issue

22 Memukhan had said. He sent scrolls to all the king's provinces, province
by province, each in its script, and people by people, each in its language –
ruling that each man be master in his home, speaking the language of his
own people.

2 1 Some time later, when King Ahasuerus' fury had subsided – he remembered

---

of the king subsided, he began to think well of her. He suddenly began to brood and doubt whether or not he should have punished her with so much cruelty: "There were mitigating circumstances that I should have taken into consideration while I sat in judgment. It was wrong, unjust, and malicious on my part." But the king cannot be guilty. He is always just. If he did something wrong, then someone else is responsible, someone misled him; someone must be liable for the mistake. Ahasuerus began to "inquire" who suggested to him to execute Vashti.

Commenting on this verse, our Sages said: "After these things, when the wrath of King Ahasuerus subsided, he sent and called to all of his chamberlains and said to them, I am not angry at Vashti; rather, I am angry at you on account of the following: If I said something, it was because of wine. But why did you incite me to kill Queen Vashti? Now I have caused her name to be erased from the kingdom. So will I kill you also and cause your names to be erased from the kingdom" (*Targum Esther* 2:1). Why did Ahasuerus blame the royal advisors for Vashti's death? Somehow Memukhan, foxy and shrewd, succeeded in convincing Ahasuerus that the royal council had advised him to kill the queen. Only Memukhan had voted in favor of clemency. No questions were asked; all denials on the part of the royal advisors were futile. The six members of the highest council were executed. Only Memukhan survived. The Megilla (3:1) tells us that Haman was elevated after these events occurred. He had persuaded Ahasuerus that he alone had defended Vashti and begged the king not to kill her. For this he was rewarded, and the rest of the council was executed. This story was known to all officialdom of the empire. Hence, they were afraid to act immediately. They did not rush to execute the royal orders. They recalled that Ahasuerus himself had changed his mind about Vashti, and that whoever was involved in the execution of Vashti was himself executed. This is the reason why our enemies were slow in acting. Meanwhile, Esther and Mordekhai had the opportunity to intercede and save the people. (*Days of Deliverance*)

כב הַמֶּלֶךְ וְהַשָּׂרִים וַיַּעַשׂ הַמֶּלֶךְ כִּדְבַר מְמוּכָן׃ וַיִּשְׁלַח סְפָרִים אֶל־כָּל־
מְדִינוֹת הַמֶּלֶךְ אֶל־מְדִינָה וּמְדִינָה כִּכְתָבָהּ וְאֶל־עַם וָעָם כִּלְשׁוֹנוֹ
ב א לִהְיוֹת כָּל־אִישׁ שֹׂרֵר בְּבֵיתוֹ וּמְדַבֵּר כִּלְשׁוֹן עַמּוֹ׃ אַחַר
הַדְּבָרִים הָאֵלֶּה כְּשֹׁךְ חֲמַת הַמֶּלֶךְ אֲחַשְׁוֵרוֹשׁ זָכַר אֶת־וַשְׁתִּי וְאֵת

Purim was made possible because of those stupid letters commanding the females to respect the males.

Everybody was commanded to be ready to execute the order on the thirteenth of Adar. In other words, the execution of the edict was postponed for eleven full months, from the first month to the twelfth. Why did the enemies wait eleven months to execute the king's order? Apparently, they were afraid of something; a certain doubt bothered their minds, and this fear dampened their malicious, fiendish enthusiasm. The previous letters sent out by the king amply demonstrated that the king lacked judgment, that he is simply stupid. They all asked themselves, How could our emperor, who rules such a vast area, whose word is law, who determines the destiny of millions of people, act like a fool and issue edicts pertaining to the intimate relationship between husband and wife? The conclusion is that the emperor is irresponsible and unreliable. If so, who can guarantee that this edict was planned properly and that the emperor and his prime minister are sane and know what they are doing? Perhaps the whole story is a hoax and we will later be punished for murder. Hence, all the hate-mongers, bigots, and killers decided not to act immediately but to wait and see, to test the validity and the genuineness of the orders. If there will be no change in the order by Adar the thirteenth, then the pogroms will start. (*Days of Deliverance*)

אַחַר הַדְּבָרִים הָאֵלֶּה...זָכַר אֶת וַשְׁתִּי *Some time later... he remembered Vashti.* When the Megilla writes, "he remembered Vashti," it uses the Hebrew word *zakhar*. Usually, the word *zakhar* means "favorably remembered." This point is made in the Talmud to explain why the verses on the theme of remembrance are called *zikhronot*, based on the term *zakhar*. The verses are not called *pikdonot*, based on the term *pakad*, which also means "remembered," because *pakad* many times is used in a negative sense (*Rosh HaShana* 32b). In contrast, *zakhar* is mostly, although not always, used in favor of the person whom one remembers. So the phrase "he remembered Vashti" should be qualified by an adverbial designation, "he remembered Vashti *favorably*." After the ire

2 Vashti and what she had done, and what had been decreed against her. The
king's pages, those who attended him daily, said, "Let beautiful young virgins
3 be sought out for the king; let the king appoint officers in all the provinces of
his realm, to gather every beautiful young virgin to the imperial city, Shushan,
to the harem, into the charge of Hegai the king's eunuch, the keeper of the
4 women, to be given their ointments there. And whichever young woman the
king likes best – let her become queen in Vashti's place!"

The suggestion pleased the king, and that is what he did.

5 ▸ Now there was a Jewish man in the imperial city of Shushan, and his name
6 was Mordekhai, son of Yair, son of Kish, of the tribe of Benjamin. ◂ He had
been exiled from Jerusalem, among the exile expelled with Jehoiachin, king of
7 Judah, who was exiled by Nebuchadnezzar, king of Babylon. And Mordekhai
had brought up Hadassa – Esther, that is – his uncle's daughter, for she had
no father or mother; and the girl was lovely, and beautiful, and when her
father and mother had died, Mordekhai had adopted her as his own child.

---

custom? In his commentary on *Shulḥan Arukh*, the Vilna Gaon cites *Sota* 30b as a source: "At the time the Israelites ascended from the Red Sea, they desired to utter a song; how did they render the song? … R. Nehemiah says: Like a school-teacher who recites the Shema in the synagogue – he begins first and they respond after him." The Gemara recounts different views about how the Song of the Sea was recited, but the common element in all of them is that of call and response. According to the Vilna Gaon, these verses of the Megilla are recited responsively because the Megilla itself is considered to be a song, and therefore contains the element of call and response.

וַיְהִי אֹמֵן אֶת הֲדַסָּה, הִיא אֶסְתֵּר בַּת דֹּדוֹ *And Mordekhai had brought up Hadassa – Esther, that is – his uncle's daughter.* Providence selected as divine agent not only Mordekhai but Esther as well. God willed that both, male and female, appear as actors on the historical stage. Judaism has never discriminated against woman. From the days of Sarah, the woman was on a par with the man as history-maker. Both Mordekhai and Esther were created in the image of God; both were endowed with dignity and majesty; both possessed great talent; both were charismatic personae; and both were called to service, to make history. God assigned equally important roles to Mordekhai and Esther because both of them were metaphysically and spiritually worthy of the task.

ב אֲשֶׁר־עָשָׂתָה וְאֵת אֲשֶׁר־נִגְזַר עָלֶיהָ׃ וַיֹּאמְרוּ נַעֲרֵי־הַמֶּלֶךְ מְשָׁרְתָיו
ג יְבַקְשׁוּ לַמֶּלֶךְ נְעָרוֹת בְּתוּלוֹת טוֹבוֹת מַרְאֶה׃ וְיַפְקֵד הַמֶּלֶךְ פְּקִידִים
בְּכָל־מְדִינוֹת מַלְכוּתוֹ וְיִקְבְּצוּ אֶת־כָּל־נַעֲרָה־בְתוּלָה טוֹבַת מַרְאֶה
אֶל־שׁוּשַׁן הַבִּירָה אֶל־בֵּית הַנָּשִׁים אֶל־יַד הֵגֶא סְרִיס הַמֶּלֶךְ שֹׁמֵר
ד הַנָּשִׁים וְנָתוֹן תַּמְרוּקֵיהֶן׃ וְהַנַּעֲרָה אֲשֶׁר תִּיטַב בְּעֵינֵי הַמֶּלֶךְ תִּמְלֹךְ
ה תַּחַת וַשְׁתִּי וַיִּיטַב הַדָּבָר בְּעֵינֵי הַמֶּלֶךְ וַיַּעַשׂ כֵּן׃ · אִישׁ
יְהוּדִי הָיָה בְּשׁוּשַׁן הַבִּירָה וּשְׁמוֹ מָרְדֳּכַי בֶּן יָאִיר בֶּן־שִׁמְעִי בֶּן־קִישׁ
ו אִישׁ יְמִינִי׃ · אֲשֶׁר הָגְלָה מִירוּשָׁלַיִם עִם־הַגֹּלָה אֲשֶׁר הָגְלְתָה עִם
ז יְכָנְיָה מֶלֶךְ־יְהוּדָה אֲשֶׁר הֶגְלָה נְבוּכַדְנֶצַּר מֶלֶךְ בָּבֶל׃ וַיְהִי אֹמֵן
אֶת־הֲדַסָּה הִיא אֶסְתֵּר בַּת־דֹּדוֹ כִּי אֵין לָהּ אָב וָאֵם וְהַנַּעֲרָה יְפַת־
תֹּאַר וְטוֹבַת מַרְאֶה וּבְמוֹת אָבִיהָ וְאִמָּהּ לְקָחָהּ מָרְדֳּכַי לוֹ לְבַת׃

אִישׁ יְהוּדִי הָיָה בְּשׁוּשַׁן הַבִּירָה *Now there was a Jewish man in the imperial city of Shushan.* How beautifully the Megilla tells us, "Now there was a Jewish man in the imperial city of Shushan." Certainly there were many Jews numerically, but there was only one *ish Yehudi*, a Jew with commitment, determination, and a sense of responsibility, ready to sacrifice, not embarrassed to protest in front of the royal palace. There were many Jews, but there was only one who proclaimed the doctrine of total and unqualified commitment of the individual to the community. Mordekhai was a lonely *ish Yehudi* who lived all his life in Shushan as an intelligent, knowledgeable, dedicated Jew, determined to perpetuate the great heritage that he brought along from Jerusalem. In this spirit he reared Esther. He inculcated in her love of and devotion to her people. That is why later when the call came through she hesitated just for a short while and she responded to the call.

אִישׁ יְהוּדִי הָיָה בְּשׁוּשַׁן הַבִּירָה וּשְׁמוֹ מָרְדֳּכַי *Now there was a Jewish man in the imperial city of Shushan, and his name was Mordekhai.* Rema (*Oraḥ Ḥayim* 690:17) records the custom according to which the congregation recites this and three other verses of redemption – 8:15, 8:16, and 10:3 – aloud during the Megilla reading, and these are then repeated by the reader. What is the basis for this

8 And when the king's word and his ruling were heard, and vast numbers of
young women were gathered in to the imperial city, Shushan, and into the
charge of Hegai – Esther too was taken to the king's palace, into the charge
of Hegai, the keeper of the women.

9 And the young woman pleased him, and she carried kindness with her, and
he hastened to her all her ointments and meals, and the seven young maids
to whom she was entitled, from the king's palace; and he treated her with
10 especial care, her and her maids, all the time that she was in the harem. Esther,
meanwhile, made no mention of her people or her birth, for Mordekhai had
11 bid her strictly not to tell. And every single day, Mordekhai would walk about
before the harem courtyard, to find out whether Esther was well, and what
was being done with her.

12 As each young woman's turn would arrive to come before King Ahasuerus,
after twelve months following her beauty regime (for that was how long
the days of their ointments lasted: six months in myrrh oil and six months
13 in perfumes and the women's ointments) – then the young woman would
come before the king: and all that she asked for would be given her, to bring
14 with her from the harem to the palace of the king. She would go in the eve-
ning, and in the morning would return to the harem again, into the charge
of Sha'ashgaz, the king's eunuch, keeper of the concubines. And then she

---

ability of man is proportionate to his greatness. The greater the success, the more vulnerable he is. Mordekhai knew that as Esther climbed up to the very heights of success, the deeper became the abyss into which she might plunge. Because of Mordekhai's humility and because of his awareness of vulnerability and caution, the great miracle happened. In sum, vulnerability leads to humility, humility to caution, and caution leads to success. (*Days of Deliverence*)

אֶל יַד שַׁעַשְׁגַז סְרִיס הַמֶּלֶךְ, שֹׁמֵר הַפִּילַגְשִׁים *into the charge of Sha'ashgaz, the king's eunuch, keeper of the concubines.* The Book of Esther did not spare words in portraying vividly, with refined artistry and sarcasm, the repugnant addiction of the king, princes, courtiers, and servants to lascivious pleasures, to the incessant pursuit of an ever-fugitive satisfaction. We read of the habits of an orgiastic society that was tired and exhausted because of satiety, yet anticipated another satiety to be tried for the sheer novelty of it. Why was it necessary to perpetuate the names of eunuchs, the harem keepers, Sha'ashgaz,

ח וַיְהִי בְּהִשָּׁמַע דְּבַר־הַמֶּלֶךְ וְדָתוֹ וּבְהִקָּבֵץ נְעָרוֹת רַבּוֹת אֶל־שׁוּשַׁן
הַבִּירָה אֶל־יַד הֵגָי וַתִּלָּקַח אֶסְתֵּר אֶל־בֵּית הַמֶּלֶךְ אֶל־יַד הֵגַי שֹׁמֵר
ט הַנָּשִׁים׃ וַתִּיטַב הַנַּעֲרָה בְעֵינָיו וַתִּשָּׂא חֶסֶד לְפָנָיו וַיְבַהֵל אֶת־
תַּמְרוּקֶיהָ וְאֶת־מָנוֹתֶהָ לָתֵת לָהּ וְאֵת שֶׁבַע הַנְּעָרוֹת הָרְאֻיוֹת לָתֶת־
י לָהּ מִבֵּית הַמֶּלֶךְ וַיְשַׁנֶּהָ וְאֶת־נַעֲרוֹתֶיהָ לְטוֹב בֵּית הַנָּשִׁים׃ לֹא־
הִגִּידָה אֶסְתֵּר אֶת־עַמָּהּ וְאֶת־מוֹלַדְתָּהּ כִּי מָרְדֳּכַי צִוָּה עָלֶיהָ אֲשֶׁר
יא לֹא־תַגִּיד׃ וּבְכָל־יוֹם וָיוֹם מָרְדֳּכַי מִתְהַלֵּךְ לִפְנֵי חֲצַר בֵּית־הַנָּשִׁים
יב לָדַעַת אֶת־שְׁלוֹם אֶסְתֵּר וּמַה־יֵּעָשֶׂה בָּהּ׃ וּבְהַגִּיעַ תֹּר נַעֲרָה וְנַעֲרָה
לָבוֹא ׀ אֶל־הַמֶּלֶךְ אֲחַשְׁוֵרוֹשׁ מִקֵּץ הֱיוֹת לָהּ כְּדָת הַנָּשִׁים שְׁנֵים
עָשָׂר חֹדֶשׁ כִּי כֵּן יִמְלְאוּ יְמֵי מְרוּקֵיהֶן שִׁשָּׁה חֳדָשִׁים בְּשֶׁמֶן הַמֹּר
יג וְשִׁשָּׁה חֳדָשִׁים בַּבְּשָׂמִים וּבְתַמְרוּקֵי הַנָּשִׁים׃ וּבָזֶה הַנַּעֲרָה בָּאָה
אֶל־הַמֶּלֶךְ אֵת כָּל־אֲשֶׁר תֹּאמַר יִנָּתֵן לָהּ לָבוֹא עִמָּהּ מִבֵּית הַנָּשִׁים
יד עַד־בֵּית הַמֶּלֶךְ׃ בָּעֶרֶב ׀ הִיא בָאָה וּבַבֹּקֶר הִיא שָׁבָה אֶל־בֵּית הַנָּשִׁים
שֵׁנִי אֶל־יַד שַׁעַשְׁגַז סְרִיס הַמֶּלֶךְ שֹׁמֵר הַפִּילַגְשִׁים לֹא־תָבוֹא עוֹד

Of course, this statement must not be misunderstood. The assignments were equal in importance but by no means identical. The assignments differed because there is a basic differentiation of the sexes, not only physiologically, but psychically and spiritually as well. A historical masculine role cannot be assigned to woman, and vice versa, a feminine task must not be imposed upon man. (*Days of Deliverance*)

לֹא הִגִּידָה אֶסְתֵּר אֶת עַמָּהּ וְאֶת מוֹלַדְתָּהּ כִּי מָרְדֳּכַי צִוָּה עָלֶיהָ אֲשֶׁר לֹא תַגִּיד *Esther, meanwhile, made no mention of her people or her birth, for Mordekhai had bid her strictly not to tell.* Had Mordekhai abandoned caution and adopted the attitude of the arrogant fool, had he let everybody know that he was related to the queen, he would have commanded their respect. However, had he been proud and vain, had he boasted that he is a relation of the queen, the whole miracle would not have happened. The miracle was made possible by Mordekhai's caution and humility. He was silent, humble; he was waiting for something to happen. He knew that the more fantastic the success story, the more vulnerable man is and the more intense is the need for prayer. Vulner-

would come no more before the king, unless he desired her, and she was called for by name.

15 And when the time came for Esther, daughter of Mordekhai's uncle, Aviḥayil, whom Mordekhai had adopted as his own child, to come before the king – she did not ask for anything, except for what Hegai the king's eunuch, keeper of the women, told her to bring. And Esther carried grace in the eyes of all who saw her.

16 Esther was taken to King Ahasuerus, to his royal palace, in the tenth month,

---

the keeper of the maidens and that of the concubines, and that the maiden who visited the king once never returned to Hegai but to Sha'ashgaz? The answer is simple. The Megilla purposely portrays the promiscuous, orgiastic, sex-crazy life of Persian upper society, with the king at its head. They had lost all standards of decency; the woman turned into a female animal. She had nothing else in her life but the gratification of the desires of the opposite sex. A madness overpowered society with Ahasuerus. What he practiced was nothing less than slavery and prostitution of the worst caliber. Modern society is not superior to the ancient Persian in this respect. Of course, in such a permissive society the very sense of beauty deteriorates and adapts itself to the taste of the voluptuary; the beauty is coarse and unredeemed. Esther did not belong to such a society. She refused to subject herself to all the treatments, unless Hegai compelled her. Those vulgar people did not understand her. Yet she fascinated everyone. She "carried grace in the eyes of all who saw her." Rabbi Akiva stated that this verse corroborates the view that the Megilla was written with divine inspiration (*Megilla* 7a). In other words, Esther herself was an inspired, charismatic person. She had within herself something divine. (*Days of Deliverance*)

וַתְּהִי אֶסְתֵּר נֹשֵׂאת חֵן בְּעֵינֵי כָּל רֹאֶיהָ *and Esther carried grace in the eyes of all who saw her.* The Hebrew word *ḥen*, grace, refers to the attribute of charm, in contradistinction to beauty. While beauty is usually a result of combinations of several physical factors, of external features, charm comes from within. It flows from the deep recesses of the spiritual personality. Charm is engendered by the presence of God in the human being. It is the reflection of the divine presence within man. One radiates charm, for the *imago Dei* is the source of charm. The symmetry of the body, the complexion, and the color of the eyes are all irrelevant to the charm-personality.

טו אֶל־הַמֶּלֶךְ כִּי אִם־חָפֵץ בָּהּ הַמֶּלֶךְ וְנִקְרְאָה בְשֵׁם׃ וּבְהַגִּיעַ תֹּר־אֶסְתֵּר
בַּת־אֲבִיחַיִל ׀ דֹּד מָרְדֳּכַי אֲשֶׁר לָקַח־לוֹ לְבַת לָבוֹא אֶל־הַמֶּלֶךְ לֹא
בִקְשָׁה דָּבָר כִּי אִם אֶת־אֲשֶׁר יֹאמַר הֵגַי סְרִיס־הַמֶּלֶךְ שֹׁמֵר הַנָּשִׁים
טז וַתְּהִי אֶסְתֵּר נֹשֵׂאת חֵן בְּעֵינֵי כָּל־רֹאֶיהָ׃ וַתִּלָּקַח אֶסְתֵּר אֶל־הַמֶּלֶךְ
אֲחַשְׁוֵרוֹשׁ אֶל־בֵּית מַלְכוּתוֹ בַּחֹדֶשׁ הָעֲשִׂירִי הוּא־חֹדֶשׁ טֵבֵת

Hegai, the brands of cosmetics used by the king's concubines, the foul and lewd habits of the king himself? The Scripture, which is tight-lipped about the lives of Moses, Abraham, and Isaac, becomes suddenly so loquacious in narrating the story of the king's wives, banquets, and the degenerate life at court. Why? Because only in a non-rational environment could irrational man-Satan rise. Only people who were pursuing pleasure – for whom values had no fixity, norms no ultimate validity – could tolerate man-Satan, irrational and destructive and cruel; only people addicted to the beautiful and pleasant could have stood by and watched the smoke rising from the chimneys of the crematoria climbing to heaven. Therefore the Megilla begins: "It happened in the days of Ahasuerus" (1:1). Do you know why all this bloody nonsense happened? Because it was the Ahasuerus era, one of *hêdonê* and freedom from the moral norm. "Some time after this, King Ahasuerus ennobled Haman" (3:1). A society of Sha'ashgaz and Hegai *must* produce a Haman. (*Days of Deliverance*)

לֹא בִקְשָׁה דָּבָר *she did not ask for anything.* The Megilla points out the paradoxical way in which Esther behaved. All the other women obtained everything they desired prior to their rendezvous with the king. The women would take advantage of their privileged position and ask for many things that they never had. But Esther did not ask for any favor, for any extra beauty treatment, with the exception of those things that Hegai imposed upon her. This she could not help. In other words, Esther neglected her looks. She did not care to impress the king. And yet she obtained favor. We do not understand the detailed description of the preparation of the maidens prior to their visit in the royal palace. The Megilla tells us about the beauty treatment they received, about the ointments and sweet perfumes and other cosmetics applied to them, and the length of time during which they were submitted to such treatment. The whole story is *prima facie* one of pagan permissiveness and voluptuousness. Why is it necessary to tell us about

17 the month of Tevet, that is, in the seventh year of his reign. And the king loved
Esther more than all the other women, and she pleased him and carried grace
and kindness with her in his eyes, more so than all the other virgins, and he
placed a royal crown upon her head, and made her queen in Vashti's place.
18 And the king made a great feast for all his ministers and courtiers: the feast
of Esther. And he granted the provinces a remission of their dues, and gifts
as great as the king's largesse.

19 As the virgins were gathered in for a second time, Mordekhai was sitting
20 at the King's Gate. And Esther had not told of her birth or of her people,
just as Mordekhai had bid her; for Esther still heeded Mordekhai's words,

---

וַיֶּאֱהַב הַמֶּלֶךְ אֶת אֶסְתֵּר מִכָּל הַנָּשִׁים, וַתִּשָּׂא חֵן וָחֶסֶד לְפָנָיו מִכָּל הַבְּתוּלוֹת *And the king loved Esther more than all the other women, and she pleased him and carried grace and kindness with her in his eyes, more so than all the other virgins.* Apparently, there was a dual aspect in the choice of Esther as the queen. There was love – plain, mundane, carnal love, which was precipitated by Esther's looks, her physical beauty. But Ahasuerus was also fascinated by something mysterious that he could not grasp, by the inner strength of Esther – her charm. He felt somehow instinctively, intuitively, that she is not an ordinary person. When he was in her presence, he felt that his whole being was more exalted, advanced, elevated to greater heights. What did the Almighty say to Moses when He said that the people had to be uplifted with judges? "I will take of the spirit that is upon you and I will put it upon them" (Num. 11:17). In your presence, they will feel differently, their minds will become brighter. You will raise them out of the depths of vulgarity and egocentricity, and you will make them soar to dizzying heights. The mere presence of a great person can accomplish this. That is what Ahasuerus felt in Esther's presence. However, he ignored this element and chose Esther for her plain beauty, in the same fashion as he had looked upon Vashti: "and he made her queen in Vashti's place." For the time being, he viewed Esther as a second Vashti. Yet, something in her intrigued him. He wanted to find out who she is and where she is from. (*Days of Deliverance*)

וּמָרְדֳּכַי יֹשֵׁב בְּשַׁעַר הַמֶּלֶךְ *Mordekhai was sitting at the King's Gate.* Do you know why Mordekhai was afraid to leave the gate? I understand it, unfortunately, because I had a similar tragic experience. Mordekhai refused to leave the gate because he feared that something horrible, something monstrous, might occur during his absence. It is a strange feeling, an absurd feeling – as if one's

יז בִּשְׁנַת־שֶׁבַע לְמַלְכוּתוֹ: וַיֶּאֱהַב הַמֶּלֶךְ אֶת־אֶסְתֵּר מִכָּל־הַנָּשִׁים
וַתִּשָּׂא־חֵן וָחֶסֶד לְפָנָיו מִכָּל־הַבְּתוּלֹת וַיָּשֶׂם כֶּתֶר־מַלְכוּת בְּרֹאשָׁהּ
יח וַיַּמְלִיכֶהָ תַּחַת וַשְׁתִּי: וַיַּעַשׂ הַמֶּלֶךְ מִשְׁתֶּה גָדוֹל לְכָל־שָׂרָיו וַעֲבָדָיו
אֵת מִשְׁתֵּה אֶסְתֵּר וַהֲנָחָה לַמְּדִינוֹת עָשָׂה וַיִּתֵּן מַשְׂאֵת כְּיַד הַמֶּלֶךְ:
יט כ וּבְהִקָּבֵץ בְּתוּלוֹת שֵׁנִית וּמָרְדֳּכַי יֹשֵׁב בְּשַׁעַר־הַמֶּלֶךְ: אֵין אֶסְתֵּר
מַגֶּדֶת מוֹלַדְתָּהּ וְאֶת־עַמָּהּ כַּאֲשֶׁר צִוָּה עָלֶיהָ מָרְדֳּכָי וְאֶת־מַאֲמַר

What is important is the divine in man. The two clauses, "The Lord was with Joseph" and "Joseph found grace in his [master's] sight," constitute an equation: Joseph found grace in Potiphar's sight *because* God was with him. The same is true of Esther. She carried grace with everyone because God was with her. She fascinated, she had an impact upon all she met. There was something different and peculiar about her. She was unique. In light of this, we can comprehend a strange verse: "Do not eat and do not drink for three whole days, day or night; I and my maids shall fast also. And so shall I come before the king" (4:16). Why did Esther fast for seventy-two hours? This fast could have had fatal results. Here she was ready to commit a crime, to violate a royal statute that no one must enter the inner court without express permission from the king. Her hope probably rested upon the fact that the king, who is in love with her, will hold out the golden scepter to her. *Prima facie,* she should have concentrated upon one aspect: to be as lovely and as physically attractive as possible. A fast of seventy-two continuous hours is hardly helpful to one's fair looks. Instead, during the last three days she should have taken care of herself, undergone beauty treatments, and planned the proper diet. Yet she acted differently. Why? Esther's attraction was not due to beauty but to charm, to inner strength, to the divine charisma (from *charis,* favor or grace) in her – things that a God-focused fast and fervent prayer might improve and enhance. How wonderfully did our Sages say: "'On the third day, Esther dressed herself in royalty' (5:1). It should have been phrased 'royal apparel'! Rather, [this teaches that] she was garbed in divine inspiration, *ruaḥ hakodesh*" (*Megilla* 14b). On the third day Esther rose from her ashes and sackcloth and she dressed in her regal garments. She was inspired; she became an exalted personality; she was wrapped in divine inspiration; she was powerful, captivating everybody's imagination. (*Days of Deliverance*)

21 just as she had when she had lived under his care. And as Mordekhai sat at
the King's Gate at that time, a fury engulfed Bigtan and Teresh, two of the
king's eunuchs, guards of the threshold, and they plotted to lay their hands
22 upon King Ahasuerus. But Mordekhai learned of the plot, and conveyed the
knowledge to Queen Esther, and Esther told the king in Mordekhai's name.
23 The matter was investigated and found to be true, and the two men were
hung up dead on a post; and the story was written down before the king in
the Scroll of the Chronicles.

3 1 Some time after this, King Ahasuerus ennobled Haman, son of Hamedata the
Agagite, and promoted him to a seat above those of all his fellow ministers.
2 And all the king's courtiers, serving at the King's Gate, would kneel and bow

---

הָאֲגָגִי *the Agagite.* The Haman episode is similar to events which took place in the wilderness when Amalek attacked. Haman was angry at Mordekhai. Why did he transfer his wrath to the whole community? The Megilla explains it in an enigmatic way: "After that Haman noticed that Mordekhai, indeed, did not kneel or bow down before him – and it filled Haman with rage." Why does the Megilla not say, "Haman was filled with rage *against Mordekhai*"? The Megilla itself explains it: "It seemed beneath his contempt to lay his hands only on Mordekhai." In other words, he considered Mordekhai's refusal to bow down as a minor incident which he would have ignored; he considered it below his dignity. However, his hate for Mordekhai's people caused him to raise the issue and to accuse the community as a whole of treason, disloyalty and being a parasitic element. We are wrong if we think that Mordekhai's refusal precipitated the hate in Haman against all Jews. The reverse is true. Because Mordekhai was a Jew, Haman was filled with anger and wrath against Mordekhai as the representative of the people. What dealings did Haman have with the Jews prior to the incident of Mordekhai's violation of the king's orders? None, and yet he hated them and tried to destroy them. The element of absurdity is visible in Haman's attempt to annihilate the people. These people never crossed his way. His action is as much understandable as the action of Amalek in the Moses era. Hate and destruction constitute a purpose *per se*. To exist means to destroy.

כא מָרְדֳּכַי אֶסְתֵּר עֹשָׂה כַּאֲשֶׁר הָיְתָה בְאָמְנָה אִתּוֹ׃ בַּיָּמִים
הָהֵם וּמָרְדֳּכַי יֹשֵׁב בְּשַׁעַר־הַמֶּלֶךְ קָצַף בִּגְתָן וָתֶרֶשׁ שְׁנֵי־סָרִיסֵי
כב הַמֶּלֶךְ מִשֹּׁמְרֵי הַסַּף וַיְבַקְשׁוּ לִשְׁלֹחַ יָד בַּמֶּלֶךְ אֲחַשְׁוֵרֹשׁ׃ וַיִּוָּדַע
הַדָּבָר לְמָרְדֳּכַי וַיַּגֵּד לְאֶסְתֵּר הַמַּלְכָּה וַתֹּאמֶר אֶסְתֵּר לַמֶּלֶךְ בְּשֵׁם
כג מָרְדֳּכָי׃ וַיְבֻקַּשׁ הַדָּבָר וַיִּמָּצֵא וַיִּתָּלוּ שְׁנֵיהֶם עַל־עֵץ וַיִּכָּתֵב בְּסֵפֶר
ג א דִּבְרֵי הַיָּמִים לִפְנֵי הַמֶּלֶךְ׃ אַחַר ׀ הַדְּבָרִים הָאֵלֶּה גִּדַּל
הַמֶּלֶךְ אֲחַשְׁוֵרוֹשׁ אֶת־הָמָן בֶּן־הַמְּדָתָא הָאֲגָגִי וַיְנַשְּׂאֵהוּ וַיָּשֶׂם אֶת־
ב כִּסְאוֹ מֵעַל כָּל־הַשָּׂרִים אֲשֶׁר אִתּוֹ׃ וְכָל־עַבְדֵי הַמֶּלֶךְ אֲשֶׁר־בְּשַׁעַר

---

presence could present the disaster from striking. You know it is wrong. I experienced a similar kind of foreboding during the illness of Mrs. Soloveitchik. I never left her sickbed. Why? It is not that she needed me. She did not need me. I knew instinctively that if I left her, death would snatch her from me before I had a chance to return. That is exactly what happened to me on Thursday, the Fast of Esther, years ago!

וַיִּוָּדַע הַדָּבָר לְמָרְדֳּכַי *But Mordekhai learned of the plot.* Two conspirators in Ahasuerus' palace, Bigtan and Teresh, hatched a plot to murder the king and to depose Haman. What did this have to do with the Jews? Yet, we read that somehow the Jew got involved. As a result, the Jewish people were involved in an internal feud between Haman and the opposition. The Jew is always involved in struggles that are completely extraneous or irrelevant to his destiny. So it was in the time of Esther. Apparently, Haman did not want to destroy the Jews for no reason; he wanted to solidify his political power. We know there were many intrigues in the royal palace. There were Bigtan and Teresh, and Ḥarvona. And, suddenly, Mordekhai got involved. "But Mordekhai would neither kneel nor bow down" (3:2). This was a good excuse for the hatred of Haman. Hitler also used the Jew as an excuse to solidify his power. So did the Communists. That is exactly what Haman utilized the Jews for. There was a political split within the Persian empire and, apparently, the opposing faction threatened Haman and Ahasuerus. In order to pacify the masses, the Jews become the internal enemy. (*Days of Deliverance*)

before Haman, for so had the king instructed – but Mordekhai would neither
3 kneel nor bow down. And so the king's courtiers would ask Mordekhai, as
they served at the King's Gate, "Why do you not obey the king's command?"

4 When, day after day, they said this to him and he took no heed, they reported
this to Haman, interested to see whether Mordekhai's word would stand – for
5 he had explained that he was a Jew. After that Haman noticed that Mordekhai,
indeed, did not kneel or bow down before him – and it filled Haman with rage.
6 It seemed beneath his contempt to lay his hands only on Mordekhai, for they
had told him who Mordekhai's people were. No: Haman's wish was to wipe
out all the Jews, all of Mordekhai's people, across all of Ahasuerus' empire.

7 And so in the first month, the month of Nisan, of the twelfth year of King
Ahasuerus' reign, a *pur* – lots, that is – were drawn before Haman; day for day
and month for month – and fell to the twelfth month: the month of Adar.

8 Haman then spoke to King Ahasuerus. "There is one people, scattered and
dispersed across all the provinces of your realm, whose laws are different from
those of all the other peoples, and who do not obey the king's own laws – and

---

ders, such as the mathematico-physical one, while he was barred from coming close to the *goral* or fate order. That is why it appears to him irregular, absurd, and hostile. However, Judaism, though it knew of and tried to understand catastrophic events that viciously destroy man, his dreams and hopes, could not accept the existence of unreasonable accidents in human life. Judaism maintains that events, which we call unreasonable and which we classify under the rubric of accident or fate, belong to a higher divine logos order into which man has not been initiated. Even the most unreasonable events may begin to reveal their structural patterns in retrospection. Retrospection sheds light upon many enigmatic, allegedly unreasonable events. When man views those absurd, freak accidents in the context of the experiences that followed them, the freakish event may appear to be a regular one. In hindsight, many events become understandable, endowed with rationality. (*Days of Deliverance*)

יֶשְׁנוֹ עַם אֶחָד *There is one people.* Haman hated not individuals, but the people as an entity. He indicted not individuals, but the nation. I interpret "*am eḥad*, one people," not in the sense of a certain people, but of one united people. Notwithstanding the fact that they are "scattered and dispersed across all the provinces of your realm," they are a united people. The fact that we live in so

הַמֶּלֶךְ כֹּרְעִים וּמִשְׁתַּחֲוִים לְהָמָן כִּי־כֵן צִוָּה־לוֹ הַמֶּלֶךְ וּמָרְדֳּכַי לֹא
ג יִכְרַע וְלֹא יִשְׁתַּחֲוֶה: וַיֹּאמְרוּ עַבְדֵי הַמֶּלֶךְ אֲשֶׁר־בְּשַׁעַר הַמֶּלֶךְ
ד לְמָרְדֳּכָי מַדּוּעַ אַתָּה עוֹבֵר אֵת מִצְוַת הַמֶּלֶךְ: וַיְהִי באמרם אֵלָיו יוֹם כְּאָמְרָם
וָיוֹם וְלֹא שָׁמַע אֲלֵיהֶם וַיַּגִּידוּ לְהָמָן לִרְאוֹת הֲיַעַמְדוּ דִּבְרֵי מָרְדֳּכַי
ה כִּי־הִגִּיד לָהֶם אֲשֶׁר־הוּא יְהוּדִי: וַיַּרְא הָמָן כִּי־אֵין מָרְדֳּכַי כֹּרֵעַ
ו וּמִשְׁתַּחֲוֶה לוֹ וַיִּמָּלֵא הָמָן חֵמָה: וַיִּבֶז בְּעֵינָיו לִשְׁלֹחַ יָד בְּמָרְדֳּכַי לְבַדּוֹ
כִּי־הִגִּידוּ לוֹ אֶת־עַם מָרְדֳּכָי וַיְבַקֵּשׁ הָמָן לְהַשְׁמִיד אֶת־כָּל־הַיְּהוּדִים
ז אֲשֶׁר בְּכָל־מַלְכוּת אֲחַשְׁוֵרוֹשׁ עַם מָרְדֳּכָי: בַּחֹדֶשׁ הָרִאשׁוֹן הוּא־
חֹדֶשׁ נִיסָן בִּשְׁנַת שְׁתֵּים עֶשְׂרֵה לַמֶּלֶךְ אֲחַשְׁוֵרוֹשׁ הִפִּיל פּוּר הוּא
הַגּוֹרָל לִפְנֵי הָמָן מִיּוֹם ׀ לְיוֹם וּמֵחֹדֶשׁ לְחֹדֶשׁ שְׁנֵים־עָשָׂר הוּא־
ח חֹדֶשׁ אֲדָר: וַיֹּאמֶר הָמָן לַמֶּלֶךְ אֲחַשְׁוֵרוֹשׁ יֶשְׁנוֹ עַם־אֶחָד

לֹא יִכְרַע וְלֹא יִשְׁתַּחֲוֶה *would neither kneel nor bow down.* These two verbs appear in the future tense. The past tense would be interpreted as recording a past event. However, by introducing the future tense the Megilla informs us about a pattern of behavior, about a characteristic feature of Mordekhai. Mordekhai is not bowing nor will he ever bow. At the beginning of the verse, the Megilla employs the present tense concerning the other courtiers who did kneel and bow. The present tense emphasizes that they were mentally fit and ready to prostrate themselves before their chief while Mordekhai found it impossible to do so. He does not worship idols not only because he was enjoined but also because he was psychologically incapable of humbling and humiliating himself. Regardless of universal interests, Mordekhai retained his unique commitment.

פּוּר הוּא הַגּוֹרָל *a pur – lots, that is.* The decree of Ahasuerus was unreasonable, absurd, an accident. Is not Purim the memorial to, and the Book of Esther the story of, human vulnerability? The ancient Greeks looked upon fate as something absurd, unalterable, and ruthless that, at best, is indifferent to the aspirations of man. We Jews have certainly rejected their mythological fate or fates. There is nothing accidental in nature. Fate and fortune belong to the creation order which God sanctioned, and as such, there is reasonableness to every event. However, man was admitted to understand certain creation or-

9 it really is not worth the king's while to leave them so. If so it please the king, let it be decreed in writing to destroy them – and I shall weigh out ten thousand talents of silver, into the hands of the bureaucrats, to be delivered to the king's treasury."

10 The king took the ring from his finger, and gave it to Haman son of Hamedata,

---

never guess their attitude toward institutions and people. They are simply unpredictable. What may occur to an inscrutable mind is impossible to foresee. One cannot gauge the psychological reactions and motivations of a Jew. Now he is loyal; tomorrow he will plot against the king. Secondly, says Haman, if the Jews decide to plot and join the underground, the king will be confronted with a menace of gigantic proportions. The danger will be great for two reasons: first, they are a united, well-organized, and disciplined people, very clannish and extremely obstinate; second, due to their dispersion and ubiquity, the Jews will carry the message of rebellion throughout your entire empire. There are Jews in every city, town, village, and hamlet. It is humanly impossible to control and watch them. They are in contact with all races and peoples throughout the far-flung lands of your Majesty. An insurrection initiated by the Jews will spread like wildfire. We all will be helpless. Suppression would be an absurdity under such circumstances. It is against the best interests of the king to permit such a status quo to continue: "it really is not worth the king's while to leave them so." Now we understand why Ahasuerus consented at once to let Haman execute his satanic plan. When a paranoiac, who lives in fear of some imaginary monster-fiend, is given an opportunity to fix the blame upon a certain person or group, then all human inhibitions and moral controls are abandoned. The paranoid person has, in such a situation, one dominant irresistible urge – to destroy, because safety can be attained only through destruction. (*Days of Deliverance*)

וַיָּסַר הַמֶּלֶךְ אֶת טַבַּעְתּוֹ מֵעַל יָדוֹ *The king took the ring from his finger.* Our Sages say, "The removal of the ring [from Ahasuerus' finger to Haman's] accomplished more than forty-eight prophets" (*Megilla* 14a). It united the people. Let us not forget that, during the First Commonwealth, the Jews were divided into two kingdoms, the Ten Tribes on the one hand and Judah and Benjamin on the other. At times their interests collided, and there was civil war. Now, for the Second Commonwealth, God wanted a united people. He did not want the

מְפֻזָּר וּמְפֹרָד בֵּין הָעַמִּים בְּכֹל מְדִינוֹת מַלְכוּתֶךָ וְדָתֵיהֶם שֹׁנוֹת
מִכָּל־עָם וְאֶת־דָּתֵי הַמֶּלֶךְ אֵינָם עֹשִׂים וְלַמֶּלֶךְ אֵין־שֹׁוֶה לְהַנִּיחָם׃
ט אִם־עַל־הַמֶּלֶךְ טוֹב יִכָּתֵב לְאַבְּדָם וַעֲשֶׂרֶת אֲלָפִים כִּכַּר־כֶּסֶף אֶשְׁקוֹל
י עַל־יְדֵי עֹשֵׂי הַמְּלָאכָה לְהָבִיא אֶל־גִּנְזֵי הַמֶּלֶךְ׃ וַיָּסַר הַמֶּלֶךְ אֶת־
טַבַּעְתּוֹ מֵעַל יָדוֹ וַיִּתְּנָהּ לְהָמָן בֶּן־הַמְּדָתָא הָאֲגָגִי צֹרֵר הַיְּהוּדִים׃

---

many countries, speak so many languages, dress in a variety of ways, have different concerns, and do not even know one another, does not deter Haman from looking upon us as a united people. (*Days of Deliverance*)

When Balaam saw the Jewish people dwelling tribe by tribe, he apprehended the mystery of the solitary mode of Jewish existence and proclaimed in a state of amazement: "הֶן עָם לְבָדָד יִשְׁכֹּן וּבַגּוֹיִם לֹא יִתְחַשָּׁב, Lo, it is a people that shall dwell alone, and shall not be reckoned among the nations" (Num. 23:9). Even if a person achieves the pinnacle of social or political success, he will still not be able to free himself from the chains of isolation. This paradoxical fate has preserved both the separateness and the uniqueness of the Jew despite his supposed integration into his foreign, non-Jewish environment. The Hebrew word for "people," *am*, is related to the Hebrew word *im* meaning "with," "togetherness." Jewish peoplehood signifies both togetherness and the uniqueness that derives from togetherness. (*Kol Dodi Dofek*)

מְפֻזָּר וּמְפֹרָד בֵּין הָעַמִּים בְּכֹל מְדִינוֹת מַלְכוּתֶךָ וְדָתֵיהֶם שֹׁנוֹת מִכָּל עָם *scattered and dispersed across all the provinces of your realm, whose laws are different from those of all the other peoples.* It was in the interests of Haman to keep the king in a state of nervous tension and restlessness, to magnify the dangers and drive the king to insanity, for a secure Ahasuerus could not have tolerated a brute like Haman. Only a sick, frightened individual could appoint Haman as the chief of staff. There is no doubt that Haman's indictment of the Jewish people aimed at arousing suspicions concerning their loyalty. Two questions arise. First, why should the king be concerned with the dispersion of the Jews throughout his empire? Second, why should the king mind the unique Jewish laws? The Megilla emphasizes several times the polyglot and multinational character of the empire. The latter was not a homogenous but a diverse community. What is wrong with a people who profess a singular faith?

The answer is simple. Since they have outlandish mores and customs, a strange mentality and incomprehensible outlook, one could

11 the Agagite, enemy of the Jews. And the king said to Haman, "The money is
yours, and so is the people; do with it as you will."

12 The king's scribes were called on the thirteenth day of the first month, and
they wrote all that Haman commanded the king's viceroys, the administra-
tors of every single province and the ministers of every single people, to
each province in its language and to each people in its tongue, written in the
13 name of King Ahasuerus and sealed with the king's ring. Scrolls were sent
out with the runners, to all the provinces of the king – ruling that they wipe
out, kill and destroy all the Jews, young and old, children and women alike,
all in one day: the thirteenth [day] of the twelfth month, which is the month
14 of Adar – leaving their wealth for plunder. The text of that letter was to lay
down law in each and every province, displayed for every people to see, that

---

in the Mishna (*Yadayim* 4:4): "Sennacherib, king of Assyria, came up and intermingled all the peoples." However, it is notable that in setting forth the commandment to wipe out Amalek (*Hilkhot Melakhim* 5:5), Maimonides does not add the phrase, "their memory has long since perished." It would appear from Maimonides' statements that Amalek is still in existence, while the seven nations have descended into the abyss of oblivion. Why didn't Maimonides apply R. Joshua's principle that "Sennacherib, king of Assyria, came up and intermingled all the peoples" to Amalek as he did to the seven nations? The answer to this question is very simple. Scripture testifies that Amalek is still in existence: "The Lord will have war with Amalek from generation to generation." It is impossible that Amalek be completely destroyed before the coming of the Messiah. Where is Amalek to be found? I once heard the following answer from my father of blessed memory, namely, that any nation that conspires to destroy *Knesset Yisrael* becomes, according to the halakha, Amalek. My father added: We have been charged with two commandments concerning Amalek. The first devolves upon every person with reference to an individual Amalekite and is set forth in the verse "You shall blot out the remembrance of Amalek" (Deut. 25:19). The second is the readiness to do battle as a community against any people which seeks to destroy us, and this battle of ours is an obligatory war (*milḥemet mitzva*) on the basis of the verse from Exodus, "The Lord will have war with Amalek from generation to generation." However, the obligation to wipe out individual Amalekites, as set forth in the verse from Deuteronomy, applies only to genealogical descendants of Amalek. (*Kol Dodi Dofek*)

יא וַיֹּאמֶר הַמֶּלֶךְ לְהָמָן הַכֶּסֶף נָתוּן לָךְ וְהָעָם לַעֲשׂוֹת בּוֹ כַּטּוֹב בְּעֵינֶיךָ׃
יב וַיִּקָּרְאוּ סֹפְרֵי הַמֶּלֶךְ בַּחֹדֶשׁ הָרִאשׁוֹן בִּשְׁלוֹשָׁה עָשָׂר יוֹם בּוֹ וַיִּכָּתֵב
כְּכָל־אֲשֶׁר־צִוָּה הָמָן אֶל אֲחַשְׁדַּרְפְּנֵי־הַמֶּלֶךְ וְאֶל־הַפַּחוֹת אֲשֶׁר ׀
עַל־מְדִינָה וּמְדִינָה וְאֶל־שָׂרֵי עַם וָעָם מְדִינָה וּמְדִינָה כִּכְתָבָהּ וְעַם
וָעָם כִּלְשׁוֹנוֹ בְּשֵׁם הַמֶּלֶךְ אֲחַשְׁוֵרֹשׁ נִכְתָּב וְנֶחְתָּם בְּטַבַּעַת הַמֶּלֶךְ׃
יג וְנִשְׁלוֹחַ סְפָרִים בְּיַד הָרָצִים אֶל־כָּל־מְדִינוֹת הַמֶּלֶךְ לְהַשְׁמִיד לַהֲרֹג
וּלְאַבֵּד אֶת־כָּל־הַיְּהוּדִים מִנַּעַר וְעַד־זָקֵן טַף וְנָשִׁים בְּיוֹם אֶחָד
בִּשְׁלוֹשָׁה עָשָׂר לְחֹדֶשׁ שְׁנֵים־עָשָׂר הוּא־חֹדֶשׁ אֲדָר וּשְׁלָלָם לָבוֹז׃
יד פַּתְשֶׁגֶן הַכְּתָב לְהִנָּתֵן דָּת בְּכָל־מְדִינָה וּמְדִינָה גָּלוּי לְכָל־הָעַמִּים

Second Commonwealth to consist of two kingdoms. Who could unite them? Haman. He taught them this idea of common destiny and the impossibility of escaping from Jewish destiny. The Megilla is the book that proclaimed the oneness of the Jewish people and their common fate and destiny. The famous message Mordekhai sent to Esther expressed this idea in the most succinct manner: "Do not imagine that you can escape to the king's palace from the fate of all the Jews" (4:13). Esther reacted with five words. If we are one people, if we are all united, if we share the same destiny, then, "Go. Gather all the Jews" (4:16). (*Days of Deliverance*)

לְהַשְׁמִיד לַהֲרֹג וּלְאַבֵּד אֶת כָּל הַיְּהוּדִים *that they wipe out, kill and destroy all the Jews.* My father, Rav Moshe Soloveitchik, said that the proclamation "The Lord will have war with Amalek from generation to generation" (Ex. 17:16) does not only translate into the communal exercise of waging obligatory war against a specific race, but includes as well the obligation to rise up as a community against any people or group that, filled with maniacal hatred, directs its enmity against *Knesset Yisrael*. When a people emblazons on its banner, "Come and let us cut them off from being a nation; that the name of Israel may be no more in remembrance" (Ps. 83:5) it becomes, thereby, Amalek. Maimonides (*Hilkhot Melakhim* 5:4) writes regarding the seven nations of Canaan: "It is a positive commandment to destroy the seven nations… But their memory has long since perished." Radbaz (in his commentary *ad loc.*) notes that the source for Maimonides' concluding comment, "But their memory has long since perished," is the statement of Rabbi Joshua

15 they should make themselves ready for that day. The runners bolted out at the
king's word, and the law was laid down in the imperial city, Shushan; and the
king and Haman sat down to drink – and the town of Shushan stood aghast
in horror.

4 1 Mordekhai understood all that had happened, and he tore his clothes, and

---

believe that human beings may act like predatory beasts of the jungle. This was a traumatic discovery for the Jews of Persia. The Jew believes intuitively in man's inherent goodness, that a divine spark inhabits every human being, even the habitual sinner and criminal. The sudden confrontation with the total Amalek-style cruelty was, therefore, a painful and rude awakening. In Haman, the Jews of Persia met a descendant of Amalek. Who is Amalek? He is the personification of total evil, for whom immorality has become the norm. Amalek is obviously more than a Bedouin tribe. He is more than a particular group, nationality, or people. He is Everyman gone berserk, who has shed his divine image for that of Satan. This is the persistent villainy that the Lord bids us combat and against which He has sworn eternal enmity. It is for this reason that there is a positive Torah commandment: "Remember what Amalek did to you when you were on your journey, after you left Egypt... Do not forget" (Deut. 25:17, 19).

וּמָרְדֳּכַי יָדַע *Mordekhai understood.* Mordekhai's foreboding prescience was correct. "Mordekhai understood" means that he knew that something monstrous was going to happen. He knew before it happened. When tragedy struck, he did not panic; clearly and objectively he arrived at the conclusion that Esther was summoned by Providence to play her part in the great drama of Israel and the nations. Suddenly, a great light went on and illuminated events that he could not connect before: Ahasuerus' madness, Vashti's execution, Esther's ascent to the throne as the Queen of Persia. These events were isolated events, which were unexplained before, but they began suddenly to fit into a historical pattern and make sense. Mordekhai immediately realized that it is Esther's turn; she and no one else had been selected by Providence as the redeemer of the Jewish people. Mordekhai was not chosen. His assignment consisted of just two things: to apprise Esther of the events that had transpired just a few hours earlier, and to make her realize that the Almighty charged her with a mission. That mission was the *raison d'être* of her paradoxical rise to queenship, for a Jewess to sit on the throne as queen of an empire. (*Days of Deliverance*)

טו לִהְי֥וֹת עֲתִדִ֖ים לַיּ֥וֹם הַזֶּֽה׃ הָֽרָצִ֞ים יָֽצְא֤וּ דְחוּפִים֙ בִּדְבַ֣ר הַמֶּ֔לֶךְ וְהַדָּ֥ת
נִתְּנָ֖ה בְּשׁוּשַׁ֣ן הַבִּירָ֑ה וְהַמֶּ֤לֶךְ וְהָמָן֙ יָשְׁב֣וּ לִשְׁתּ֔וֹת וְהָעִ֥יר שׁוּשָׁ֖ן
ד א נָבֽוֹכָה׃ וּמָרְדֳּכַ֗י יָדַע֙ אֶת־כָּל־אֲשֶׁ֣ר נַעֲשָׂ֔ה וַיִּקְרַ֤ע מָרְדֳּכַי֙

וְהַמֶּלֶךְ וְהָמָן יָשְׁבוּ לִשְׁתּוֹת *and the king and Haman sat down to drink.* If not watched and supervised carefully, man may become a beauty addict. He is prone to succumb to beauty, to become intoxicated with a lovely face and an attractive sight, to the extent of abandoning all other commitments. Beauty itself is in need of redemption. There is so much primitive, cold, cruel, scheming and treacherously false beauty around that it is comical to speak about the high potential of remedial energy in beauty. Does not the Book of Esther tell us so much about the developed sense of beauty of King Ahasuerus, who was a connoisseur in enjoying food and women? Would we say that his relationship to women was humane, decent, and ethical? Was there an element of genuine love, devotion, and understanding? Is beauty good, and art cathartic by its very nature? Let me put aside philosophic abstractions and relate to you a small incident which took place in Vilna during the German occupation. I have heard that there was a Gestapo officer there who was an accomplished musician, an expert on Beethoven and Mozart. He was also an expert in killing children. He particularly liked to engage in both of his hobbies simultaneously. While he sat at a piano or organ in the courtyard of the Gestapo headquarters in Vilna, the Gestapo officers used to line up little babies and children. Ambidextrous, he played Beethoven's *Moonlight Sonata* with his right hand, while the left hand was busy shooting innocent babies, one by one. If you investigate the background of Hitler and his entourage, which consisted of psychopaths and maniacs, you will find among them many people with a developed sense of beauty: accomplished musicians, art critics, and the like. They loved beauty and had succumbed to beauty. But they also liked spilling blood, particularly Jewish blood. Somehow, beauty did not protect them from murder. (*Festival of Freedom*)

וְהָעִיר שׁוּשָׁן נָבוֹכָה *the town of Shushan stood aghast in horror.* Our faith in man's goodness should not blind us to the latent demonic in man. Evidently, civilized men can become the personification of evil. "The town of Shushan stood aghast in horror" due to the traditional naivete of the Jew who cannot

dressed himself in sackcloth and ash; and he walked out across the town,
2 crying out, a great and bitter cry. He came as far as the entrance to the
3 King's Gate – for no one enters the King's Gate dressed in sackcloth. And
in every single province, wherever the king's word and law extended, deep
mourning prevailed among the Jews, and fasting and weeping and grief,
the multitudes lying down upon sackcloth and ash.

4 Esther's young maids and her eunuchs came and told her of this – and the
queen's whole body shook. And she sent clothes for Mordekhai to put on,
5 to lay aside the sackcloth he was wearing – but he would not accept them. So
Esther called Hatakh, the king's eunuch employed for her service; and she
bid him go and speak to Mordekhai, to find out what all this was, and why.
6 Hatakh went out to Mordekhai, to the town square just before the King's
7 Gate; and Mordekhai told him all that had happened to him, and all about
the money that Haman had promised to have weighed out to the king's
8 treasury in return for the Jews, to destroy them. And he gave him the text
of the decree that had been issued in Shushan to have them wiped out,
telling him to show it to Esther and to speak to her, bidding her strictly
to go to the king and plead with him, to entreat with him on her people's
9 10 behalf. Hatakh came and told Esther what Mordekhai had said. Esther

---

vice: one is continuous – one serves God as long as he lives – and one is timely – man should serve when a special, urgent summons is addressed by God to man. Such an appeal was addressed to Abraham, "Take now your son" (Gen. 22:2). Such a request was made of Esther by Mordekhai: "Bidding her strictly to go to the king and plead with him, to entreat with him on her people's behalf," even at the risk of losing her life. Such a "petition" is submitted to each individual once in his life. The day-by-day service has the universal character to which Micah referred when he asked his famous question, "What does the Lord require of you?" (Mic. 6:8). The one-timely service that the individual is called upon to perform is singular; only the individual who received the call is capable of rendering it. In this service, one finds fulfillment. The service requested of Esther was of a singular nature, one that only she could accomplish: "And who can say; could it not be for just such a time as this that you came into royalty?" (4:14). Many events that at first glance seem completely irrelevant may transpire in order to give the individual an opportunity to perform his mission. He is catapulted into the strangest place, since only there it is possible for him to serve. (*Days of Deliverance*)

אֶת־בְּגָדָיו וַיִּלְבַּשׁ שַׂק וָאֵפֶר וַיֵּצֵא בְּתוֹךְ הָעִיר וַיִּזְעַק זְעָקָה גְדוֹלָה
ב וּמָרָה׃ וַיָּבוֹא עַד לִפְנֵי שַׁעַר־הַמֶּלֶךְ כִּי אֵין לָבוֹא אֶל־שַׁעַר הַמֶּלֶךְ
ג בִּלְבוּשׁ שָׂק׃ וּבְכָל־מְדִינָה וּמְדִינָה מְקוֹם אֲשֶׁר דְּבַר־הַמֶּלֶךְ וְדָתוֹ
מַגִּיעַ אֵבֶל גָּדוֹל לַיְּהוּדִים וְצוֹם וּבְכִי וּמִסְפֵּד שַׂק וָאֵפֶר יֻצַּע לָרַבִּים׃
ד ותבואינה נַעֲרוֹת אֶסְתֵּר וְסָרִיסֶיהָ וַיַּגִּידוּ לָהּ וַתִּתְחַלְחַל הַמַּלְכָּה וַתָּבוֹאנָה
מְאֹד וַתִּשְׁלַח בְּגָדִים לְהַלְבִּישׁ אֶת־מָרְדֳּכַי וּלְהָסִיר שַׂקּוֹ מֵעָלָיו וְלֹא
ה קִבֵּל׃ וַתִּקְרָא אֶסְתֵּר לַהֲתָךְ מִסָּרִיסֵי הַמֶּלֶךְ אֲשֶׁר הֶעֱמִיד לְפָנֶיהָ
ו וַתְּצַוֵּהוּ עַל־מָרְדֳּכָי לָדַעַת מַה־זֶּה וְעַל־מַה־זֶּה׃ וַיֵּצֵא הֲתָךְ אֶל־
ז מָרְדֳּכָי אֶל־רְחוֹב הָעִיר אֲשֶׁר לִפְנֵי שַׁעַר־הַמֶּלֶךְ׃ וַיַּגֶּד־לוֹ מָרְדֳּכַי אֵת
כָּל־אֲשֶׁר קָרָהוּ וְאֵת ׀ פָּרָשַׁת הַכֶּסֶף אֲשֶׁר אָמַר הָמָן לִשְׁקוֹל עַל־גִּנְזֵי
ח הַמֶּלֶךְ ביהודיים לְאַבְּדָם׃ וְאֶת־פַּתְשֶׁגֶן כְּתָב־הַדָּת אֲשֶׁר־נִתַּן בְּשׁוּשָׁן בַּיְּהוּדִים
לְהַשְׁמִידָם נָתַן לוֹ לְהַרְאוֹת אֶת־אֶסְתֵּר וּלְהַגִּיד לָהּ וּלְצַוּוֹת עָלֶיהָ
ט לָבוֹא אֶל־הַמֶּלֶךְ לְהִתְחַנֶּן־לוֹ וּלְבַקֵּשׁ מִלְּפָנָיו עַל־עַמָּהּ׃ וַיָּבוֹא הֲתָךְ
י וַיַּגֵּד לְאֶסְתֵּר אֵת דִּבְרֵי מָרְדֳּכָי׃ וַתֹּאמֶר אֶסְתֵּר לַהֲתָךְ וַתְּצַוֵּהוּ אֶל־

וַיִּזְעַק זְעָקָה גְדוֹלָה וּמָרָה *crying out, a great and bitter cry.* Is a loud prayer more acceptable to God than a silent prayer? Does God measure the sound waves? The cry was loud and bitter because Mordekhai was not a single person but a people; it was as loud as the cry of millions, and as bitter as the accumulated tears of millions. His cry was the sum total of all individual prayers. He incarnated the people. Through him and with him the nation cried. Haman, in his blind hatred, intuited this. The Mordekhai who defies him is not just an individual, a lonely, single Jew, but Mordekhai the people, Mordekhai the nation, Mordekhai the multitude. Therefore "Haman sought to destroy all the Jews … the people of Mordekhai" (3:6). The same is true of Esther. When she fasts, the whole community fasts with her; when she is clothed in royal garments, the whole community feels that salvation is just a step away. Esther was the nation; Esther was the people. She was Israel. (*Days of Deliverance*)

לָבוֹא אֶל הַמֶּלֶךְ לְהִתְחַנֶּן לוֹ וּלְבַקֵּשׁ מִלְּפָנָיו עַל עַמָּהּ *to go to the king and plead with him, to entreat with him on her people's behalf.* There are two kinds of ser-

11 told Hatakh, bidding him repeat it to Mordekhai, "All the king's courtiers,
and all the people of his provinces know, that there is only one law for
any man or woman who comes before the king, into the inner courtyard,
without being called: to be killed. Unless, that is, the king extends the
golden scepter towards him, that he live on. And as for me – I have not
12 been called to come before the king these thirty days past." And Mordekhai
was told what Esther had said.

13 Mordekhai sent back reply to Esther – "Do not imagine that you can escape
14 to the king's palace from the fate of all the Jews. For if you keep your silence
at this time, relief and salvation will come forth for the Jews from some
other place – but you and your father's house will be lost forever. And
who can say; could it not be for just such a time as this that you came into
royalty?"

---

the same mission was placed upon the frail shoulders of a delicate and lonely young woman who steadily lived in the shadow of rejection and death. She was burdened with a gigantic task. She was a queen not because Ahasuerus crowned her but on account of the great assignment entrusted her. Second, in the face of human failure, betrayal, or indifference, God's will nonetheless will be done. The assignment will be carried out – if not by the individual, then by someone else. "For if you keep your silence at this time, relief and salvation will come forth for the Jews from some other place." Third, the individual who did not answer the call of history, did not respond to the challenge, did not carry out his assignment – such a person is a traitor and his sin is unpardonable. "But you and your father's house will be lost forever." (*Vision and Leadership*)

וּמִי יוֹדֵעַ אִם לְעֵת כָּזֹאת הִגַּעַתְּ לַמַּלְכוּת *And who can say; could it not be for just such a time as this that you came into royalty?* The Megilla contains the story of events that occurred in the twilight hour of Jewish history. It marks the passing of a bright, beautiful, summer day, full of song, color and joy, a day on which God's word was on many tongues and His spirit in many hearts. It ushers in a dark, dreary, autumnal night of silence and fear, a night in the course of which God stopped speaking to His people. At that time, the covenantal community was losing, slowly but surely, the most precious of all gifts: prophecy. The great covenantal dialogue between man and God that had commenced with Abraham was about to be terminated,

יא מׇרְדֳּכָי: כׇּל־עַבְדֵי הַמֶּלֶךְ וְעַם מְדִינוֹת הַמֶּלֶךְ יֹדְעִים אֲשֶׁר כׇּל־אִישׁ
וְאִשָּׁה אֲשֶׁר־יָבוֹא אֶל־הַמֶּלֶךְ אֶל־הֶחָצֵר הַפְּנִימִית אֲשֶׁר לֹא־יִקָּרֵא
אַחַת דָּתוֹ לְהָמִית לְבַד מֵאֲשֶׁר יוֹשִׁיט־לוֹ הַמֶּלֶךְ אֶת־שַׁרְבִיט הַזָּהָב
יב וְחָיָה וַאֲנִי לֹא נִקְרֵאתִי לָבוֹא אֶל־הַמֶּלֶךְ זֶה שְׁלוֹשִׁים יוֹם: וַיַּגִּידוּ
יג לְמׇרְדֳּכָי אֵת דִּבְרֵי אֶסְתֵּר: וַיֹּאמֶר מׇרְדֳּכַי לְהָשִׁיב אֶל־אֶסְתֵּר אַל־
יד תְּדַמִּי בְנַפְשֵׁךְ לְהִמָּלֵט בֵּית־הַמֶּלֶךְ מִכׇּל־הַיְּהוּדִים: כִּי אִם־הַחֲרֵשׁ
תַּחֲרִישִׁי בָּעֵת הַזֹּאת רֶוַח וְהַצָּלָה יַעֲמוֹד לַיְּהוּדִים מִמָּקוֹם אַחֵר
וְאַתְּ וּבֵית־אָבִיךְ תֹּאבֵדוּ וּמִי יוֹדֵעַ אִם־לָעֵת כָּזֹאת הִגַּעַתְּ לַמַּלְכוּת:

אַל תְּדַמִּי בְנַפְשֵׁךְ לְהִמָּלֵט בֵּית הַמֶּלֶךְ מִכׇּל הַיְּהוּדִים *Do not imagine that you can escape to the king's palace from the fate of all the Jews.* Our fate does not distinguish between aristocrats and common folk, between rich and poor, between a prince garbed in the royal purple and a pauper begging from door to door, between a pietist and an assimilationist. Even though we speak a plethora of languages, even though we are inhabitants of different lands, even though we look different – one may be short and dark, the other tall and blond – even though we live in varying and unequal social and economic conditions – one may dwell in a magnificent palace, the other in a miserable hovel – we still share the same fate. If the Jew in the hovel is beaten, then the security of the Jew in the palace is endangered. "Do not imagine that you can escape to the king's palace from the fate of all the Jews." Both Queen Esther, garbed in royal apparel, and Mordekhai the Jew, clad in sackcloth, were caught in the same web of historical circumstances. "*Ḥaverim kol Yisrael,* All Israel are knit together" – we will all be pursued unto death or we will all be redeemed with an eternal salvation. (*Kol Dodi Dofek*)

וְאַתְּ וּבֵית אָבִיךְ תֹּאבֵדוּ *but you and your father's house will be lost forever.* Here we encounter Judaism's doctrine of assignment. It consists of three basic component parts, all of them spelled out by Mordekhai. First, each individual is assigned a task which he must implement, and which does not transcend his ability. The mission of saving the people was once placed squarely upon the strong shoulders of David and his commander-in-chief Joab. And now

15 Esther sent back word to Mordekhai – "Go. Gather all the Jews in Shushan,
16 and fast for me, do not eat and do not drink for three whole days, day or

---

The answer to this question is more a statement of facts than an explanation. Even during the non-prophetic era, at a time when the divine countenance is hidden (*hester panim*), man is elected by God to carry on, to make decisions, to undertake difficult tasks courageously and implement them superbly. Of course, it is a superhuman task for a young, inexperienced maiden. However, the spirit of God will descend on her and inspire her to defy danger and to make the right decisions. God asks of man to reach maturity and independence. He wills man to act with courage and wisdom, allegedly as his own master. "This song shall answer" (Deut. 31:21); the song of the Torah will never be terminated. All communities, prophetic and non-prophetic, will join in. (*Days of Deliverance*)

לֵךְ כְּנוֹס אֶת כׇּל הַיְּהוּדִים הַנִּמְצְאִים בְּשׁוּשָׁן וְצוּמוּ עָלַי *Go. Gather all the Jews in Shushan, and fast for me.* Esther taught Mordekhai and the Jews how to pray and how to fast in times of distress and crisis. The inspired-charismatic woman is superior to inspired-charismatic man in two areas: the area of applied, practical thinking and the area of prayer. The woman knows something that man does not know. Was not Hannah the great, charismatic teacher who taught the entire congregation of Israel how to pray and how to confront God with petition? Our Sages said, "Many important rules can be derived from the verses relating to Hannah's prayer" (*Berakhot* 31a). While Hannah taught the individual, the lonely man or woman, how to pour out his or her soul in times of distress and vexation, Esther taught Mordekhai, the Jews, and all future generations how to pray in assembly, in community, when disaster strikes the nation. The gesture of cunning and that of prayer represent two opposite aspects of the human personality, which find their reconciliation in woman. Cunning, in contrast to slyness, is an art that only the adult is capable of mastering. Only mature people, toughened by experiences, have the ability of planning strategy, of devising schemes, of not overlooking the smallest detail and not dismissing the most farfetched possibilities. An immature person cannot engage in the art of diplomacy or military strategy. Providence appointed Esther to the most sensitive diplomatic post. It is clear that she had all the attributes indispensable for such a mission. On the other hand, prayer is an art that the child knows best. The mature person is a cynic, a skeptic, too practical-minded, too tough and insensitive. Maturity ennobles and corrupts man at the same time. When is man

טו טז וַתֹּ֥אמֶר אֶסְתֵּ֖ר לְהָשִׁ֥יב אֶֽל־מָרְדֳּכָֽי׃ לֵךְ֩ כְּנ֨וֹס אֶת־כָּל־הַיְּהוּדִ֜ים
הַנִּמְצְאִ֣ים בְּשׁוּשָׁ֗ן וְצ֣וּמוּ עָ֠לַי וְאַל־תֹּאכְל֨וּ וְאַל־תִּשְׁתּ֜וּ שְׁלֹ֤שֶׁת יָמִים֙

---

and the prophetic community faced a stark, ruthless reality – a non-prophetic existence. With the transition from a prophetic to a non-prophetic community, the Jewish historical experience changed completely. The mission with which Moses was charged was precisely defined. There was no alternative but to act in a strictly prescribed manner. Moses did not enjoy freedom of decision and action. He received specific instructions, what to do and how to accomplish it. "Speak to the children of Israel that they go forward. Lift up your rod and stretch out your hand over the sea" (Ex. 14:15-16). Mordekhai, in contrast to this kind of agency, received not a clearly defined but a multifaceted mandate. It was left to him how to interpret and implement this mandate. Mordekhai was confronted with a number of alternatives. The choice was his. He exercised free judgment. In Egypt, God acted; man was an onlooker. In Persia, God summoned man to act freely and wisely, under God's supervision and watchful eyes.

Of course, God was in communication with man in both eras. However, the nature of the communication is not the same. In the prophetic era, the communication is clear and understandable; in the non-prophetic era, the communications are laconic and enigmatic, consisting of mysterious hints and signs, bright, dazzling flashes and intimations that mystify man, who is often lonely and feels forsaken. He is under the impression, however incorrect, that God has abandoned and deserted him. A frightening silence envelops everybody and everything.

"Where is there an allusion to Esther in the Pentateuch?" asks the Talmud (*Ḥullin* 139b). The answer is given immediately: "And I shall hide (*haster astir*) My countenance on that day" (Deut. 31:18). What did the Talmud mean to express by this question and answer? The Pentateuch tells us the story of the prophetic community at the hour of triumph, at the hour of unusual revelation and direct contact with God. But what kind of message does the Pentateuch have for the non-prophetic community at an hour of distress? Where is there in the Torah an allusion to the silent, mute confrontation between mighty historical events and the Jew in the Diaspora, between a wicked, cruel monster and a lonely Jewish maiden on whose frail shoulders Providence placed the heavy load of historical responsibility? How can the Jew triumph over his adversaries and enemies if God has stopped speaking to him, if the cryptic messages he receives remain unintelligible and incomprehensible?

night; I and my maids shall fast also. And so shall I come before the king, in defiance of the law – and if I am lost – I am lost."

17 Then Mordekhai walked on, and did all that Esther had bid him.

---

before You") are recited and a mood of solemn penitence prevails. The Fast of Esther and Purim are integrally connected – unlike Passover and the Fast of the Firstborn, where the latter does not form part of the festival and is an extraneous addendum. The Fast of Esther, however, is a genuine Purim day; it reflects the foreboding fear and prayer of the Jews on the thirteenth of Adar as they gave battle to their enemies. Purim day itself celebrates the victory which followed, the sudden miraculous salvation of the people. The joining of a fast day and a feast day bespeaks the dual character of Purim. Perhaps the common feature to both Purim and Yom Kippur is that aspect of Purim which is a call for divine compassion and intercession, a mood of petition arising out of great distress. While the Fast of Esther reflects the terror of the threatening physical extinction of the people, the prayerful mood of Yom Kippur emerges out of a sense of spiritual anxiety and the desperate need for reconciliation with God.

וְכַאֲשֶׁר אָבַדְתִּי, אָבָדְתִּי *and if I am lost – I am lost.* May an individual sacrifice his life in order to save the community? This problem arose quite frequently throughout Jewish history. At the beginning of the eighteenth century in Vilna, there was an apostate who had been excommunicated and expelled from the Jewish community and wanted to take revenge. In Vilna was a famous cathedral in which was contained a famous icon. The apostate stole the icon and hid it in the *Aron Kodesh* of the Old Synagogue. (He probably colluded with some priest or some other member of the clergy. Otherwise, he could never have gained access to the cathedral.) He went to the Archbishop and informed him that on Hoshana Raba the Jews will take the icon, place the icon on the altar, and take turns striking it with bushels of reeds. He suggested that they send someone to the Old Synagogue to find the icon hidden in the ark and to search a few Jewish homes for the reeds. That is exactly what happened. The thirty members of the Jewish council were arrested. Naturally, the verdict was a foregone conclusion. It meant simply that they would be tortured and burned at the stake. A certain individual, Rav Man ben Rav Man, approached Rav Shmuel *Aharon*, the last rabbi of Vilna and a contemporary of the Vilna Gaon. He

לַיְלָה וָיוֹם גַּם־אֲנִי וְנַעֲרֹתַי אָצוּם כֵּן וּבְכֵן אָבוֹא אֶל־הַמֶּלֶךְ אֲשֶׁר
יז לֹא־כַדָּת וְכַאֲשֶׁר אָבַדְתִּי אָבָדְתִּי׃ וַיַּעֲבֹר מָרְדֳּכָי וַיַּעַשׂ כְּכֹל אֲשֶׁר־

---

summoned to pray? When he is completely overpowered by emotions, by black despair or dazzling joy; when he is under the impression that his world has disintegrated and is in shambles; or when he feels himself a conqueror, when he is enraptured with himself and the world, when he is delirious with joy. Prayer is an expression of either complete resignation or ecstasy. Prayer requires the individual's absolute identification with an emotional state. An adult usually does not experience emotions of unlimited intensity and all-powerful dynamics. When he meets with adversity, he tries to console himself by saying that it is just a temporary experience; when he is triumphant he tells himself that triumph quite often leads to defeat. The adult tries to protect himself against the onslaught of the tidal wave of emotions. The child responds spontaneously to his emotions; he fluctuates quite often between despair and joy. He never tries to censor them. The distress of a child is boundless, and there is no limit to his happiness. He knows how to pray "from the depths" and at the same time how to thank and serenade God, how to sing praises to Him. The Jew should be adult and child, grown up and immature at the same time. When called upon to act as divine agent, to be a history-maker, the Jew must be mature, courageous, and intellectually developed. When it is time to pray, the Jew must shed his maturity and reach out for either the enthusiasm or the grief of the child. The woman is more of an expert in playing this double role. Esther performed it magnificently. She knew how to be cunning and how to pray. Therefore, the Megilla is named for Esther. (*Days of Deliverance*)

וּבְכֵן אָבוֹא אֶל הַמֶּלֶךְ *And so shall I come before the king.* We usually think of Purim in terms of indulgence and merrymaking, to the point of forgetfulness and the dulling of the senses. Actually, Purim is also a day of introspection and prayerful meditation. The Megilla is both a book of thanksgiving and a book of distress and petition. The narrative relates two stories, of a people in a terrifying predicament and also of their great exhilaration at their sudden deliverance. Since it is impossible to juxtapose contradictory moods into one day, our Sages instituted the Fast of Esther for the thirteenth of Adar in anticipation of Purim. They advanced the supplication aspect of Purim to the preceding day, when *seliḥot* and *Avinu Malkenu* ("Our Father, our King, we have sinned

5 1 On the third day, Esther dressed herself in royalty, and came to stand in the inner courtyard of the king's palace, facing the palace, while the king sat upon his royal throne in the great hall, facing the palace entrance.

וַיַּעַשׂ כְּכֹל אֲשֶׁר צִוְּתָה עָלָיו אֶסְתֵּר *and did all that Esther had bid him.* Mordekhai's task had been to watch over Esther and to inspire and influence her. He had been Esther's teacher for many years. He had raised her. At this stage, the man is the leader, the woman the follower; the man is the teacher, the woman the disciple. The voice of God addressed itself through Mordekhai. He was bold, aggressive, and initiated action. He knew first; he conveyed the news to Esther. Suddenly, the scene changes; roles are shifted. The man-actor is demoted to a less prominent position, and the central role is turned over to the figure whom, until now, had played a lesser role. At this juncture, Esther takes over; she is the mistress, Mordekhai the follower. She issues orders, gives instructions. Mordekhai is the subordinate, submissive and obedient. He performs the errands for her. The very moment Esther said that she was ready to go to the king, ready to face torture and death, the spotlight shifted from him to her. Providence wanted the woman to be the divine agent, the messenger of the Almighty, and man to remain in the wings. Why? The first intellectual judgment, the first intuitive flash, the primordial revelation of truth belongs frequently to man. However, when it comes to implementation, the woman is the master. The implementation of any plan is a technological feat that consists in the selection and employment of the most effective means for the sake of achieving a desired end. This is cunning, which is the forte of the woman. Our Sages said: "Woman was endowed by the Holy One, blessed be He, with supplemental intuition, *bina yeteira*" (*Nidda* 45b). She is more incisive and has better practical judgment than the man. Esther became the main actor. Mordekhai had to listen to her. (*Days of Deliverance*)

וַיְהִי בַּיּוֹם הַשְּׁלִישִׁי, וַתִּלְבַּשׁ אֶסְתֵּר מַלְכוּת *On the third day, Esther dressed herself in royalty.* Judaism disliked cowardice or the exaggerated caution that tells man that he must not begin unless he knows for sure that he will be able to finish. Courageous action is motivated not by pragmatic, mercantile, discursive, logical reasoning, but by convincing, intuitive insights, by spiritual perceptions that are beyond the reach of logical-formal analysis. As a matter of fact, the most important decisions in one's life are reached in the intuitive rather than in the logical dimension. The Jew of old defying Haman was guided not by syllogistic inferences. Had he inquired of the strict, slightly pompous logos,

ה א צִוְּתָה עָלָיו אֶסְתֵּר׃ וַיְהִי ׀ בַּיּוֹם הַשְּׁלִישִׁי וַתִּלְבַּשׁ אֶסְתֵּר מַלְכוּת
וַתַּעֲמֹד בַּחֲצַר בֵּית־הַמֶּלֶךְ הַפְּנִימִית נֹכַח בֵּית הַמֶּלֶךְ וְהַמֶּלֶךְ יוֹשֵׁב

---

said that he was willing to accept the blame upon himself to save the community. He would tell the Archbishop that he had stolen the icon and that the reeds were just an annual Jewish ritual which had nothing in common with the theft of the icon. He knew that he would be executed, but he was willing to do so in order to save the lives of thirty people. He asked Rav Shmuel whether he was permitted to do so or not. Rav Shmuel answered that he wished to consult with the Vilna Gaon since it was a very serious question. He asked Rav Man to return in a few hours. We know that Rav Shmuel consulted with the Gaon, but we do not know what the Gaon told him. Later that night, on the night of Shemini Atzeret, Rav Shmuel asked someone to bring Rav Man to his home.

Rav Man came to the house and told Rav Shmuel that he had decided what to do. Rav Shmuel was flabbergasted. He told Rav Man that he had advised him not to make any decisions until after he consulted with the Gaon. Rav Man said that there is no need for the Vilna Gaon; there was no need for anyone else to render a decision. He had decided what to do based on the precedent established by Esther in Megillat Esther. Rav Man went that same night and surrendered to the authorities. The *parnasim* of the community were freed immediately. Rav Man was tortured for many months and was executed on the first day of Shavuot in front of the cathedral. After his death, a practice was established that all synagogues in Vilna recite *E-l malei raḥamim* for HaKadosh Rav Man ben Rav Man twice a year, on Hoshana Raba, and the second day of Shavuot. I myself heard this recited a number of times.

This is the central halakha contained in Megillat Esther. It is the duty of the individual to sacrifice his life if the destiny and the future of the community are at stake. This is what the soldiers in *Eretz Yisrael* practiced in the wars fought with the Arab nations. Many of the soldiers could have been excused from serving in the army; they were not compelled to serve. Yet, seven hundred individuals sacrificed their young lives in the Six-Day War to protect the community of two-and-a-half-million people. It is the same story. While in Megillat Esther it was the story of one frail woman, in 1967, it was the story of an army, of seven hundred individuals who sacrificed their lives. This is the primary lesson derived from Megillat Esther. Let us hope and pray that this issue need not be addressed again.

2 And when the king noticed Queen Esther standing in the courtyard,
she carried grace in his eyes, and the king extended the golden scepter
in his hand towards Esther, and Esther came forward and touched the
3 scepter's end. And the king said to her, "What brings you, Esther my
queen? And what would you ask? Be it even half my kingdom, it shall be
yours."

4 Esther said, "If it so please Your Majesty, may the king come today, with
Haman, to the feast that I have prepared for him."

5 And the king called out, "Hurry – fetch Haman to carry out Esther's word!"

6 So the king and Haman come to the feast that Esther had prepared. And
at that drinking feast, the king said to Esther, "What is your desire, then?
It shall be yours. And what would you ask? Be it even half my kingdom, it
shall be done."

7 8 So Esther answered and replied, "This is my desire and my request: if I am
pleasing to the king, and if it so please the king, to grant what I desire, to give
me my request – let the king and Haman come again to the feast that I shall
prepare for them. And tomorrow I shall do whatever the king asks."

---

has something queenly about her that does not need the crown to corroborate. She has always been a queen. He tells her, You are a queen *per se,* in your own right. You were a queen before you were elevated to queenship by me. (*Days of Deliverance*)

עַד חֲצִי הַמַּלְכוּת וְתֵעָשׂ *Be it even half my kingdom, it shall be yours.* Responding to her indomitable charm, Ahasuerus holds the scepter out and uses a strange phrase: "And what would you ask? Be it even half my kingdom, it shall be yours." Why half the kingdom? Because, says Ahasuerus, you are an equal partner of mine. Half the kingdom belongs to you. Esther's personality and nature were the precise opposite of that of Ahasuerus. The king was a usurper and vulgarian, one who felt truly at home with the wild masses of Shushan. Yet Esther was regal in her essence; she had a noble, refined nature. Ahasuerus indulged repeatedly in voluptuous feasting. Esther in the royal palace refused every favor, every beauty treatment, except that which Hegai forced upon her. Ahasuerus demonstrated his volatile temper and poor judgment, while Esther manifested an inner strength and steadfastness, never revealing her identity and origin. Most important, while the king's actions displayed a self-centered egocentricity, Esther was a model of sacrificial action. Esther was the true queen. (*Days of Deliverance*)

ב על־כסא מלכותו בבית המלכות נכח פתח הבית: ויהי כראות
המלך את־אסתר המלכה עמדת בחצר נשאה חן בעיניו ויושט
המלך לאסתר את־שרביט הזהב אשר בידו ותקרב אסתר ותגע
ג בראש השרביט: ויאמר לה המלך מה־לך אסתר המלכה ומה־
ד בקשתך עד־חצי המלכות וינתן לך: ותאמר אסתר אם־על־המלך
ה טוב יבוא המלך והמן היום אל־המשתה אשר־עשיתי לו: ויאמר
המלך מהרו את־המן לעשות את־דבר אסתר ויבא המלך והמן
ו אל־המשתה אשר־עשתה אסתר: ויאמר המלך לאסתר במשתה
היין מה־שאלתך וינתן לך ומה־בקשתך עד־חצי המלכות ותעש:
ז ח ויען אסתר ותאמר שאלתי ובקשתי: אם־מצאתי חן בעיני המלך
ואם־על־המלך טוב לתת את־שאלתי ולעשות את־בקשתי יבוא
המלך והמן אל־המשתה אשר אעשה להם ומחר אעשה כדבר

---

he would have received an answer in the negative. From a logico-rational viewpoint, those actions are absurd, plainly suicidal. Mordekhai's defiance of Haman, Esther risking her life and with it the lives of millions of Jews, these were logically unwarranted. She did so because, "On the third day, Esther dressed herself in royalty"; the spirit of God descended upon her (*Megilla* 14b). She was inspired. (*Days of Deliverance*)

ויהי כראות המלך את אסתר המלכה עמדת בחצר נשאה חן בעיניו *And when the king noticed Queen Esther standing in the courtyard, she carried grace in his eyes.* Esther refused to betray her people and her origin. The king tried hard to get the secret out of her. He failed. She was "queen in Vashti's place," and at the same time she was not Vashti's successor. She was singular, distinct. She radiated serenity, peace, cleanliness of spirit, power, and kindness. All that struck Ahasuerus on that fateful day when she appeared unbidden in the inner court. She is not Vashti. The latter might have been more beautiful than she. However, some strange light emanates from Esther's eyes that the other one never had. She is called "Esther the queen." The king suddenly notices the queen in Esther. She is a queen in her own right. The strange charm she radiates is invincible; I must hold out the scepter to her, for she is indeed a queen. Sitting on the throne in his full regalia, Ahasuerus realizes that Esther

9 Haman went out on that day, happy and buoyant of heart. But when he saw
Mordekhai at the King's Gate, and the latter did not stand up and did not
10 tremble in his presence, Haman was filled with rage against Mordekhai. Yet
Haman restrained himself until he reached his home, and there he sent for
11 all his friends and his wife, Zeresh. And Haman told them of his glorious
wealth and the great number of his sons, and all the ways the king had ele-
vated him, and raised him above all the ministers and the courtiers of the king.
12 And finally Haman said, "And Esther brought no one else with the king to her
13 feast but me, and tomorrow too I am invited to her along with the king. Yet
all this is worth nothing to me, whenever I see that Jew Mordekhai, sitting
there at the King's Gate."

14 Zeresh, his wife, replied, with all his friends: "Let a post be erected, full fifty
cubits high. And in the morning, just say the word to the king and Mordekhai
shall be hung up on it, and then you will go happy with the king to the
feast." The idea pleased Haman, and he erected the post.

6 1 The king slept fitfully that night. And he called for the scroll of the records,
the Chronicles of the Realm, to be brought to him, to be read out before the
2 king. There it was found written that Mordekhai had reported Bigtan and
Teresh, two of the king's eunuchs, guards of the threshold, who had planned
3 to lay hands upon King Ahasuerus. The king said, "What honor or greatness
has been granted Mordekhai for doing this?" and the king's pages, those who
were attending him, said, "Nothing has been done for him at all."

4 "Who is in the courtyard?" asked the king. And Haman had come to the outer
courtyard of the king's palace, to speak to the king about hanging Mordekhai

---

It could boomerang. This is the reason for Esther's procrastination and slowness. She dreaded the results of an unsuccessful attack on Haman. She took a wait-and-see attitude. She waited for something to happen, for an event to occur. The twenty-four hour intermission between the first and second feast is the most destiny-charged and most crucial period in the whole story. The question was, Will something happen or not? And indeed something happened: "The king slept fitfully that night. And he called for the scroll of the records, the Chronicles of the Realm, to be brought to him, to be read out before the king." (*Days of Deliverance*)

ט הַמֶּלֶךְ: וַיֵּצֵא הָמָן בַּיּוֹם הַהוּא שָׂמֵחַ וְטוֹב לֵב וְכִרְאוֹת הָמָן אֶת־
מָרְדֳּכַי בְּשַׁעַר הַמֶּלֶךְ וְלֹא־קָם וְלֹא־זָע מִמֶּנּוּ וַיִּמָּלֵא הָמָן עַל־מָרְדֳּכַי
י חֵמָה: וַיִּתְאַפַּק הָמָן וַיָּבוֹא אֶל־בֵּיתוֹ וַיִּשְׁלַח וַיָּבֵא אֶת־אֹהֲבָיו וְאֶת־
יא זֶרֶשׁ אִשְׁתּוֹ: וַיְסַפֵּר לָהֶם הָמָן אֶת־כְּבוֹד עָשְׁרוֹ וְרֹב בָּנָיו וְאֵת כָּל־
יב אֲשֶׁר גִּדְּלוֹ הַמֶּלֶךְ וְאֵת אֲשֶׁר נִשְּׂאוֹ עַל־הַשָּׂרִים וְעַבְדֵי הַמֶּלֶךְ: וַיֹּאמֶר
הָמָן אַף לֹא־הֵבִיאָה אֶסְתֵּר הַמַּלְכָּה עִם־הַמֶּלֶךְ אֶל־הַמִּשְׁתֶּה אֲשֶׁר־
יג עָשָׂתָה כִּי אִם־אוֹתִי וְגַם־לְמָחָר אֲנִי קָרוּא־לָהּ עִם־הַמֶּלֶךְ: וְכָל־
זֶה אֵינֶנּוּ שֹׁוֶה לִי בְּכָל־עֵת אֲשֶׁר אֲנִי רֹאֶה אֶת־מָרְדֳּכַי הַיְּהוּדִי יוֹשֵׁב
יד בְּשַׁעַר הַמֶּלֶךְ: וַתֹּאמֶר לוֹ זֶרֶשׁ אִשְׁתּוֹ וְכָל־אֹהֲבָיו יַעֲשׂוּ־עֵץ גָּבֹהַּ
חֲמִשִּׁים אַמָּה וּבַבֹּקֶר ׀ אֱמֹר לַמֶּלֶךְ וְיִתְלוּ אֶת־מָרְדֳּכַי עָלָיו וּבֹא
עִם־הַמֶּלֶךְ אֶל־הַמִּשְׁתֶּה שָׂמֵחַ וַיִּיטַב הַדָּבָר לִפְנֵי הָמָן וַיַּעַשׂ
ו א הָעֵץ: בַּלַּיְלָה הַהוּא נָדְדָה שְׁנַת הַמֶּלֶךְ וַיֹּאמֶר לְהָבִיא
ב אֶת־סֵפֶר הַזִּכְרֹנוֹת דִּבְרֵי הַיָּמִים וַיִּהְיוּ נִקְרָאִים לִפְנֵי הַמֶּלֶךְ: וַיִּמָּצֵא
כָתוּב אֲשֶׁר הִגִּיד מָרְדֳּכַי עַל־בִּגְתָנָא וָתֶרֶשׁ שְׁנֵי סָרִיסֵי הַמֶּלֶךְ
ג מִשֹּׁמְרֵי הַסַּף אֲשֶׁר בִּקְשׁוּ לִשְׁלֹחַ יָד בַּמֶּלֶךְ אֲחַשְׁוֵרוֹשׁ: וַיֹּאמֶר הַמֶּלֶךְ
מַה־נַּעֲשָׂה יְקָר וּגְדוּלָּה לְמָרְדֳּכַי עַל־זֶה וַיֹּאמְרוּ נַעֲרֵי הַמֶּלֶךְ מְשָׁרְתָיו
ד לֹא־נַעֲשָׂה עִמּוֹ דָּבָר: וַיֹּאמֶר הַמֶּלֶךְ מִי בֶחָצֵר וְהָמָן בָּא לַחֲצַר בֵּית־
הַמֶּלֶךְ הַחִיצוֹנָה לֵאמֹר לַמֶּלֶךְ לִתְלוֹת אֶת־מָרְדֳּכַי עַל־הָעֵץ אֲשֶׁר־

בַּלַּיְלָה הַהוּא נָדְדָה שְׁנַת הַמֶּלֶךְ *The king slept fitfully that night.* Esther, with her incisive intelligence, understood that no plea addressed to the king would produce any results. Hysterical crying, supplication, begging, would at best be ineffectual. At worst, they may cause the infliction of more harm. Esther could avail herself of one method only, namely, to turn the tables on Haman, to accuse him of plotting against the king and the empire, to arouse doubts in the sick king's mind concerning Haman's loyalty and devotion. However, leveling such a charge against Haman entailed tremendous risks.

5 on the post he had prepared for him. The king's pages said to him, "Ah, there
is Haman standing in the courtyard," and the king said, "Show him in!"

6 In came Haman, and the king asked him, "What should be done for a man
the king wishes to honor?" Said Haman to himself, "Who could the king
wish to honor more than me?"

7 8 So Haman told the king, "The man the king wishes to honor – well, let the
clothes of royalty be brought forth, clothes that the king himself has worn,
and a horse on which the king has ridden, with a royal crown placed upon
9 its head; and let these clothes and the horse be entrusted to one of the king's
noble ministers, to dress the man whom the king has a wish to honor. And
let him lead that man, riding on the horse, across the town square, crying
out before him as they go, '*This is what is done for the man the king wishes to
honor!*'"

10 "Hurry now!" said the king to Haman; "Take the clothes and the horse as
you have said, and do just that for Mordekhai the Jew, who sits at the King's
Gate – let no detail fall short of what you have described!"

11 So Haman took the clothes and the horse and dressed Mordekhai, and led
him across the town square, crying out before him as they went, "*This is what
is done for the man the king wishes to honor!*"

12 And then Mordekhai returned to the King's Gate, and Haman bolted back to
13 his house, grief-stricken, covering his face. Haman told his wife, Zeresh, and
all his friends, all that had happened to him, and his wise men, with his wife,
Zeresh, said to him, "If this Mordekhai you have begun to fall before is of
Jewish blood, you will not overcome him; you will fall, must fall before him –"

---

responsibility of rewarding those people who deserved a reward and whose names were inscribed in the chronicles. The fact that Haman was derelict in his patriotic duty to reward a person who saved the king cast a shadow of doubt on Haman's integrity, on his sincere commitment to the king. As a matter of fact, there is no need for a solid argument in order to change the mind of a paranoiac; he reverses his relationship to people at the slightest provocation. Be that as it may, Esther could easily charge Haman with treason at the second reception. Ahasuerus was waiting for such an accusation. Esther easily convinced the king that Haman was a traitor and revolutionary who plotted against the king. (*Days of Deliverance*)

ה הַכִּ֣ין ל֑וֹ׃ וַ֠יֹּאמְרוּ נַעֲרֵ֤י הַמֶּ֙לֶךְ֙ אֵלָ֔יו הִנֵּ֥ה הָמָ֖ן עֹמֵ֣ד בֶּחָצֵ֑ר וַיֹּ֥אמֶר
ו הַמֶּ֖לֶךְ יָבֽוֹא׃ וַיָּבוֹא֮ הָמָן֒ וַיֹּ֤אמֶר לוֹ֙ הַמֶּ֔לֶךְ מַה־לַּֽעֲשׂ֕וֹת בָּאִ֕ישׁ אֲשֶׁ֥ר
הַמֶּ֖לֶךְ חָפֵ֣ץ בִּיקָר֑וֹ וַיֹּ֤אמֶר הָמָן֙ בְּלִבּ֔וֹ לְמִ֞י יַחְפֹּ֥ץ הַמֶּ֛לֶךְ לַעֲשׂ֥וֹת יְקָ֖ר
ז יוֹתֵ֥ר מִמֶּֽנִּי׃ וַיֹּ֥אמֶר הָמָ֖ן אֶל־הַמֶּ֑לֶךְ אִ֕ישׁ אֲשֶׁ֥ר הַמֶּ֖לֶךְ חָפֵ֥ץ בִּיקָרֽוֹ׃
ח יָבִ֙יאוּ֙ לְב֣וּשׁ מַלְכ֔וּת אֲשֶׁ֥ר לָֽבַשׁ־בּ֖וֹ הַמֶּ֑לֶךְ וְס֗וּס אֲשֶׁ֨ר רָכַ֤ב עָלָיו֙
ט הַמֶּ֔לֶךְ וַאֲשֶׁ֥ר נִתַּ֛ן כֶּ֥תֶר מַלְכ֖וּת בְּרֹאשֽׁוֹ׃ וְנָת֨וֹן הַלְּב֜וּשׁ וְהַסּ֗וּס עַל־
יַד־אִ֞ישׁ מִשָּׂרֵ֤י הַמֶּ֙לֶךְ֙ הַֽפַּרְתְּמִ֔ים וְהִלְבִּ֙ישׁוּ֙ אֶת־הָאִ֔ישׁ אֲשֶׁ֥ר הַמֶּ֖לֶךְ
חָפֵ֣ץ בִּיקָר֑וֹ וְהִרְכִּיבֻ֤הוּ עַל־הַסּוּס֙ בִּרְח֣וֹב הָעִ֔יר וְקָרְא֣וּ לְפָנָ֔יו כָּ֚כָה
י יֵעָשֶׂ֣ה לָאִ֔ישׁ אֲשֶׁ֥ר הַמֶּ֖לֶךְ חָפֵ֥ץ בִּיקָרֽוֹ׃ וַיֹּ֨אמֶר הַמֶּ֜לֶךְ לְהָמָ֗ן מַ֠הֵר
קַ֣ח אֶת־הַלְּב֤וּשׁ וְאֶת־הַסּוּס֙ כַּאֲשֶׁ֣ר דִּבַּ֔רְתָּ וַעֲשֵׂה־כֵן֙ לְמָרְדֳּכַ֣י הַיְּהוּדִ֔י
יא הַיּוֹשֵׁ֖ב בְּשַׁ֣עַר הַמֶּ֑לֶךְ אַל־תַּפֵּ֣ל דָּבָ֔ר מִכֹּ֖ל אֲשֶׁ֥ר דִּבַּֽרְתָּ׃ וַיִּקַּ֤ח הָמָן֙
אֶת־הַלְּב֣וּשׁ וְאֶת־הַסּ֔וּס וַיַּלְבֵּ֖שׁ אֶֽת־מָרְדֳּכָ֑י וַיַּרְכִּיבֵ֙הוּ֙ בִּרְח֣וֹב הָעִ֔יר
יב וַיִּקְרָ֣א לְפָנָ֔יו כָּ֚כָה יֵעָשֶׂ֣ה לָאִ֔ישׁ אֲשֶׁ֥ר הַמֶּ֖לֶךְ חָפֵ֥ץ בִּיקָרֽוֹ׃ וַיָּ֥שָׁב
מָרְדֳּכַ֖י אֶל־שַׁ֣עַר הַמֶּ֑לֶךְ וְהָמָן֙ נִדְחַ֣ף אֶל־בֵּית֔וֹ אָבֵ֖ל וַחֲפ֥וּי רֹֽאשׁ׃
יג וַיְסַפֵּ֨ר הָמָ֜ן לְזֶ֤רֶשׁ אִשְׁתּוֹ֙ וּלְכָל־אֹ֣הֲבָ֔יו אֵ֖ת כָּל־אֲשֶׁ֣ר קָרָ֑הוּ וַיֹּ֨אמְרוּ
ל֜וֹ חֲכָמָ֗יו וְזֶ֤רֶשׁ אִשְׁתּוֹ֙ אִ֣ם מִזֶּ֣רַע הַיְּהוּדִ֗ים מָרְדֳּכַ֞י אֲשֶׁ֨ר הַחִלּ֜וֹת

מַהֵר *Hurry now!* Let us understand what actually happened that night. The most significant aspect was not the public humiliation of Haman or the public recognition accorded to Mordekhai, but the sudden loss of confidence on the part of the king in Haman's loyalty. While reading the story, you can feel the king's irritation and anger: "Hurry now! Take the clothes and the horse as you have said, and do just that for Mordekhai the Jew, who sits at the King's gate." This laconic order is indicative of an about-face and a change of attitude on the part of the king toward Haman. There is obvious viciousness and malice to the order. Ahasuerus enjoyed Haman's humiliation. Why? Our Sages explained that Haman's mention of the crown upset Ahasuerus (*Pirkei DeRabbi Eliezer* 50). I believe that there is also another reason. As the highest executive officer in the empire, the prime minister was charged with the

14 But they were still speaking when the king's eunuchs arrived, to fetch Haman,
with terrible haste, to the feast that Esther had prepared.

7 1 So the king and Haman arrived to drink with Queen Esther. And on that
2 second day also, at the drinking feast, the king said to Esther, "What is your
desire, Esther my queen? It shall be yours. And what would you ask? Be it
even half my kingdom, it shall be done."

3 And Queen Esther answered: "If I have your favor, my king," she said, "and if
so it please your majesty – let me have my life at my desire; my people at my
4 request. For we have been sold – I and my people – to be wiped out, killed
and destroyed. Had we but been sold away as slaves and bondwomen, I would
have kept my silence; for that anguish is not worth any loss to the king."

5 And King Ahasuerus spoke: he said to Esther the queen, "Who is this and
where is he, who has put it into his heart to do such a thing?"

6 "It is a foe, an enemy," said Esther, "this vicious man, Haman!" And Haman
7 was suddenly terrified before the king and queen. The king rose up in his
fury and left the wine feast for the palace garden, as Haman stood up to
entreat for his life with Esther the queen, for he saw that the king was already
8 set upon his downfall. By the time the king came back from the palace
garden to the feasting chamber, Haman had thrown himself onto Esther's

---

he recommended physical liquidation of the Jews. Why? The reason, Esther went on, is obvious. He wanted to arm his cohorts, who are conspiring against the king. He purposely proposed to the king the method of physical extermination in order to make the government open its magazines and arsenals and start giving weapons to all those who are ready to participate in the bloody spectacle. After all, the government will have to provide the would-be killers with ammunition; otherwise the royal decree "to be wiped out, killed and destroyed" could not be implemented. Once the arms will be under control of Haman's followers, Esther continued to argue, they will effect a volte-face and turn against the king, plunging the empire inexorably into a civil war. Haman is not interested in the safety of the king. He is promoting single-mindedly the cause of revolution and anarchy. He is the most dangerous enemy of the king. When she, pointing her accusing finger at Haman, said in a loud voice, "It is a foe, an enemy, this vicious man, Haman!" (7:6), she meant that Haman is the adversary and enemy of the king. (*Days of Deliverance*)

יד לִנְפֹּ֣ל לְפָנָ֔יו לֹֽא־תוּכַ֣ל ל֔וֹ כִּֽי־נָפ֥וֹל תִּפּ֖וֹל לְפָנָֽיו׃ עוֹדָם֙ מְדַבְּרִ֣ים עִמּ֔וֹ
וְסָרִיסֵ֥י הַמֶּ֖לֶךְ הִגִּ֑יעוּ וַיַּבְהִ֙לוּ֙ לְהָבִ֣יא אֶת־הָמָ֔ן אֶל־הַמִּשְׁתֶּ֖ה אֲשֶׁר־
ז א עָשְׂתָ֥ה אֶסְתֵּֽר׃ וַיָּבֹ֤א הַמֶּ֙לֶךְ֙ וְהָמָ֔ן לִשְׁתּ֖וֹת עִם־אֶסְתֵּ֥ר הַמַּלְכָּֽה׃
ב וַיֹּאמֶר֩ הַמֶּ֨לֶךְ לְאֶסְתֵּ֜ר גַּ֣ם בַּיּ֤וֹם הַשֵּׁנִי֙ בְּמִשְׁתֵּ֣ה הַיַּ֔יִן מַה־שְּׁאֵלָתֵ֛ךְ
אֶסְתֵּ֥ר הַמַּלְכָּ֖ה וְתִנָּ֣תֵֽן לָ֑ךְ וּמַה־בַּקָּשָׁתֵ֛ךְ עַד־חֲצִ֥י הַמַּלְכ֖וּת וְתֵעָֽשׂ׃
ג וַתַּ֨עַן אֶסְתֵּ֤ר הַמַּלְכָּה֙ וַתֹּאמַ֔ר אִם־מָצָ֨אתִי חֵ֤ן בְּעֵינֶ֙יךָ֙ הַמֶּ֔לֶךְ וְאִם־
ד עַל־הַמֶּ֖לֶךְ ט֑וֹב תִּנָּֽתֶן־לִ֤י נַפְשִׁי֙ בִּשְׁאֵ֣לָתִ֔י וְעַמִּ֖י בְּבַקָּשָׁתִֽי׃ כִּ֤י נִמְכַּ֙רְנוּ֙
אֲנִ֣י וְעַמִּ֔י לְהַשְׁמִ֖יד לַהֲר֣וֹג וּלְאַבֵּ֑ד וְ֠אִלּוּ לַעֲבָדִ֨ים וְלִשְׁפָח֤וֹת נִמְכַּ֙רְנוּ֙
ה הֶחֱרַ֔שְׁתִּי כִּ֣י אֵ֥ין הַצָּ֛ר שֹׁוֶ֖ה בְּנֵ֥זֶק הַמֶּֽלֶךְ׃ וַיֹּ֙אמֶר֙ הַמֶּ֣לֶךְ
אֲחַשְׁוֵר֔וֹשׁ וַיֹּ֖אמֶר לְאֶסְתֵּ֣ר הַמַּלְכָּ֑ה מִ֣י ה֥וּא זֶה֙ וְאֵֽי־זֶ֣ה ה֔וּא אֲשֶׁר־
ו מְלָא֥וֹ לִבּ֖וֹ לַעֲשׂ֥וֹת כֵּֽן׃ וַתֹּ֣אמֶר אֶסְתֵּ֔ר אִ֚ישׁ צַ֣ר וְאוֹיֵ֔ב הָמָ֥ן הָרָ֖ע הַזֶּ֑ה
ז וְהָמָ֣ן נִבְעַ֔ת מִלִּפְנֵ֥י הַמֶּ֖לֶךְ וְהַמַּלְכָּֽה׃ וְהַמֶּ֜לֶךְ קָ֤ם בַּחֲמָתוֹ֙ מִמִּשְׁתֵּ֣ה
הַיַּ֔יִן אֶל־גִּנַּ֖ת הַבִּיתָ֑ן וְהָמָ֣ן עָמַ֗ד לְבַקֵּ֤שׁ עַל־נַפְשׁוֹ֙ מֵאֶסְתֵּ֣ר הַמַּלְכָּ֔ה
ח כִּ֣י רָאָ֔ה כִּֽי־כָלְתָ֥ה אֵלָ֛יו הָרָעָ֖ה מֵאֵ֥ת הַמֶּֽלֶךְ׃ וְהַמֶּ֡לֶךְ שָׁ֠ב מִגִּנַּ֨ת הַבִּיתָ֜ן
אֶל־בֵּ֣ית ׀ מִשְׁתֵּ֣ה הַיַּ֗יִן וְהָמָן֙ נֹפֵ֔ל עַל־הַמִּטָּה֙ אֲשֶׁ֣ר אֶסְתֵּ֣ר עָלֶ֔יהָ

וְאִלּוּ לַעֲבָדִים וְלִשְׁפָחוֹת נִמְכַּרְנוּ הֶחֱרַשְׁתִּי כִּי אֵין הַצָּר שֹׁוֶה בְּנֵזֶק הַמֶּלֶךְ *Had we but been sold away as slaves and bondwomen, I would have kept my silence; for that anguish is not worth any loss to the king.* With these enigmatic words, Esther tried to prove to the king that Haman was not concerned with the welfare of the king. She argued that Haman should have suggested another method to protect the king. He should have advised the king that all Jews be interned in slave-labor camps, treated like prisoners of war. The king would thus have gained two objectives: there would be no menace to the safety of the king, because the Jews would be confined within prescribed limits; and the economy of the land would be strengthened.

Now we understand why Esther said, "Had we but been sold away as slaves and bondwomen, I would have kept my silence." Had Haman suggested this method, I would have kept quiet. Interning the Jews would have been more profitable economically, and just as efficacious in terms of security. However,

couch – "What!" said the king, "Would you take the queen too, and with me in the palace?" And the servants stepped forward to cover Haman's face.

9 And one of the eunuchs, Ḥarvona, said to the king, "You know, the post Haman prepared for Mordekhai, who spoke up well for the king, is standing now in Haman's house, fifty cubits high…" And the king said, "Hang him upon it!"

10 Thus was Haman hung up, on the very post he had prepared for Mordekhai; and the king's fury subsided.

8 1 On that day, King Ahasuerus granted Queen Esther the estate of Haman,
enemy of the Jews; and Mordekhai came before the king, for Esther had
2 finally revealed what he was to her. The king took off the very ring that he
had once given over to Haman, and gave it instead to Mordekhai; and Esther
appointed Mordekhai over Haman's estate.

3 But then Esther spoke to the king again, falling down at his feet, weeping and pleading with him to overturn the wickedness of Haman the Agagite,

---

believed in such a possibility, in the merger of the I with the multitude. The charismatic woman upon whom God let His spirit descend and upon whom God placed the burden of becoming the people; this woman-nation emerged victorious. Yes, Mordekhai was the initiator, the teacher, the first messenger; he awakened her, he fired her imagination and sensitized her heart. Through him came the inspired word to her. Yet the strategy was hers, the critical decisions how and when to do it were hers. She could not consult Mordekhai; and, even if she could, she would not have accepted advice from him. Providence wanted her to do everything on her own, all by herself. God's spirit descended upon her and she attained victory. (*Days of Deliverance*)

וַתּוֹסֶף אֶסְתֵּר וַתְּדַבֵּר לִפְנֵי הַמֶּלֶךְ, וַתִּפֹּל לִפְנֵי רַגְלָיו וַתֵּבְךְּ וַתִּתְחַנֶּן לוֹ *But then Esther spoke to the king again, falling down at his feet, weeping and pleading with him.* We do not say Hallel on Purim. One opinion in the Gemara explains that this is due to the fact that on Purim, the miracle was not final: "Can we say, 'Praise, O servants of the Lord,' who are no longer the servants of Ahasuerus? We are still the servants of Ahasuerus" (*Megilla* 14a). What happened on Purim was not of a permanent nature. They were saved, of course. However, no one could guarantee that the next day the same story would not repeat itself. That is why there is no Hallel.

וַיֹּאמֶר הַמֶּלֶךְ הֲגַם לִכְבּוֹשׁ אֶת־הַמַּלְכָּה עִמִּי בַּבָּיִת הַדָּבָר יָצָא
ט מִפִּי הַמֶּלֶךְ וּפְנֵי הָמָן חָפוּ׃ וַיֹּאמֶר חַרְבוֹנָה אֶחָד מִן־הַסָּרִיסִים
לִפְנֵי הַמֶּלֶךְ גַּם הִנֵּה־הָעֵץ אֲשֶׁר־עָשָׂה הָמָן לְמָרְדֳּכַי אֲשֶׁר דִּבֶּר־
טוֹב עַל־הַמֶּלֶךְ עֹמֵד בְּבֵית הָמָן גָּבֹהַּ חֲמִשִּׁים אַמָּה וַיֹּאמֶר הַמֶּלֶךְ
י תְּלֻהוּ עָלָיו׃ וַיִּתְלוּ אֶת־הָמָן עַל־הָעֵץ אֲשֶׁר־הֵכִין לְמָרְדֳּכָי וַחֲמַת
ח א הַמֶּלֶךְ שָׁכָכָה׃ בַּיּוֹם הַהוּא נָתַן הַמֶּלֶךְ אֲחַשְׁוֵרוֹשׁ לְאֶסְתֵּר
הַמַּלְכָּה אֶת־בֵּית הָמָן צֹרֵר היהודיים וּמָרְדֳּכַי בָּא לִפְנֵי הַמֶּלֶךְ הַיְּהוּדִים
ב כִּי־הִגִּידָה אֶסְתֵּר מַה הוּא־לָהּ׃ וַיָּסַר הַמֶּלֶךְ אֶת־טַבַּעְתּוֹ אֲשֶׁר
הֶעֱבִיר מֵהָמָן וַיִּתְּנָהּ לְמָרְדֳּכָי וַתָּשֶׂם אֶסְתֵּר אֶת־מָרְדֳּכַי עַל־בֵּית
ג הָמָן׃ וַתּוֹסֶף אֶסְתֵּר וַתְּדַבֵּר לִפְנֵי הַמֶּלֶךְ וַתִּפֹּל לִפְנֵי רַגְלָיו
וַתֵּבְךְּ וַתִּתְחַנֶּן־לוֹ לְהַעֲבִיר אֶת־רָעַת הָמָן הָאֲגָגִי וְאֵת מַחֲשַׁבְתּוֹ

הֲגַם לִכְבּוֹשׁ אֶת הַמַּלְכָּה עִמִּי בַּבָּיִת *Would you take the queen too, and with me in the palace?* The miracle happened: Esther succeeded in convincing the king that Haman and his cohorts, not the Jews, are a menace to his safety and security. When Ahasuerus returned from his walk in the garden into Esther's chambers and found Haman fallen upon the couch whereon Esther was, his exclamation tells the whole story: "Would you take the queen too, and with me in the palace?" Esther succeeded in convincing Ahasuerus that Haman was plotting against him. The proof of this is the expression "הֲגַם, too." In other words, Haman wants to take away something besides the kingdom, namely, the queen; הֲגַם stresses that this is the second item Haman wishes to conquer. Taking away the queen was the ultimate sign of revolt, as when Absalom raped David's concubines (II Sam. 16:21–22). This is exactly what Ahasuerus suspected of Haman, namely, that he wanted to rape Esther in order to demonstrate disobedience against the king.

Esther succeeded. A young, frail maiden, the daughter of immigrants, defeated the most powerful prime minister in the annals of Persia. Can an individual turn into a people, a single person into a nation, one man into a community, a woman into a kingdom of priests? Judaism held that this is not absurd. Of course, it is a strange metamorphosis, a frightening equation: individual equals people. It is a mysterious identity. And yet Judaism

4 and the plot that he had thought up against the Jews. The king extended his
golden scepter to Esther, and Esther raised herself up and stood before the
5 king. And she said, "If so it please the king, and if I have his favor, and if it
seems right to the king and I am pleasing in his eyes – let the decree be writ-
ten to revoke the scrolls that were the plot of Haman, son of Hamedata the
Agagite, who wrote to destroy all the Jews that are in all the king's provinces.
6 For how can I live to see the evil that will come upon my people; how can I
live to see the loss of those I am born of?"

7 King Ahasuerus said to Queen Esther and to Mordekhai the Jew, "Look, I
have given Haman's house to Esther, and he has been hung up on the post
8 for putting out his hand against the Jews. Now, write whatever you like about
the Jews in the king's name, and seal it with the king's ring – but no writing
that has been written in the name of the king and sealed with the king's seal
can ever be revoked."

---

need to ask for mercy that He will redeem us now as He did then" (*Tur, Oraḥ Ḥayim* 693). We rejoice in the miracle that took place, and we pray that God will continue to guard and protect us from our enemies. There is not only one Haman; there are many more who rise up against us. As a matter of fact, there is a controversy about how much of the Megilla should be read on Purim: "From where does one read the Megilla and thereby fulfill his obligation? Rabbi Meir says: All of it. Rabbi Judah says: From 'Now there was a Jewish man…' (2:5). Rabbi Yosi says: From 'Some time after this [King Ahasuerus ennobled Haman]…' (3:1)" (*Megilla* 19a). If the Megilla is just a story of Hallel – to celebrate our victory over Haman – then we should begin with: "The king slept fitfully that night" (6:1). This is indeed, the opinion of Rabbi Simeon bar Yohai (*Megilla* 19a). This is the turning point, the first defeat of Haman. The fortune of the Jews began to change that night. However, others felt one should begin at an earlier point in the Megilla. The Megilla is not just the story of triumph; it is also a book of despair, of human insecurity – particularly, Jewish insecurity and instability. (*Days of Deliverance*)

כִּי אֵיכָכָה אוּכַל וְרָאִיתִי בָּרָעָה *For how can I live to see the evil.* The word וְרָאִיתִי means has the implication of "stand still and watch." So too in Psalms 37:25, "I was young and am now old, *velo ra'iti* the righteous forsaken or his children begging for bread." It means that I never merely stood still and watched while the righteous was forsaken or his children were begging for bread.

ד אֲשֶׁר חָשַׁב עַל־הַיְּהוּדִים׃ וַיּוֹשֶׁט הַמֶּלֶךְ לְאֶסְתֵּר אֵת שַׁרְבִט הַזָּהָב
ה וַתָּקָם אֶסְתֵּר וַתַּעֲמֹד לִפְנֵי הַמֶּלֶךְ׃ וַתֹּאמֶר אִם־עַל־הַמֶּלֶךְ טוֹב
וְאִם־מָצָאתִי חֵן לְפָנָיו וְכָשֵׁר הַדָּבָר לִפְנֵי הַמֶּלֶךְ וְטוֹבָה אֲנִי בְּעֵינָיו
יִכָּתֵב לְהָשִׁיב אֶת־הַסְּפָרִים מַחֲשֶׁבֶת הָמָן בֶּן־הַמְּדָתָא הָאֲגָגִי
ו אֲשֶׁר כָּתַב לְאַבֵּד אֶת־הַיְּהוּדִים אֲשֶׁר בְּכָל־מְדִינוֹת הַמֶּלֶךְ׃ כִּי
אֵיכָכָה אוּכַל וְרָאִיתִי בָּרָעָה אֲשֶׁר־יִמְצָא אֶת־עַמִּי וְאֵיכָכָה אוּכַל
ז וְרָאִיתִי בְּאָבְדַן מוֹלַדְתִּי׃ וַיֹּאמֶר הַמֶּלֶךְ אֲחַשְׁוֵרֹשׁ לְאֶסְתֵּר
הַמַּלְכָּה וּלְמָרְדֳּכַי הַיְּהוּדִי הִנֵּה בֵית־הָמָן נָתַתִּי לְאֶסְתֵּר וְאֹתוֹ תָּלוּ
ח עַל־הָעֵץ עַל אֲשֶׁר־שָׁלַח יָדוֹ ביהודיים׃ וְאַתֶּם כִּתְבוּ עַל־הַיְּהוּדִים בַּיְּהוּדִים
כַּטּוֹב בְּעֵינֵיכֶם בְּשֵׁם הַמֶּלֶךְ וְחִתְמוּ בְּטַבַּעַת הַמֶּלֶךְ כִּי־כְתָב אֲשֶׁר־

There is another reason given for not reciting Hallel on Purim: "*Keriyata zo hallela,* The reading [of the Megilla] is to be equated with the recital of Hallel" (*Megilla* 14a). But surely we read the Torah on Pesaḥ, too. Why don't we say that the reading of the story of the Exodus substitutes for the recital of Hallel, that *keriyata zo hallela*? The answer is that the Megilla has an additional special message. It is a story of triumph and salvation, but also the book of Jewish tragedy and the peculiar Jewish destiny. It is a book of Jewish insecurity: "But then Esther spoke to the king again, falling down at his feet, weeping and pleading with him to overturn the wickedness of Haman the Agagite, and the plot that he had thought up against the Jews… And she said, 'If so it please the king, and if I have his favor, and if it seems right to the king and I am pleasing in his eyes…'" This is not the way that Moses addressed Pharaoh. This was not the way Jews acted during their sojourn in the Land of Israel, when they composed an independent commonwealth. Rav Amram Gaon records a very strange custom: "It is customary in the *yeshivot* [on Purim] for the reciters to descend before the Gaon and the heads of the rabbinic court and the leaders and the entire yeshiva, and to plead profusely and to recite *Taḥanun*" (*Seder Rav Amram Gaon,* II, 72).

The *Tur* cites his opinion as follows: "Rav Amram Gaon, of blessed memory, wrote that it is a custom in the two *yeshivot* to recite *Taḥanun* [on Purim]; because it is a day of miracles on which they were redeemed, we

9 And so, at that time, the king's scribes were called – on the twenty-third
day of the third month, the month of Sivan, that is – and they wrote down
all that Mordekhai dictated, to the Jews and to the viceroys, the adminis-
trators and the ministers of all the provinces from India to Ethiopia, one
hundred and twenty-seven provinces, to each province in its script and
to each people in its language, and to the Jews also, in their script and in
10 their language. It was written in the name of King Ahasuerus and sealed
with the king's seal, and the scrolls were sent with the horseback runners,
11 riding the swift horses of the royal stable, young of the royal mares – to
convey that the king had granted the Jews in every single town the right
to come together to stand up and defend their lives, to wipe out, kill and
destroy all the armed hordes of the peoples and provinces who threat-
ened them, even their children and women, and to loot their plunder,
12 all on one day, the thirteenth day of the twelfth month – the month of
13 Adar, that is – in all the provinces of King Ahasuerus. The text of that
decree was to lay down law in every single province, displayed for every
people to see, that the Jews should make themselves ready for that day, to
14 wreak vengeance on their enemies. The runners, riding the swift horses of
the royal service, bolted out at great speed, spurred on at the king's word,
and the law was laid down in the imperial city, Shushan.

15 ▸ So Mordekhai left the king's presence in royal clothes of sky-blue wool
and fine white fabric, wearing a great coronet of gold, and a mantle of finest
linen and scarlet; and the town of Shushan was filled with jubilation and
16 happiness. ◂ ▸ And the Jews basked in light and happiness, joy and great
17 honor. ◂ And in each and every province, in each and every town, as far
as the king's word and law reached, happiness and joy touched the Jews,

---

is not just an individual, a single person. What was he? God reached a covenant with Abraham. It is self-evident that God was not concerned with an individual but with a people, with a community that He willed to enter into a covenantal relationship with Him. Similarly, God sent Moses to take the Jews out of Egypt. He stated distinctly that He was concerned "with My people, the children of Israel" (Ex. 3:10). Judaism thought very highly of the role of the individual in history. But in contradistinction to Thomas Carlyle, Judaism did not glorify the individual; it never made a hero or demi-god of the great man. Instead, Judaism brought forth a new identity: individual-people, single-many, lonely man-community.

ט נִכְתָּב בְּשֵׁם־הַמֶּלֶךְ וְנַחְתּוֹם בְּטַבַּעַת הַמֶּלֶךְ אֵין לְהָשִׁיב׃ וַיִּקָּרְאוּ
סֹפְרֵי־הַמֶּלֶךְ בָּעֵת־הַהִיא בַּחֹדֶשׁ הַשְּׁלִישִׁי הוּא־חֹדֶשׁ סִיוָן בִּשְׁלוֹשָׁה
וְעֶשְׂרִים בּוֹ וַיִּכָּתֵב כְּכָל־אֲשֶׁר־צִוָּה מָרְדֳּכַי אֶל־הַיְּהוּדִים וְאֶל
הָאֲחַשְׁדַּרְפְּנִים וְהַפַּחוֹת וְשָׂרֵי הַמְּדִינוֹת אֲשֶׁר ׀ מֵהֹדּוּ וְעַד־כּוּשׁ שֶׁבַע
וְעֶשְׂרִים וּמֵאָה מְדִינָה מְדִינָה וּמְדִינָה כִּכְתָבָהּ וְעַם וָעָם כִּלְשֹׁנוֹ
י וְאֶל־הַיְּהוּדִים כִּכְתָבָם וְכִלְשׁוֹנָם׃ וַיִּכְתֹּב בְּשֵׁם הַמֶּלֶךְ אֲחַשְׁוֵרֹשׁ
וַיַּחְתֹּם בְּטַבַּעַת הַמֶּלֶךְ וַיִּשְׁלַח סְפָרִים בְּיַד הָרָצִים בַּסּוּסִים רֹכְבֵי
יא הָרֶכֶשׁ הָאֲחַשְׁתְּרָנִים בְּנֵי הָרַמָּכִים׃ אֲשֶׁר נָתַן הַמֶּלֶךְ לַיְּהוּדִים ׀ אֲשֶׁר ׀
בְּכָל־עִיר וָעִיר לְהִקָּהֵל וְלַעֲמֹד עַל־נַפְשָׁם לְהַשְׁמִיד וְלַהֲרֹג וּלְאַבֵּד
יב אֶת־כָּל־חֵיל עַם וּמְדִינָה הַצָּרִים אֹתָם טַף וְנָשִׁים וּשְׁלָלָם לָבוֹז׃ בְּיוֹם
אֶחָד בְּכָל־מְדִינוֹת הַמֶּלֶךְ אֲחַשְׁוֵרוֹשׁ בִּשְׁלוֹשָׁה עָשָׂר לְחֹדֶשׁ שְׁנֵים־
יג עָשָׂר הוּא־חֹדֶשׁ אֲדָר׃ פַּתְשֶׁגֶן הַכְּתָב לְהִנָּתֵן דָּת בְּכָל־מְדִינָה וּמְדִינָה
גָּלוּי לְכָל־הָעַמִּים וְלִהְיוֹת היהודיים עתודים לַיּוֹם הַזֶּה לְהִנָּקֵם
הַיְּהוּדִים עֲתִידִים
יד מֵאֹיְבֵיהֶם׃ הָרָצִים רֹכְבֵי הָרֶכֶשׁ הָאֲחַשְׁתְּרָנִים יָצְאוּ מְבֹהָלִים וּדְחוּפִים
טו בִּדְבַר הַמֶּלֶךְ וְהַדָּת נִתְּנָה בְּשׁוּשַׁן הַבִּירָה׃ וּמָרְדֳּכַי יָצָא ׀
מִלִּפְנֵי הַמֶּלֶךְ בִּלְבוּשׁ מַלְכוּת תְּכֵלֶת וָחוּר וַעֲטֶרֶת זָהָב גְּדוֹלָה
טז וְתַכְרִיךְ בּוּץ וְאַרְגָּמָן וְהָעִיר שׁוּשָׁן צָהֲלָה וְשָׂמֵחָה׃ לַיְּהוּדִים

וְהָעִיר שׁוּשָׁן צָהֲלָה וְשָׂמֵחָה *and the town of Shushan was filled with jubilation and happiness.* Mordekhai was most probably an elderly Jew at the time at which the events of the Megilla occurred; he was the son of poor immigrants, an exile. No one knew of his existence. He lived in anonymity. And yet we read in the Megilla that, when Mordekhai cried a loud and bitter cry, the Jews throughout the empire cried with him; all of Shushan was aghast and in horror (3:15). When Mordekhai appeared on the streets of Shushan clothed in purple and velvet, with a crown of gold on his head, the whole city was delirious with joy. Something strange comes to mind while reading and meditating about the mysterious bond between Mordekhai and the people. Mordekhai

feasting, a holiday; and many of the local people joined with the Jews, for
a terror of the Jews had fallen upon them.

9 1 And on the thirteenth day of the twelfth month, the month of Adar, when
the king's word and his law were to come into effect: on the day when the
Jews' enemies had hoped to overcome them – it was all turned over, for
2 the Jews themselves overcame those who hated them. For the Jews came
together in their cities, throughout the provinces of King Ahasuerus, to lay
hands upon those who sought their harm; and no man could stand before
3 them, for their terror had fallen upon all the nations. And the ministers of
the provinces, the viceroys and the administrators, and the bureaucrats of
the king's court, all supported the Jews, for a fear of Mordekhai had fallen

---

the Jews did not accept upon themselves the prohibition of *melakha*. Subsequently, the Gemara states that in a place where the custom is to refrain from *melakha* on Purim, one must follow the custom. The Gemara again questions R. Yehuda HaNasi's planting of a sapling on Purim, but now responds that since this was planted for a joyous occasion, it was permitted. Apparently, planting a sapling of joy can be permitted only once it has been established that the prohibition of *melakha* is merely a custom dependent on locale. Were there to be a prohibition across the board, stemming from a communal acceptance of Purim as a Yom Tov, then even plantings of joy would be forbidden, just as on any other Yom Tov, and the prohibition would not have been suspended for joyous plantings. Apparently, once the Gemara establishes that *melakha* is prohibited only by local custom, it follows that the nature of the prohibition is not akin to Yom Tov. Rather, the custom to abstain from *melakha* stems from the mitzva to rejoice on Purim, and performing *melakha* undermines rejoicing. Thus, plantings of joy are permitted, as they do not stand in the way of the day's *simḥa*. We now return to our original question: Does the prohibition of *melakha* on Purim apply even at night? The Gemara derives from the words "יְמֵי מִשְׁתֶּה וְשִׂמְחָה, days of feasting and happiness" (9:22), that one who eats his Purim feast at night has not fulfilled his obligation. Based on the same verse, it would seem that the mitzva of *simḥa* does not apply on Purim night. Since the custom to abstain from *melakha* is based on the obligation of *simḥa*, it follows that this custom does not apply at night.

יז הָֽיְתָ֥ה אוֹרָ֖ה וְשִׂמְחָ֑ה וְשָׂשֹׂ֖ן וִיקָֽר׃ · וּבְכָל־מְדִינָ֨ה וּמְדִינָ֜ה וּבְכָל־עִ֣יר
וָעִ֗יר מְקוֹם֙ אֲשֶׁ֨ר דְּבַר־הַמֶּ֤לֶךְ וְדָתוֹ֙ מַגִּ֔יעַ שִׂמְחָ֤ה וְשָׂשׂוֹן֙ לַיְּהוּדִ֔ים
מִשְׁתֶּ֖ה וְי֣וֹם ט֑וֹב וְרַבִּ֞ים מֵעַמֵּ֤י הָאָ֙רֶץ֙ מִֽתְיַהֲדִ֔ים כִּֽי־נָפַ֥ל פַּֽחַד־
ט א הַיְּהוּדִ֖ים עֲלֵיהֶֽם׃ וּבִשְׁנֵים֩ עָשָׂ֨ר חֹ֜דֶשׁ הוּא־חֹ֣דֶשׁ אֲדָ֗ר בִּשְׁלוֹשָׁ֨ה
עָשָׂ֥ר יוֹם֙ בּ֔וֹ אֲשֶׁ֨ר הִגִּ֧יעַ דְּבַר־הַמֶּ֛לֶךְ וְדָת֖וֹ לְהֵעָשׂ֑וֹת בַּיּ֗וֹם אֲשֶׁ֨ר
שִׂבְּר֜וּ אֹיְבֵ֤י הַיְּהוּדִים֙ לִשְׁל֣וֹט בָּהֶ֔ם וְנַהֲפ֣וֹךְ ה֔וּא אֲשֶׁ֨ר יִשְׁלְט֧וּ
ב הַיְּהוּדִ֛ים הֵ֖מָּה בְּשֹׂנְאֵיהֶֽם׃ נִקְהֲל֨וּ הַיְּהוּדִ֜ים בְּעָרֵיהֶ֗ם בְּכָל־מְדִינוֹת֙
הַמֶּ֣לֶךְ אֲחַשְׁוֵר֔וֹשׁ לִשְׁלֹ֣חַ יָ֔ד בִּמְבַקְשֵׁ֖י רָֽעָתָ֑ם וְאִישׁ֙ לֹא־עָמַ֣ד לִפְנֵיהֶ֔ם
ג כִּֽי־נָפַ֥ל פַּחְדָּ֖ם עַל־כָּל־הָעַמִּֽים׃ וְכָל־שָׂרֵ֨י הַמְּדִינ֜וֹת וְהָֽאֲחַשְׁדַּרְפְּנִ֗ים
וְהַפַּחוֹת֙ וְעֹשֵׂ֣י הַמְּלָאכָ֔ה אֲשֶׁ֣ר לַמֶּ֔לֶךְ מְנַשְּׂאִ֖ים אֶת־הַיְּהוּדִ֑ים

God addressed Himself to such strange personalities. He dealt with them, reached covenants with them, and established relationships with them: Abraham, Isaac, Jacob, Moses, Aaron, David. Our Sages said, "Jacob our father did not die" (*Ta'anit* 5b); "Moses did not die" (*Sota* 13b); "David, king of Israel, continues to live" (*Rosh HaShana* 25a). All those individuals – people in whom a multitude, a community, resided – did not die. They live on forever. These divine agents belonged to the people and the people belonged to them; their love was boundless and their thoughts encompassed all dimensions of time. The individual becomes the abode of the millions. If the individual can prepare within himself an abode for God, the infinite and eternal – "Let them make Me a sanctuary, that I may dwell among them" (Ex. 25:8) – he certainly can invite the millions to abide in him. (*Days of Deliverance*)

וְיוֹם טוֹב *a holiday. Shulḥan Arukh* (*Oraḥ Ḥayim* 696:1) rules that in places where the custom is to abstain from *melakha* on Purim, *melakha* is forbidden. The question arises as to whether this custom applies on Purim night as well (see *Be'ur Halakha ibid.* who cites a dispute of the *Aḥaronim* on this matter). The Gemara (*Megilla* 5b) records that R. Yehuda HaNasi planted a sapling on Purim, seemingly a clear demonstration that *melakha* is permitted. The Gemara concludes, based on the omission of the words *yom tov* in verse 17 of chapter 9, that although Mordekhai originally intended Purim to be a full-fledged day of Yom Tov, including the prohibition of *melakha*,

4 on them. For Mordekhai was great now, in the king's palace, and word
of him was spreading to all the provinces: the man, this Mordekhai, was
becoming ever greater.

5 The Jews dealt all their enemies a terrible blow, of sword and of slaughter and
6 destruction; they did whatever they pleased to those who hated them. And in
the imperial city of Shushan the Jews killed and destroyed ▸ five hundred men;
7 and they killed Parshandata and
Dalfon, and
8 Aspata, and
Porata, and
Adaliya and
9 Aridata, and
Parmashta, and
Arisai, and
Aridai, and
10 Vayzata, the ten ◂
sons of Haman, son of Hamedata, enemy of the Jews – but they did not
even touch the plunder.

11 On that same day, the number of those killed in the imperial city, Shushan,
12 was brought to the king, and the king said to Queen Esther, "The Jews
have killed five hundred men in the imperial city of Shushan, alone, as well
as Haman's ten sons – what must they have done in the rest of the king's
provinces? And now – what is your desire? It shall be yours. And what

---

publicize the miracle. Likewise, with respect to the law of reading the names of Haman's ten sons in one breath, Maimonides (*ibid.*) writes, "The reader must read the names of Haman's ten sons in one breath in order to inform the public that they all were hanged and killed as one." This implies that the law of reciting the names in one breath applies only when the Megilla is read with a *tzibur*, where there is a public to inform, but not when read individually. Thus, reciting the names of Haman's sons in one breath isn't defined as a condition in the Megilla's reading, which would be required of an individual as well. Rather, it too is a fulfillment of publicizing the miracle which is only applicable in the context of a *tzibur*.

ד כִּי־נָפַל פַּחַד־מָרְדֳּכַי עֲלֵיהֶם: כִּי־גָדוֹל מָרְדֳּכַי בְּבֵית הַמֶּלֶךְ
ה וְשָׁמְעוֹ הוֹלֵךְ בְּכָל־הַמְּדִינוֹת כִּי־הָאִישׁ מָרְדֳּכַי הוֹלֵךְ וְגָדוֹל: וַיַּכּוּ
הַיְּהוּדִים בְּכָל־אֹיְבֵיהֶם מַכַּת־חֶרֶב וְהֶרֶג וְאַבְדָן וַיַּעֲשׂוּ בְשֹׂנְאֵיהֶם
ו כִּרְצוֹנָם: וּבְשׁוּשַׁן הַבִּירָה הָרְגוּ הַיְּהוּדִים וְאַבֵּד · חֲמֵשׁ מֵאוֹת
ז אִישׁ: וְאֵת ׀
פַּרְשַׁנְדָּתָא וְאֵת ׀
דַּלְפוֹן וְאֵת ׀
ח אַסְפָּתָא: וְאֵת ׀
פּוֹרָתָא וְאֵת ׀
אֲדַלְיָא וְאֵת ׀
ט אֲרִידָתָא: וְאֵת ׀
פַּרְמַשְׁתָּא וְאֵת ׀
אֲרִיסַי וְאֵת ׀
אֲרִידַי וְאֵת ׀
י וַיְזָתָא: עֲשֶׂרֶת ·
בְּנֵי הָמָן בֶּן־הַמְּדָתָא צֹרֵר הַיְּהוּדִים הָרָגוּ וּבַבִּזָּה לֹא שָׁלְחוּ אֶת־יָדָם:
יא יב בַּיּוֹם הַהוּא בָּא מִסְפַּר הַהֲרוּגִים בְּשׁוּשַׁן הַבִּירָה לִפְנֵי הַמֶּלֶךְ: וַיֹּאמֶר
הַמֶּלֶךְ לְאֶסְתֵּר הַמַּלְכָּה בְּשׁוּשַׁן הַבִּירָה הָרְגוּ הַיְּהוּדִים וְאַבֵּד חֲמֵשׁ
מֵאוֹת אִישׁ וְאֵת עֲשֶׂרֶת בְּנֵי־הָמָן בִּשְׁאָר מְדִינוֹת הַמֶּלֶךְ מֶה עָשׂוּ

עֲשֶׂרֶת בְּנֵי הָמָן *the ten sons of Haman.* Maimonides (*Hilkhot Megilla* 2:12) implies that the custom of spreading out the Megilla as a letter only applies when read with a *tzibur* (see *Ateret Zekenim* 690:17). Maimonides also maintains that one spreads out the Megilla in the form of a letter only upon completion of the reading. According to Maimonides, this custom is not part of the conditions of the reading (in which case, it would be done when read in private as well). Rather, the custom is to display the scroll to an audience in order to

13 would you ask further? It shall be done." And Esther said, "If so it please
the king, may the Jews of Shushan be granted tomorrow also, to do as they
14 did today. And let Haman's ten sons be hung up on the post." And thus the
king commanded; the law was laid down in the imperial city, Shushan, and
15 Haman's ten sons were hung up. And the Jews of Shushan gathered on the
fourteenth day of Adar also, and killed three hundred men in Shushan, never
once touching the plunder.

16 Meanwhile, the rest of the Jews in the king's provinces, having come together
and stood up to defend their lives, found rest from their enemies, killing
seventy-five thousand of those who hated them, though they did not touch
17 the plunder. That was on the thirteenth day of the month – and on the four-
teenth they rested, and made it a day of feasting and happiness.

18 And the Jews who were in Shushan came together both on the thirteenth
and on the fourteenth, and rested on the fifteenth, and made that a day of
19 feasting and happiness. Thus it came about that provincial Jews, living in
unwalled towns, make the fourteenth day of the month of Adar a day of
happiness, of feasting and festivity, and of sending one another good things
to eat.

20 Mordekhai wrote all this down, and sent scrolls to all the Jews in all the

---

the singularity of each Jew, but the common destiny of all Jews. Individual and community are not only metaphysical, existential terms, but also historical terms. When an individual is immersed in the community, he knows that he is no exception to the rule. If the community suffers, so does he.

On Purim and Ḥanukka, the *reshut harabbim*, the public domain, reigns supreme. It was not the individual but the entire community that was the target of hatred, hostility, and persecution. The individual cannot escape the destiny of the collective, and salvation, when it comes, includes the many. Man's role often expresses itself in total involvement with the community, in the readiness to sacrifice. This was true of Esther, and it was true of the Hasmoneans. Therefore, in commemorating the victory, we do not celebrate the event alone, as individuals, but, on the contrary, celebrate the event by merging the individual with the community. The symbol of the day is not the prohibition against work; it is not disengagement and withdrawal. On the contrary, the symbol of the day is joining with the community and seeing oneself as an integral part of a greater community with which God has concluded a covenant. (*Days of Deliverance*)

יג וּמַה־שְּׁאֵלָתֵךְ וְיִנָּתֵן לָךְ וּמַה־בַּקָּשָׁתֵךְ עוֹד וְתֵעָשׂ׃ וַתֹּאמֶר אֶסְתֵּר
אִם־עַל־הַמֶּלֶךְ טוֹב יִנָּתֵן גַּם־מָחָר לַיְּהוּדִים אֲשֶׁר בְּשׁוּשָׁן לַעֲשׂוֹת
יד כְּדָת הַיּוֹם וְאֵת עֲשֶׂרֶת בְּנֵי־הָמָן יִתְלוּ עַל־הָעֵץ׃ וַיֹּאמֶר הַמֶּלֶךְ
טו לְהֵעָשׂוֹת כֵּן וַתִּנָּתֵן דָּת בְּשׁוּשָׁן וְאֵת עֲשֶׂרֶת בְּנֵי־הָמָן תָּלוּ׃ וַיִּקָּהֲלוּ
היהודיים אֲשֶׁר־בְּשׁוּשָׁן גַּם בְּיוֹם אַרְבָּעָה עָשָׂר לְחֹדֶשׁ אֲדָר וַיַּהַרְגוּ הַיְּהוּדִים
טז בְשׁוּשָׁן שְׁלֹשׁ מֵאוֹת אִישׁ וּבַבִּזָּה לֹא שָׁלְחוּ אֶת־יָדָם׃ וּשְׁאָר הַיְּהוּדִים
אֲשֶׁר בִּמְדִינוֹת הַמֶּלֶךְ נִקְהֲלוּ ׀ וְעָמֹד עַל־נַפְשָׁם וְנוֹחַ מֵאֹיְבֵיהֶם וְהָרוֹג
יז בְּשֹׂנְאֵיהֶם חֲמִשָּׁה וְשִׁבְעִים אָלֶף וּבַבִּזָּה לֹא שָׁלְחוּ אֶת־יָדָם׃ בְּיוֹם־
שְׁלוֹשָׁה עָשָׂר לְחֹדֶשׁ אֲדָר וְנוֹחַ בְּאַרְבָּעָה עָשָׂר בּוֹ וְעָשֹׂה אֹתוֹ יוֹם
יח מִשְׁתֶּה וְשִׂמְחָה׃ והיהודיים אֲשֶׁר־בְּשׁוּשָׁן נִקְהֲלוּ בִּשְׁלוֹשָׁה עָשָׂר וְהַיְּהוּדִים
בּוֹ וּבְאַרְבָּעָה עָשָׂר בּוֹ וְנוֹחַ בַּחֲמִשָּׁה עָשָׂר בּוֹ וְעָשֹׂה אֹתוֹ יוֹם מִשְׁתֶּה
יט וְשִׂמְחָה׃ עַל־כֵּן הַיְּהוּדִים הפרוזים הַיֹּשְׁבִים בְּעָרֵי הַפְּרָזוֹת עֹשִׂים הַפְּרָזִים
אֵת יוֹם אַרְבָּעָה עָשָׂר לְחֹדֶשׁ אֲדָר שִׂמְחָה וּמִשְׁתֶּה וְיוֹם טוֹב וּמִשְׁלֹחַ
כ מָנוֹת אִישׁ לְרֵעֵהוּ׃ וַיִּכְתֹּב מָרְדֳּכַי אֶת־הַדְּבָרִים הָאֵלֶּה וַיִּשְׁלַח סְפָרִים

וְעָשֹׂה אֹתוֹ יוֹם מִשְׁתֶּה וְשִׂמְחָה *and made it a day of feasting and happiness.* Spontaneously, the next day they celebrated, before any legislation was passed. The situation in which Israel found itself before the 1967 war was similarly unimaginable. Simply, they were trapped like an animal with all routes of escape sealed off. In the best case they expected 60,000-75,000 casualties. The day after the Six-Day War, there was ecstasy and spontaneous celebration.

שִׂמְחָה וּמִשְׁתֶּה וְיוֹם טוֹב וּמִשְׁלֹחַ מָנוֹת אִישׁ לְרֵעֵהוּ *of happiness, of feasting and festivity, and of sending one another good things to eat.* The Megilla urges the people to celebrate Purim by feasting, by sending gifts to acquaintances and, particularly, presents to the poor. Purim is a day of sharing. Ḥanukka also involves sharing – not sharing of material goods but of Hallel, sharing in the joy of the miracle. The Ḥanukka candle is always kindled in the doorway or window. *Ner Ḥanukka* must be seen, because *simḥa vehallel* can be achieved only if man is ready to share whatever he has. Purim and Ḥanukka manifest not human aloneness, but the unity of the individual and the community; not

21 provinces of King Ahasuerus, near and far, to establish among them that
they should mark the fourteenth and fifteenth days of Adar every single
22 year: the days when the Jews rested from their enemies – the month that
was turned over for them from sorrow to happiness, from mourning to
celebration – to make them days of feasting and happiness, and for sending

---

In the Temple, the joy of Rosh Ḥodesh is manifested in song and trumpets (Num. 10:10; Naḥmanides' glosses to *Sefer HaMitzvot, shoresh* 1). Outside of the Temple, however, there is no positive commandment mandating joy on Rosh Ḥodesh, but only an obligation to abstain from eulogizing and fasting.

Based on the foregoing, we can resolve another difficulty. Maimonides (*Hilkhot Ḥanukka* 3:4) states that fasting and eulogies are forbidden on the eight days of Ḥanukka, "like the days of Purim." Why does Maimonides compare Ḥanukka's prohibition to that of Purim? Furthermore, why does Maimonides refer to Purim as "the days of Purim," instead of simply as "Purim"? By referring to Purim as "the days of Purim," Maimonides alludes to a law mentioned earlier (*Hilkhot Megilla* 2:13) which prohibits eulogizing and fasting not only on the day which one observes as Purim (either the fourteenth or fifteenth of Adar), but on both days, regardless of the day observed. One may have imagined that the prohibition against eulogizing and fasting on Purim stems from its status as יְמֵי מִשְׁתֶּה וְשִׂמְחָה; as such, the prohibition would not apply to Ḥanukka which does not share this status. Maimonides thus hints that the prohibition against eulogizing and fasting on Ḥanukka relates to the passive aspect of Purim which applies to both the fourteenth and fifteenth of Adar, regardless of the day being observed. Although Ḥanukka does not possess a positive manifestation of joy, it is nevertheless like Purim with regard to the passive aspect.

לַעֲשׂוֹת אוֹתָם יְמֵי מִשְׁתֶּה וְשִׂמְחָה *to make them days of feasting and happiness.* Maimonides (*Hilkhot Megilla* 2:17) writes that it is better for a person to spend more resources on giving *matanot la'evyonim* than on dining and giving *mishloaḥ manot,* "for there is no greater and grander joy than to gladden the hearts of the poor, the orphans, the widows, and the converts." Similarly, Maimonides writes elsewhere (*Hilkhot Yom Tov* 6:18), regarding the mitzva of *simḥat yom tov,* "As he eats and drinks he must feed the convert, orphan, and widow together with the poor. But one who locks the doors to his home… this is not rejoicing of mitzva but rejoicing of his stomach." Why is it, however,

אֶל־כָּל־הַיְּהוּדִים אֲשֶׁר בְּכָל־מְדִינוֹת הַמֶּלֶךְ אֲחַשְׁוֵרוֹשׁ הַקְּרוֹבִים
כא וְהָרְחוֹקִים׃ לְקַיֵּם עֲלֵיהֶם לִהְיוֹת עֹשִׂים אֵת יוֹם אַרְבָּעָה עָשָׂר לְחֹדֶשׁ
כב אֲדָר וְאֵת יוֹם־חֲמִשָּׁה עָשָׂר בּוֹ בְּכָל־שָׁנָה וְשָׁנָה׃ כַּיָּמִים אֲשֶׁר־נָחוּ
בָהֶם הַיְּהוּדִים מֵאֽוֹיְבֵיהֶם וְהַחֹדֶשׁ אֲשֶׁר נֶהְפַּךְ לָהֶם מִיָּגוֹן לְשִׂמְחָה
וּמֵאֵבֶל לְיוֹם טוֹב לַעֲשׂוֹת אוֹתָם יְמֵי מִשְׁתֶּה וְשִׂמְחָה וּמִשְׁלֹחַ מָנוֹת

אֵת יוֹם אַרְבָּעָה עָשָׂר לְחֹדֶשׁ אֲדָר וְאֵת יוֹם חֲמִשָּׁה עָשָׂר בּוֹ *the fourteenth and fifteenth days of Adar.* When there are two months of Adar, we read the Megilla in the second Adar (*Megilla* 6b). What is the status of the fourteenth and fifteenth of the first Adar? The Gemara (*ibid.*) states that fasting and eulogizing are prohibited in the first Adar as well, and this is how Maimonides rules (*Hilkhot Megilla* 2:13). However, Rosh (*Megilla* 1:7) denies this entirely. He explains that the Gemara addresses only the period when the months were sanctified by *beit din,* when it was not known if there would be a second Adar by the fourteenth of the first. But in our time, when we know in advance whether there will be a second Adar, the fourteenth and fifteenth of the first month have no significance. According to Maimonides, these days have the status of Purim but only with regard to passive halakhot – fasting and eulogizing are prohibited, but the active mitzvot of Megilla, *mishloaḥ manot,* etc., cannot be fulfilled. There is a third view, cited by Rema (*Oraḥ Ḥayim* 697:1): "Some say that one should increase feasting and joy on the fourteenth of the first Adar, but we do not practice this. Nevertheless, one should increase his meal slightly to fulfill the stringent opinion. 'And he that is of a merry heart has a continual feast' [Prov. 15:15]." According to this view, the first Adar has an active obligation of feasting as well.

לִהְיוֹת עֹשִׂים אֵת יוֹם אַרְבָּעָה עָשָׂר לְחֹדֶשׁ אֲדָר וְאֵת יוֹם חֲמִשָּׁה עָשָׂר בּוֹ בְּכָל שָׁנָה וְשָׁנָה *that they should mark the fourteenth and fifteenth days of Adar every single year.* This verse and the following one reflect two aspects of Purim. In this verse, "that they should mark the fourteenth and fifteenth days of Adar every single year," Purim is marked only as a passive commemoration, which is reflected in a prohibition against fasting and eulogizing but containing no active obligations. In the next verse, we find that Purim is marked as a holiday of active celebration as well: "לַעֲשׂוֹת אוֹתָם יְמֵי מִשְׁתֶּה וְשִׂמְחָה, to make them days of feasting and happiness." Rosh Ḥodesh too contains these two aspects.

23 one another good things to eat, and giving gifts to the poor. And so the Jews
accepted upon themselves what they had already begun to perform, just as
Mordekhai had written.

24 For Haman, son of Hamedata the Agagite, enemy of all the Jews, had plotted
against the Jews to destroy them, and had drawn the *pur* – the lot, that is – to
25 consume and to destroy them. And when Esther came before the king, he
declared, by the scroll, that the evil plot Haman had hatched against the Jews
must come down upon his own head – and he and his sons must be hung up

---

near and far" (9:20), to tell them: You may not have been exposed to danger, but solidarity is something very important among the Jews. There is neither a poor Jew nor a rich Jew, a protected Jew nor a defenseless Jew; there is neither an aristocratic Jew nor a plebian Jew. All Jews are involved in one destiny. This was the idea of Mordekhai. While you celebrate, you cannot forget about your brother who cannot afford to celebrate the holiday properly. Therefore, he introduced *matanot la'evyonim.*

וְקִבֵּל הַיְּהוּדִים אֵת אֲשֶׁר הֵחֵלּוּ לַעֲשׂוֹת *And so the Jews accepted upon themselves what they had already begun to perform.* Why is it that the festival of Purim takes place on the fourteenth of Adar, the day following the victorious battle of the Jews against their enemies, whereas Ḥanukka begins on the twenty-fifth of Kislev, the very same day on which the Jews defeated their enemies? The answer lies in a difference between Purim and all other ordinances of *Ḥazal.* Purim did not originate as the result of a rabbinic ruling, but rather through the actions of the Jewish people themselves. As the verse relates, "And so the Jews accepted upon themselves what they had already begun to perform" – it was the Jewish people who undertook the observance of Purim as a festival, and only afterwards did Mordekhai commit them to their own observance. It is for this reason that Purim was set for future generations on the fourteenth of Adar, as during the first year of its observance the Jews were fighting on the thirteenth of Adar, and could therefore celebrate only on the day following the battle. Mordekhai, in turn, committed the nation for future generations to follow the observance which they had begun. Ḥanukka, on the other hand, was not established through the actions of the Jewish people themselves, but through the enactment of the Rabbis, who saw fit to begin the holiday on the very day on which the miracle took place.

כג אִישׁ לְרֵעֵהוּ וּמַתָּנוֹת לָאֶבְיוֹנִים׃ וְקִבֵּל הַיְּהוּדִים אֵת אֲשֶׁר־הֵחֵלּוּ
כד לַעֲשׂוֹת וְאֵת אֲשֶׁר־כָּתַב מָרְדֳּכַי אֲלֵיהֶם׃ כִּי הָמָן בֶּן־הַמְּדָתָא הָאֲגָגִי
צֹרֵר כָּל־הַיְּהוּדִים חָשַׁב עַל־הַיְּהוּדִים לְאַבְּדָם וְהִפִּל פּוּר הוּא הַגּוֹרָל
כה לְהֻמָּם וּלְאַבְּדָם׃ וּבְבֹאָהּ לִפְנֵי הַמֶּלֶךְ אָמַר עִם־הַסֵּפֶר יָשׁוּב מַחֲשַׁבְתּוֹ
הָרָעָה אֲשֶׁר־חָשַׁב עַל־הַיְּהוּדִים עַל־רֹאשׁוֹ וְתָלוּ אֹתוֹ וְאֶת־בָּנָיו

---

that the resulting joy establishes the precedence of *matanot la'evyonim*? Maimonides is clearly teaching that all three of these mitzvot – *seuda, mishloaḥ manot* and *matanot la'evyonim* – are all manifestations of the central mitzva of *simḥat Purim*. It is for this reason that the mitzva of *matanot la'evyonim*, which is a "greater and grander" joy, takes precedence over the other two mitzvot.

וּמַתָּנוֹת לָאֶבְיוֹנִים *and giving gifts to the poor.* Whenever the Torah speaks about civil law and disputes, it uses the term "רֵעֵהוּ, your neighbor," but when the Torah speaks of *tzedaka*, charity, it uses instead the word "אָחִיךָ, your brother" (see Lev. 25:25-47; Deut. 15:7-14). What is the difference between these two terms? First of all, the term רֵעֵהוּ refers to something transient, something which doesn't endure. Brotherhood, on the other hand, has an element of permanency; brothers, in the normal fashion, never part. And secondly, the word אָחִיךָ connotes a common destiny; brothers share a common past and they anticipate a common future. The Torah uses the word אָחִיךָ with regard to *tzedaka* because *tzedaka* is always the symbol of solidarity.

Initially, Purim was celebrated only by the Jews in the unwalled cities who had seen themselves as vulnerable, and their observance did not include *matanot la'evyonim* (9:19). When Mordekhai pressed for the holiday of Purim, his primary concern was not that each Jew should celebrate that he was saved. Mordekhai wished to implant in the Jews a deep awareness of solidarity, that we are all brothers. Many American Jews ask why we should celebrate Yom HaAtzma'ut. We were not in *Eretz Yisrael*, we were not involved. And, in fact, the Jew who lives in Boston was not involved. This was the mentality of the Jews in the walled cities, who did not see themselves as vulnerable and therefore did not wish to celebrate Purim. Mordekhai's enactment included the walled cities in the observance of Purim to emphasize the common destiny of all Jews. Only in this subsequent enactment was *matanot la'evyonim* added. Mordekhai "sent scrolls to all the Jews in all the provinces of King Ahasuerus,

26 on the post. And so these days were named Purim, after the *pur*. So, following
the words of the letter, and what they had seen, and what had befallen them,
27 they established and accepted, for themselves and for their children, and for
all who would ever come to join their ranks, never to be neglected – that they
keep these two days as they are prescribed and in their right times, every single
28 year. And indeed, these days are remembered and marked in every single
generation, family by family, province upon province, town upon town; nor
will these days of Purim ever be neglected by the Jews, nor their memory ever
cease to be among their children.

---

stand condemned before his Maker. The mitigation of His judgment is due to God's recognition that man is subject to pressures and temptations, and is gullible, easily persuaded. One individual may be saintly because he was reared in noble surroundings; another succumbs to evil because his home background lacked moral instruction and inspiration. The two may be as alike as twins, with similar dispositions, but the difference in their environments has affected their personalities. Should all sinners, then, be deemed equally guilty? Is not much of man's waywardness due to his susceptibility to external pressures? Despite his free will and his accountability for his deeds, man enters his plea before the Almighty, claiming that he is not the author and designer of the worldly pressures that were too powerful for him to resist. These subverting temptations were thrust upon him by *goral* circumstances. Yom Kippur is in this respect like Purim, both involving a *goral*. The compelling intrusion of the unknown and irrational is basic to man's existential condition and it is precisely this weakness which qualifies him to receive God's compassionate forgiveness.

מִשְׁפָּחָה וּמִשְׁפָּחָה מְדִינָה וּמְדִינָה וְעִיר וָעִיר *family by family, province upon province, town upon town.* Maimonides rules (*Hilkhot Megilla* 1:1), "All are obligated in reading [the Megilla]: men, women, converts, and freed slaves." Maimonides, following the Tosefta (*Megilla* 2:4), specifies that "freed slaves" are obligated in Megilla reading, implying that slaves who have not been freed are exempt. Why is it that Megilla reading differs from other mitzvot in which slaves, regardless of whether they were freed, share the same obligations as women? There is an additional difficulty which relates to this one. Maimonides specifically mentions the obligation of converts to read the Megilla as well. In fact, the Megilla itself includes the obligation of converts: "and for all who

כו עַל־הָעֵץ׃ עַל־כֵּן קָרְאוּ לַיָּמִים הָאֵלֶּה פוּרִים עַל־שֵׁם הַפּוּר עַל־כֵּן
עַל־כָּל־דִּבְרֵי הָאִגֶּרֶת הַזֹּאת וּמָה־רָאוּ עַל־כָּכָה וּמָה הִגִּיעַ אֲלֵיהֶם׃
כז קִיְּמוּ וְקִבְּלֻ הַיְּהוּדִים ׀ עֲלֵיהֶם ׀ וְעַל־זַרְעָם וְעַל כָּל־הַנִּלְוִים עֲלֵיהֶם
וְלֹא יַעֲבוֹר לִהְיוֹת עֹשִׂים אֵת־שְׁנֵי הַיָּמִים הָאֵלֶּה כִּכְתָבָם וְכִזְמַנָּם
כח בְּכָל־שָׁנָה וְשָׁנָה׃ וְהַיָּמִים הָאֵלֶּה נִזְכָּרִים וְנַעֲשִׂים בְּכָל־דּוֹר וָדוֹר
מִשְׁפָּחָה וּמִשְׁפָּחָה מְדִינָה וּמְדִינָה וְעִיר וָעִיר וִימֵי הַפּוּרִים הָאֵלֶּה לֹא

עַל כֵּן קָרְאוּ לַיָּמִים הָאֵלֶּה פוּרִים, עַל שֵׁם הַפּוּר *And so these days were named Purim, after the pur.* The *ba'alei hakabbala* discovered mystical associations between Purim and Yom Kippurim, the only difference between the two in the Hebrew spelling being the initial *kaf* in Kippurim. Yom Kippurim, then, would signify "a day like Purim." A strange association! To suggest that Yom Kippur is like Purim, to compare the boisterous Purim to the awesome Yom Kippur, a raucous celebration to a solemn observance! In what way, then, does Yom Kippur resemble Purim?

Purim and Yom Kippur are alike in that both involve the casting of lots (*goral*), a characteristic of games of chance. The Purim *goral* determined the date chosen by Haman for the destruction of the Jews (3:7). Indeed, the very name Purim means "lots." What is so significant about the method that Haman employed to choose a date? Why should the holiday itself be so named?

The Megilla is a book of contradictions. It is filled with events that are unreasonable, even absurd, coincidental, pure chance. At one moment, the Jews live in security in Persia; at the next, they face destruction. Mordekhai is threatened with execution; then, suddenly, he is the prime minister. Irrational events and moods transform fear into festivity, and entire situations are suddenly reversed. Purim, therefore, epitomizes the instability, uncertainty, and vulnerability which characterize the Jews. Thus, the name Purim expresses the erratic capriciousness of events. It alerts the Jew to the sudden turns of fortune, lurking dangers, the fickleness of life, even as the *goral* itself seems to operate through blind chance. Theologically, God forgives man's sinfulness precisely because He acknowledges human vulnerability to changing fortunes, pressing circumstances, and the intrusion of the unexpected. Otherwise, sinful man would always

29 And Esther, daughter of Aviḥayil, the queen, together with Mordekhai the
Jew, wrote with all their authority, for this second letter of Purim to be
30 confirmed. And they sent out scrolls to all the Jews, across one hundred
and twenty-seven provinces, all of Ahasuerus' realm – words of peace and
31 truth. The scrolls were to confirm these days of Purim in their times, just as
Mordekhai the Jew and Esther the queen had fixed them; and, indeed, as
they had all fixed their fast days and entreaties, for themselves and for their
32 children. And so, Esther's word confirmed this practice of Purim; and it was
written down in the scroll.

Maimonides describes is akin to *hagbaha* performed after *Keriat HaTorah* as described by Rema (*Oraḥ Ḥayim* 133:2). The mitzva of Megilla contains two components: publicizing the miracle, and *Keriat Ketuvim*, reading from Scripture. The second component, *Keriat Ketuvim*, is the basis for the blessing of *al mikra megilla*, which is recited before reading all of the five Megillot (*Masekhet Sofrim* 14:3). According to Maimonides, the Megilla is read as a rolled scroll, consistent with the manner of reading other parts of *Ketuvim*, and is only spread as a letter, in fulfillment of *pirsumei nisa*, upon completion of the reading.

לְקַיֵּם אֵת אִגֶּרֶת הַפּוּרִים הַזֹּאת הַשֵּׁנִית *for this second letter of Purim to be confirmed.* In this context, the word לְקַיֵּם must mean to confirm. The word לְקַיֵּם in this verse is used in the sense of confirming the absolute and true character of this scroll, this letter of Purim. Esther wanted to raise the scroll to the level of Scripture, to elevate what was an *iggeret*, a letter, into a *sefer*, a book of Tanakh. Likewise, in the verse "קִיְּמוּ וְקִבְּלוּ הַיְּהוּדִים...לִהְיוֹת עֹשִׂים אֵת שְׁנֵי הַיָּמִים הָאֵלֶּה, they established and accepted … that they keep these two days" (9:27), the word קִיְּמוּ means that they confirmed and certified the veracity, the truthfulness, the importance, and the significance of the holiday of Purim. The Jews agreed to celebrate Purim not just as a festival of rabbinic origin, but as an institution which is mentioned in Scripture. Purim itself was elevated to a holiday whose existence, validity and obligatory character are explicitly mentioned in Tanakh.

דִּבְרֵי הַצֹּמוֹת וְזַעֲקָתָם *their fast days and entreaties. Ḥazal* detected a sense of insecurity in the Megilla: "One is obligated to read the Megilla at night and to repeat it in the day; as it says (Ps. 22:3), 'O my God, I call by day but You answer not, and at night and there is no surcease for me'" (*Megilla* 4a). What does this verse have to do with the Megilla? The Megilla is, on the contrary,

כט יעברו מתוך היהודים וזכרם לא־יסוף מזרעם: ותכתב
אסתר המלכה בת־אביחיל ומרדכי היהודי את־כל־תקף לקים
ל את אגרת הפרים הזאת השנית: וישלח ספרים אל־כל־היהודים
אל־שבע ועשרים ומאה מדינה מלכות אחשורוש דברי שלום
לא ואמת: לקים את־ימי הפרים האלה בזמניהם כאשר קים עליהם
מרדכי היהודי ואסתר המלכה וכאשר קימו על־נפשם ועל־זרעם
לב דברי הצומות וזעקתם: ומאמר אסתר קים דברי הפרים האלה

---

would ever come to join their ranks" (9:27). The fact that a verse is needed to obligate converts points to the fact that Megilla reading differs from other mitzvot, and this too requires explanation.

The solution to these problems can be found in the verse, "And indeed, these days are remembered and marked in every single generation, family by family, province upon province, town upon town." Whereas most rabbinic mitzvot were enacted for the entire Jewish people as one unified entity, the mitzva of reading the Megilla was enacted upon every family, every province, and every town. This explains why different types of cities read the Megilla on different days – the mitzva of Megilla devolves upon distinct units within the nation, not upon the nation as a whole. For this reason, the Megilla needed to specifically include converts in the mitzva, as converts were not part of an existing Jewish family at the time of the Megilla, and would therefore have been excluded from the mitzva which falls upon families. Likewise, according to Maimonides, slaves are not obligated in Megilla reading because "slaves do not have family relationships" (*Yevamot* 62a). [This also explains why the Tosefta (*ibid.*) enumerates those who are disqualified from marrying as obligated in the mitzva of Megilla – since the mitzva devolves on family units, we may otherwise have exempted these individuals. – *Ed.*]

אגרת הפרים *letter of Purim.* Maimonides writes (*Hilkhot Megilla* 2:12), "It is the custom that the reader reads and spreads it like a letter, in order to publicize the miracle. Upon completion of the reading, he rolls back the Megilla and says the blessing." While it is our custom to first unfold the Megilla and then read it so that the reading is from a Megilla in the appearance of a letter, according to Maimonides the custom is for the reader to display the Megilla as a letter upon completion of the reading. The process

10 1 As for King Ahasuerus, he levied a tribute from the people of all the land and
2 of the islands of the sea. And the full account of his authority and might, and
all the greatness of Mordekhai, whom the king exalted – are they not already
3 written in the Scroll of the Chronicles of the Kings of Medea and Persia? ▸ For
Mordekhai the Jew was second-in-command to King Ahasuerus, and revered
too among the Jews – beloved of all the multitudes of his brothers, working
for the good of his people, and speaking words of peace for all his children. ◂

---

epistle does narrate; yet its main task is to explain. It not only describes but also interprets. It links up events, sets them up against their proper causal background, and points out their fundamental patterns of development. In short, at this stage, a descriptive chronicle or story turns into interpretive history. Our Rabbis said: "[The Megilla] is called an epistle in order to teach that if one sewed it with three threads of tendons – it is fit for use" (*Megilla* 19a). The scrolls must be held together by three stitches at least. Of course, the stitches symbolize the unity of the tale, the causative unfolding of events. A book, *sefer*, in contradistinction to *iggeret* at both levels, signifies a text written under the impact of divine inspiration. A book moves events from the particular and transient toward the universal, omnipresent, and dynamic in the great drama of human destiny. At this point, the idea of truth transcends that of factual observation as well as that of causalistic interpretation and reaches into the realm of inspiration. Truth at this stage is of a predictive nature; to be truthful means to be inspired, to enjoy clairvoyance, to see in every individual fact the fingerprints of universality, in each passing phenomenon what Leopold von Ranke called the "great trends of the centuries," the traces of the eternal and the inevitable, and in each plot the manifestation of the *élan vital*. The truth of the book is revealed, not discovered; it is beheld as a vision, not just inferred by logical judgment. In short, it is "the declaration of him that hears the sayings of God, who sees the vision of the Almighty, falling down but having his eyes uncovered" (Num. 24:4). The conclusion, therefore, is obvious. If the book of Esther is an integral part of the Holy Scriptures, then its relevance is not limited to the narration of events, to the plot that took place once upon a time. In short, the Megilla is a halakhic book, replete with rules, principles, and criteria that should guide us as human beings and Jews participating in the unfolding of the great historical drama in general and our unique national destiny in particular. (*Days of Deliverance*)

הֲלוֹא הֵם כְּתוּבִים עַל סֵפֶר דִּבְרֵי הַיָּמִים לְמַלְכֵי מָדַי וּפָרָס *are they not already written in the Scroll of the Chronicles of the Kings of Medea and Persia?* A courageous life

י א וְנִכְתָּב בַּסֵּפֶר: וַיָּשֶׂם הַמֶּלֶךְ אחשרש ׀ מַס עַל־הָאָרֶץ אֲחַשְׁוֵרוֹשׁ
ב וְאִיֵּי הַיָּם: וְכָל־מַעֲשֵׂה תָקְפּוֹ וּגְבוּרָתוֹ וּפָרָשַׁת גְּדֻלַּת מָרְדֳּכַי אֲשֶׁר
גִּדְּלוֹ הַמֶּלֶךְ הֲלוֹא־הֵם כְּתוּבִים עַל־סֵפֶר דִּבְרֵי הַיָּמִים לְמַלְכֵי מָדַי
ג וּפָרָס: כִּי ׀ מָרְדֳּכַי הַיְּהוּדִי מִשְׁנֶה לַמֶּלֶךְ אֲחַשְׁוֵרוֹשׁ וְגָדוֹל לַיְּהוּדִים
וְרָצוּי לְרֹב אֶחָיו דֹּרֵשׁ טוֹב לְעַמּוֹ וְדֹבֵר שָׁלוֹם לְכָל־זַרְעוֹ:

Hallel, a hymn. Apparently, *Ḥazal* identified the Megilla not only with a hymn, but with a great prayer as well – a prayer which rises *mima'amakim,* from the depths, from a person in despair. (*Days of Deliverance*)

The Gemara (*Megilla* 2b) states that the thirteenth of Adar is considered *zeman kehilla lakol,* a time of assembly for all, and therefore when the Megilla is read before the fourteenth of Adar it can be read on this day. Rashi explains that on this day, the Jewish people assembled to take revenge on their enemies, which allows for reading of the Megilla on this day as an expression of gratitude for the miracle which occurred. Rabbenu Tam (cited by Rosh, *Megilla* 1:1), however, explains that the thirteenth is considered *zeman kehilla lakol* because all gather on this day to observe Ta'anit Esther. According to Rabbenu Tam, what then about the thirteenth of Adar allows us to read the Megilla? The answer is based on the Gemara (*Megilla* 4a) which relates to the reading of the Megilla not only as a commemoration of our salvation, but also of our distress. Ta'anit Esther is a commemoration of the anxiety and distress experienced by the protagonists at the time of the first Purim. The thirteenth of Adar is a day of Megilla reading because the Megilla is not only a document of thanksgiving but also one of distress and supplication.

וְנִכְתָּב בַּסֵּפֶר *and it was written down in the scroll.* An epistle, an *iggeret,* is simply a chronicle, a tale of events. Its excellence consists in honest, objective, and precise recording. The truth of the epistle is the kind of truth to which we expect witnesses to conform in the case of litigation or court proceedings. The truthfulness of the witness is of a descriptive, matter-of-fact nature, concerned with exact, impartial, and detailed observation. However, the epistle is more than a tale, a descriptive chronicle recording dry facts, naked, isolated events in chronological order. An epistle contains not just a dead *story,* but a living *history*. An epistle not only informs but instructs as well. It addresses itself not only to a platitudinous, fact-prying, gossip-enjoying instinct, but also to our knowledge-questing, inquisitive mind. Of course, even at this level an

The scroll is rolled up and, if a minyan is present, the Reader continues:

בָּרוּךְ Blessed are You, Lord our God, King of the Universe,
who pleads our cause, judges our claim, avenges our wrong,
brings retribution to our enemies, and punishes our foes.
Blessed are You, Lord, who on behalf of His people Israel,
exacts punishment from all their foes, the God who brings salvation.

אֲשֶׁר הֵנִיא [God] frustrated the plan of the nations,
thwarted the intentions of the crafty.
An evil man rose up against us,
an arrogant branch of Amalek's tree,
haughty, rich, he dug his own pit.
His hubris became his own snare.
He was trapped in the trap he set for others.
Seeking to destroy, he was destroyed.
Haman shared his ancestors' hate,
and stirred against children the hostility of brothers.

---

as long as he is the Messiah, the anointed one, consecrated to the covenantal community. The very moment he finishes his job, the lights are dimmed and he disappears from sight. What does the Megilla tell us about Mordekhai the Jew and Esther the queen before and after the Haman episode? Nothing! The Megilla refers us to the history books of Medea and Persia. Only the activities during a short period of time are memorialized. The rest is enveloped in mystery. (*Days of Deliverance*)

הָרָב אֶת רִיבֵנוּ *who pleads our cause.* According to some, this blessing should be recited by each individual and one should not rely on the reader's blessing. According to this view, the rule of *shome'a ke'oneh,* listening to a recitation is equivalent to reciting it oneself, applies only to shared obligations, based on the principle that all Jews are responsible for one another (*kol Yisrael arevim zeh lazeh*). For this reason, one can recite blessings over mitzvot for another, even if one has already fulfilled the mitzva, as well as blessings over food, when one partakes of the food and is thus also obligated to recite a blessing. But reciting the blessing of הָרָב אֶת רִיבֵנוּ, *who pleads our cause,* is merely customary, and there is therefore no shared obligation which creates the framework for *shome'a ke'oneh.*

The scroll is rolled up and, if a מנין *is present, the* קורא *continues:*

בָּרוּךְ אַתָּה יהוה אֱלֹהֵינוּ מֶלֶךְ הָעוֹלָם
הָרָב אֶת רִיבֵנוּ, וְהַדָּן אֶת דִּינֵנוּ, וְהַנּוֹקֵם אֶת נִקְמָתֵנוּ
וְהַמְשַׁלֵּם גְּמוּל לְכָל אוֹיְבֵי נַפְשֵׁנוּ, וְהַנִּפְרָע לָנוּ מִצָּרֵינוּ.
בָּרוּךְ אַתָּה יהוה
הַנִּפְרָע לְעַמּוֹ יִשְׂרָאֵל מִכָּל צָרֵיהֶם, הָאֵל הַמּוֹשִׁיעַ.

אֲשֶׁר הֵנִיא עֲצַת גּוֹיִם, וַיָּפֶר מַחְשְׁבוֹת עֲרוּמִים.
בְּקוּם עָלֵינוּ אָדָם רָשָׁע, נֵצֶר זָדוֹן מִזֶּרַע עֲמָלֵק.
גָּאָה בְעָשְׁרוֹ וְכָרָה לוֹ בּוֹר, וּגְדֻלָּתוֹ יָקְשָׁה לוֹ לָכֶד.
דִּמָּה בְנַפְשׁוֹ לִלְכֹּד וְנִלְכַּד, בִּקֵּשׁ לְהַשְׁמִיד וְנִשְׁמַד מְהֵרָה.
הָמָן הוֹדִיעַ אֵיבַת אֲבוֹתָיו, וְעוֹרֵר שִׂנְאַת אַחִים לַבָּנִים.

---

means a sacrificial life. The highest form of sacrifice is readiness to leave the stage after one has played the part assigned to him and to vanish in anonymity and oblivion. Both the pragmatic society as well as the tyrannical society attempt to overcome human finiteness by the perpetuity of the historical. Public memory is the substitute for metaphysical immortality. Judaism did not accept this. On the contrary, it considered the quest to have one's deeds recorded to be vanity.

The individual as such can never become a historical figure. Only the covenantal community has a claim on perpetuity. The service that the individual provides to the community is recorded. The very moment his service is completed, history is not concerned with him anymore. The ideal cathartic experience is that of anonymity. How many facts did the Torah record of the lives of the Patriarchs or of Moses? Only those periods were recorded that are directly intertwined with the service that they rendered to the covenantal community. God requires of man the highest of sacrifices – anonymity, humility. God hates glamour, fame, external glitter, and vainglory. He loves the actor who appears on the stage for a short while, plays his or her part humbly, and disappears immediately without receiving applause. Man stands in the limelight

He did not remember Saul's act of mercy,
his pity for Agag, through which a new enemy was born.
The wicked planned to cut off the righteous,
but the impure was defeated by the pure.
[Mordekhai's] goodness overcame the father's [Saul's] error,
but the evil [Haman] piled sin upon sin.
He hid in his heart his cunning schemes,intent on his evildoing.
He stretched out his hand against God's holy ones;
he spent his wealth to destroy every memory of them.
When Mordekhai saw the wrath go forth,
and Haman's decrees issued in Shushan,
he put on sackcloth, wrapped himself in mourning,
decreed a fast and sat on ashes.
"Who will arise to atone for error,
and find forgiveness for our ancestors' sins?"
A flower blossomed from the palm tree;
Hadassa arose to wake those who slept.
Her servants hastened Haman to come,
to serve him wine with the venom of serpents.
He had risen by his wealth, but fell by his evil.
He made the very gallows by which he was hanged.
All the inhabitants of the world were amazed
when Haman's ploy (*pur*) became our joy (*Purim*).
The righteous one was saved from evil hands,
the perpetrator suffered the fate of his intended victim.
They undertook to celebrate Purim,
and to rejoice on it year after year.
You heeded the prayer of Mordekhai and Esther;
and Haman and his sons were hanged on the gallows.

שׁוֹשַׁנַּת יַעֲקֹב The lily of Jacob rejoiced and was glad,
when, together, they saw Mordekhai robed in royal blue.
You have been their eternal salvation, their hope in every generation;
to make known that all who hope in You will not be put to shame,
all who trust in You will never be humiliated.

Cursed be Haman who sought to destroy me.
Blessed be Mordekhai the Yehudi.
Cursed be Zeresh, wife of the one who terrified me.
Blessed be Esther [whose actions saved] me.
Cursed be all the wicked;
blessed be all Israel.
And may Ḥarvona, too, be remembered for good.

וְלֹא זָכַר רַחֲמֵי שָׁאוּל, כִּי בְחֶמְלָתוֹ עַל אֲגָג נוֹלַד אוֹיֵב.
זָמַם רָשָׁע לְהַכְרִית צַדִּיק, וְנִלְכַּד טָמֵא בִּידֵי טָהוֹר.
חֶסֶד גָּבַר עַל שִׁגְגַת אָב, וְרָשָׁע הוֹסִיף חֵטְא עַל חֲטָאָיו.
טָמַן בְּלִבּוֹ מַחְשְׁבוֹת עֲרוּמָיו, וַיִּתְמַכֵּר לַעֲשׂוֹת רָעָה.
יָדוֹ שָׁלַח בִּקְדוֹשֵׁי אֵל, כַּסְפּוֹ נָתַן לְהַכְרִית זִכְרָם.
כִּרְאוֹת מָרְדֳּכַי כִּי יָצָא קֶצֶף, וְדָתֵי הָמָן נִתְּנוּ בְשׁוּשָׁן.
לָבַשׁ שַׂק וְקָשַׁר מִסְפֵּד וְגָזַר צוֹם וַיֵּשֶׁב עַל הָאֵפֶר.
מִי זֶה יַעֲמֹד לְכַפֵּר שְׁגָגָה, וְלִמְחֹל חַטַּאת עֲוֹן אֲבוֹתֵינוּ.
נֵץ פָּרַח מִלּוּלָב, הֵן הֲדַסָּה עָמְדָה לְעוֹרֵר יְשֵׁנִים.
סָרִיסֶיהָ הִבְהִילוּ לְהָמָן, לְהַשְׁקוֹתוֹ יֵין חֲמַת תַּנִּינִים.
עָמַד בְּעָשְׁרוֹ וְנָפַל בְּרִשְׁעוֹ, עָשָׂה לּוֹ עֵץ וְנִתְלָה עָלָיו.
פִּיהֶם פָּתְחוּ כָּל יוֹשְׁבֵי תֵבֵל, כִּי פוּר הָמָן נֶהְפַּךְ לְפוּרֵנוּ.
צַדִּיק נֶחֱלַץ מִיַּד רָשָׁע, אוֹיֵב נִתַּן תַּחַת נַפְשׁוֹ.
קִיְּמוּ עֲלֵיהֶם לַעֲשׂוֹת פּוּרִים וְלִשְׂמֹחַ בְּכָל שָׁנָה וְשָׁנָה.
רָאִיתָ אֶת תְּפִלַּת מָרְדֳּכַי וְאֶסְתֵּר, הָמָן וּבָנָיו עַל הָעֵץ תָּלִיתָ.

שׁוֹשַׁנַּת יַעֲקֹב צָהֲלָה וְשָׂמֵחָה בִּרְאוֹתָם יַחַד תְּכֵלֶת מָרְדֳּכָי.
תְּשׁוּעָתָם הָיִיתָ לָנֶצַח, וְתִקְוָתָם בְּכָל דּוֹר וָדוֹר.
לְהוֹדִיעַ שֶׁכָּל קֹוֶיךָ לֹא יֵבֹשׁוּ, וְלֹא יִכָּלְמוּ לָנֶצַח כָּל הַחוֹסִים בָּךְ.

אָרוּר הָמָן אֲשֶׁר בִּקֵּשׁ לְאַבְּדִי
בָּרוּךְ מָרְדֳּכַי הַיְּהוּדִי.
אֲרוּרָה זֶרֶשׁ אֵשֶׁת מַפְחִידִי
בְּרוּכָה אֶסְתֵּר בַּעֲדִי.
אֲרוּרִים כָּל הָרְשָׁעִים
בְּרוּכִים כָּל יִשְׂרָאֵל
וְגַם חַרְבוֹנָה זָכוּר לַטּוֹב.

On Motza'ei Shabbat, continue with "May the pleasantness" on page 142.
On other days, continue with "You are the Holy One."

▸ You are the Holy One, enthroned on the praises of Israel. *Ps. 22*
And [the angels] call to one another, saying, "Holy, holy, holy *Is. 6*
is the LORD of hosts; the whole world is filled with His glory."

And they receive permission from one another, saying: *Targum Yonatan Is. 6*
"Holy in the highest heavens, home of His Presence; holy on earth,
the work of His strength; holy for ever and all time is the LORD of hosts;
the whole earth is full of His radiant glory."

▸ Then a wind lifted me up and I heard behind me the sound of a great noise, saying, "Blessed is the LORD's glory from His place." *Ezek. 3*

Then a wind lifted me up and I heard behind me *Targum Yonatan Ezek. 3*
the sound of a great tempest of those who uttered praise, saying,
"Blessed is the LORD's glory from the place of the home of His Presence."

The LORD shall reign for ever and all time. *Ex. 15*

The LORD's kingdom is established for ever and all time. *Targum Onkelos Ex. 15*

יהוה LORD, God of Abraham, Isaac and Yisrael, our ancestors, may You keep this for ever so that it forms the thoughts in Your people's heart, and directs their heart toward You. He is compassionate. He forgives iniquity and does not destroy. Repeatedly He suppresses *1 Chr. 29* *Ps. 78*

---

the *Shekhina*. Since *Taḥanun* is an extension of the Amida, we defer the full Kaddish until after *Ve'Ata Kadosh*. On Purim night, however, *Ve'Ata Kadosh* is not an expression of *Taḥanun*. We recite *Ve'Ata Kadosh* following the Megilla because, according to our tradition, Esther recited it when she entered Ahasuerus' chamber (*Yoma* 29a; see the essay "*Ve'Ata Kadosh*: Hallel of the Hidden God" in this volume). Since *Ve'Ata Kadosh* on Purim night is not recited as *Taḥanun* and is not an integral part of the Amida, it is unnecessary to defer the full Kaddish until after *Ve'Ata Kadosh*. This explains the view of Tosafot. Avudraham apparently reasoned that regardless of the occasion, *Ve'Ata Kadosh* is always related to the Amida and becomes one entity with it. As such, the full Kaddish is always deferred until after *Ve'Ata Kadosh*.

On מוצאי שבת*, continue with* וִיהִי נֹעַם *on page 143.*
On other days, continue with וְאַתָּה קָדוֹשׁ

תהלים כב ◂ וְאַתָּה קָדוֹשׁ יוֹשֵׁב תְּהִלּוֹת יִשְׂרָאֵל: וְקָרָא זֶה אֶל־זֶה וְאָמַר
ישעיה ו קָדוֹשׁ, קָדוֹשׁ, קָדוֹשׁ, יהוה צְבָאוֹת, מְלֹא כָל־הָאָרֶץ כְּבוֹדוֹ:
תרגום יונתן ישעיה ו וּמְקַבְּלִין דֵּין מִן דֵּין וְאָמְרִין, קַדִּישׁ בִּשְׁמֵי מְרוֹמָא עִלָּאָה בֵּית שְׁכִינְתֵּהּ
קַדִּישׁ עַל אַרְעָא עוֹבַד גְּבוּרְתֵּהּ, קַדִּישׁ לְעָלַם וּלְעָלְמֵי עָלְמַיָּא
יהוה צְבָאוֹת, מַלְיָא כָל אַרְעָא זִיו יְקָרֵהּ.

יחזקאל ג ◂ וַתִּשָּׂאֵנִי רוּחַ, וָאֶשְׁמַע אַחֲרַי קוֹל רַעַשׁ גָּדוֹל
בָּרוּךְ כְּבוֹד־יהוה מִמְּקוֹמוֹ:
תרגום יונתן יחזקאל ג וּנְטָלַתְנִי רוּחָא, וּשְׁמָעִית בַּתְרַי קָל זִיעַ סַגִּיא, דִּמְשַׁבְּחִין וְאָמְרִין
בְּרִיךְ יְקָרָא דַיהוה מֵאֲתַר בֵּית שְׁכִינְתֵּהּ.

שמות טו יהוה יִמְלֹךְ לְעֹלָם וָעֶד:
תרגום אונקלוס שמות טו יהוה מַלְכוּתֵהּ קָאֵם לְעָלַם וּלְעָלְמֵי עָלְמַיָּא.

דברי הימים א׳ כט יהוה אֱלֹהֵי אַבְרָהָם יִצְחָק וְיִשְׂרָאֵל אֲבֹתֵינוּ, שָׁמְרָה־זֹּאת לְעוֹלָם
תהלים עח לְיֵצֶר מַחְשְׁבוֹת לְבַב עַמֶּךָ, וְהָכֵן לְבָבָם אֵלֶיךָ: וְהוּא רַחוּם יְכַפֵּר
עָוֹן וְלֹא־יַשְׁחִית, וְהִרְבָּה לְהָשִׁיב אַפּוֹ, וְלֹא־יָעִיר כָּל־חֲמָתוֹ:

וְאַתָּה קָדוֹשׁ *You are the Holy One.* There is a dispute about when on Purim night we recite the full Kaddish, which includes the request of "תִּתְקַבַּל צְלוֹתְהוֹן וּבָעוּתְהוֹן דְּכָל בֵּית יִשְׂרָאֵל, May the prayers and pleas of all of Israel be accepted." Tosafot (*Megilla* 4a s.v. *pasak*) maintain that we recite the full Kaddish immediately following the Amida, while Avudraham (cited by *Magen Avraham* 693:1) holds that following the Amida we recite only half Kaddish, and defer the full Kaddish until after *Ve'Ata Kadosh*. What does this dispute depend on? On an ordinary Motza'ei Shabbat, we recite the full Kaddish only after *Ve'Ata Kadosh*. Motza'ei Shabbat is, in certain respects, a time of distress because of the additional "soul" of Shabbat which is lost. We recite *Ve'Ata Kadosh* on Motza'ei Shabbat as a form of *Taḥanun* for the loss of communion with

His anger, not rousing His full wrath. For You, my Lord, are good Ps. 86
and forgiving, abundantly kind to all who call on You. Your righ- Ps. 119
teousness is eternally righteous, and Your Torah is truth. Grant Micah 7
truth to Jacob, loving-kindness to Abraham, as You promised our
ancestors in ancient times. Blessed is my Lord for day after day He Ps. 68
burdens us [with His blessings]; God is our salvation, Selah! The Ps. 46
Lord of hosts is with us; the God of Jacob is our refuge, Selah!
Lord of hosts, happy is the one who trusts in You. Lord, save! Ps. 84 Ps. 20
May the King answer us on the day we call.

בָּרוּךְ Blessed is He, our God, who created us for His glory, separating us from those who go astray; who gave us the Torah of truth, planting within us eternal life. May He open our heart to His Torah, imbuing our heart with the love and awe of Him, that we may do His will and serve Him with a perfect heart, so that we neither toil in vain nor give birth to confusion.

יְהִי רָצוֹן May it be Your will, O Lord our God and God of our ancestors, that we keep Your laws in this world, and thus be worthy to live, see and inherit goodness and blessing in the Messianic Age and in
the life of the World to Come. So that my soul may sing to You and Ps. 30
not be silent. Lord, my God, for ever I will thank You. Blessed is Jer. 17
the man who trusts in the Lord, whose trust is in the Lord alone.
Trust in the Lord for evermore, for God, the Lord, is an everlast- Is. 26
ing Rock. ▸ Those who know Your name trust in You, for You, Lord, Ps. 9
do not forsake those who seek You. The Lord desired, for the sake Is. 42
of Israel's merit, to make the Torah great and glorious.

---

ing attributes were fused into the attribute of *tiferet,* as represented by Jacob. It is interesting to note that only Abraham and Jacob are mentioned in this verse, along with the divine attributes that they represent. Isaac's name and attribute were omitted, consistent with the very theme of withdrawal which he personifies.

כִּי־אַתָּה אֲדֹנָי טוֹב וְסַלָּח, וְרַב־חֶסֶד לְכָל־קֹרְאֶיךָ: צִדְקָתְךָ תהלים פו / תהלים קיט
צֶדֶק לְעוֹלָם וְתוֹרָתְךָ אֱמֶת: תִּתֵּן אֱמֶת לְיַעֲקֹב, חֶסֶד לְאַבְרָהָם, מיכה ז
אֲשֶׁר־נִשְׁבַּעְתָּ לַאֲבֹתֵינוּ מִימֵי קֶדֶם: בָּרוּךְ אֲדֹנָי יוֹם יוֹם יַעֲמָס־ תהלים סח
לָנוּ, הָאֵל יְשׁוּעָתֵנוּ סֶלָה: יהוה צְבָאוֹת עִמָּנוּ, מִשְׂגָּב לָנוּ אֱלֹהֵי תהלים מו
יַעֲקֹב סֶלָה: יהוה צְבָאוֹת, אַשְׁרֵי אָדָם בֹּטֵחַ בָּךְ: יהוה הוֹשִׁיעָה, תהלים פד / תהלים כ
הַמֶּלֶךְ יַעֲנֵנוּ בְיוֹם־קָרְאֵנוּ:

בָּרוּךְ הוּא אֱלֹהֵינוּ שֶׁבְּרָאָנוּ לִכְבוֹדוֹ, וְהִבְדִּילָנוּ מִן הַתּוֹעִים, וְנָתַן לָנוּ תּוֹרַת אֱמֶת, וְחַיֵּי עוֹלָם נָטַע בְּתוֹכֵנוּ. הוּא יִפְתַּח לִבֵּנוּ בְּתוֹרָתוֹ, וְיָשֵׂם בְּלִבֵּנוּ אַהֲבָתוֹ וְיִרְאָתוֹ וְלַעֲשׂוֹת רְצוֹנוֹ וּלְעָבְדוֹ בְּלֵבָב שָׁלֵם, לְמַעַן לֹא נִיגַע לָרִיק וְלֹא נֵלֵד לַבֶּהָלָה.

יְהִי רָצוֹן מִלְּפָנֶיךָ יהוה אֱלֹהֵינוּ וֵאלֹהֵי אֲבוֹתֵינוּ, שֶׁנִּשְׁמֹר חֻקֶּיךָ
בָּעוֹלָם הַזֶּה, וְנִזְכֶּה וְנִחְיֶה וְנִרְאֶה וְנִירַשׁ טוֹבָה וּבְרָכָה, לִשְׁנֵי
יְמוֹת הַמָּשִׁיחַ וּלְחַיֵּי הָעוֹלָם הַבָּא. לְמַעַן יְזַמֶּרְךָ כָבוֹד וְלֹא יִדֹּם, תהלים ל
יהוה אֱלֹהַי, לְעוֹלָם אוֹדֶךָּ: בָּרוּךְ הַגֶּבֶר אֲשֶׁר יִבְטַח בַּיהוה, ירמיה יז
וְהָיָה יהוה מִבְטַחוֹ: בִּטְחוּ בַיהוה עֲדֵי־עַד, כִּי בְּיָהּ יהוה צוּר ישעיה כו
עוֹלָמִים: › וְיִבְטְחוּ בְךָ יוֹדְעֵי שְׁמֶךָ, כִּי לֹא־עָזַבְתָּ דֹרְשֶׁיךָ, יהוה: תהלים ט
יהוה חָפֵץ לְמַעַן צִדְקוֹ, יַגְדִּיל תּוֹרָה וְיַאְדִּיר: ישעיה מב

תִּתֵּן אֱמֶת לְיַעֲקֹב, חֶסֶד לְאַבְרָהָם *Grant truth to Jacob, loving-kindness to Abraham.* Each of our forefathers represented a different attribute of the Almighty. Abraham represented *ḥesed,* loving-kindness; Isaac represented *gevura,* strength; and Jacob represented *tiferet,* glory, or *emet,* truth. *Ḥesed* expresses itself in an outward motion of expansion, because in *ḥesed,* one shares with others. In contrast, *gevura* involves retreat, an act of withdrawal. These oppos-

FULL KADDISH

Leader: יִתְגַּדַּל Magnified and sanctified may His great name be,
in the world He created by His will.
May He establish His kingdom in your lifetime
and in your days,
and in the lifetime of all the house of Israel,
swiftly and soon –
and say: Amen.

All: May His great name be blessed for ever and all time.

Leader: Blessed and praised,
glorified and exalted,
raised and honored,
uplifted and lauded be
the name of the Holy One,
blessed be He,
beyond any blessing,
song, praise and consolation uttered in the world –
and say: Amen.

The line beginning with "Titkabel" is omitted.

May there be great peace from heaven,
and life for us and all Israel –
and say: Amen.

Bow, take three steps back, as if taking leave of the Divine Presence, then bow, first left, then right, then center, while saying:

May He who makes peace in His high places,
make peace for us and all Israel –
and say: Amen.

קדיש שלם

ש״ץ: יִתְגַּדַּל וְיִתְקַדַּשׁ שְׁמֵהּ רַבָּא (קהל: אָמֵן)
בְּעָלְמָא דִּי בְרָא כִרְעוּתֵהּ
וְיַמְלִיךְ מַלְכוּתֵהּ
בְּחַיֵּיכוֹן וּבְיוֹמֵיכוֹן וּבְחַיֵּי דְכָל בֵּית יִשְׂרָאֵל
בַּעֲגָלָא וּבִזְמַן קָרִיב
וְאִמְרוּ אָמֵן. (קהל: אָמֵן)

קהל וש״ץ: יְהֵא שְׁמֵהּ רַבָּא מְבָרַךְ לְעָלַם וּלְעָלְמֵי עָלְמַיָּא.

ש״ץ: יִתְבָּרַךְ וְיִשְׁתַּבַּח וְיִתְפָּאַר
וְיִתְרוֹמַם וְיִתְנַשֵּׂא וְיִתְהַדָּר וְיִתְעַלֶּה וְיִתְהַלָּל
שְׁמֵהּ דְּקֻדְשָׁא בְּרִיךְ הוּא (קהל: בְּרִיךְ הוּא)
לְעֵלָּא מִן כָּל בִּרְכָתָא וְשִׁירָתָא, תֻּשְׁבְּחָתָא וְנֶחֱמָתָא
דַּאֲמִירָן בְּעָלְמָא
וְאִמְרוּ אָמֵן. (קהל: אָמֵן)

The line beginning with תִּתְקַבַּל *is omitted.*

יְהֵא שְׁלָמָא רַבָּא מִן שְׁמַיָּא
וְחַיִּים, עָלֵינוּ וְעַל כָּל יִשְׂרָאֵל
וְאִמְרוּ אָמֵן. (קהל: אָמֵן)

Bow, take three steps back, as if taking leave of the Divine Presence, then bow, first left, then right, then center, while saying:

עֹשֶׂה שָׁלוֹם בִּמְרוֹמָיו
הוּא יַעֲשֶׂה שָׁלוֹם עָלֵינוּ וְעַל כָּל יִשְׂרָאֵל
וְאִמְרוּ אָמֵן. (קהל: אָמֵן)

Stand while saying Aleinu. Bow at ▾.

עָלֵינוּ It is our duty to praise the Master of all,
and ascribe greatness to the Author of creation,
who has not made us like the nations of the lands
nor placed us like the families of the earth;
who has not made our portion like theirs,
nor our destiny like all their multitudes.
(For they worship vanity and emptiness,
and pray to a god who cannot save.)
▾But we bow in worship
and thank the Supreme King of kings,
the Holy One, blessed be He,
who extends the heavens and establishes the earth,
whose throne of glory is in the heavens above,
and whose power's Presence is in the highest of heights.
He is our God; there is no other.
Truly He is our King, there is none else,
as it is written in His Torah:
"You shall know and take to heart this day *Deut. 4*
that the LORD is God,
in heaven above and on earth below. There is no other."

"יְסוֹד הַיְסוֹדוֹת וְעַמּוּד הַחָכְמוֹת, לֵידַע שֶׁיֵּשׁ שָׁם מָצוּי רִאשׁוֹן וְהוּא מַמְצִיא כָּל הַנִּמְצָא, The foundation of foundations and pillar of all wisdom is to know that there is a First Being who is the Creator of all." Maimonides does not write "to believe," but rather "to know." Our conviction regarding the existence of God should be a continuous awareness of His reality, a constant level of consciousness. "To believe" does not carry this connotation because belief can wax and wane depending on circumstances. "To know," however, means that God should be a living reality that one cannot forget even momentarily. In every budding flower, in every rose opening its petals, in every ray of light and in every drop of rain, one must "know that there is a First Being."

Stand while saying עָלֵינוּ. *Bow at* ▾.

עָלֵינוּ לְשַׁבֵּחַ לַאֲדוֹן הַכֹּל, לָתֵת גְּדֻלָּה לְיוֹצֵר בְּרֵאשִׁית
שֶׁלֹּא עָשָׂנוּ כְּגוֹיֵי הָאֲרָצוֹת, וְלֹא שָׂמָנוּ כְּמִשְׁפְּחוֹת הָאֲדָמָה
שֶׁלֹּא שָׂם חֶלְקֵנוּ כָּהֶם וְגוֹרָלֵנוּ כְּכָל הֲמוֹנָם.
(שֶׁהֵם מִשְׁתַּחֲוִים לְהֶבֶל וָרִיק וּמִתְפַּלְלִים אֶל אֵל לֹא יוֹשִׁיעַ.)
▾וַאֲנַחְנוּ כּוֹרְעִים וּמִשְׁתַּחֲוִים וּמוֹדִים
לִפְנֵי מֶלֶךְ מַלְכֵי הַמְּלָכִים, הַקָּדוֹשׁ בָּרוּךְ הוּא
שֶׁהוּא נוֹטֶה שָׁמַיִם וְיוֹסֵד אָרֶץ
וּמוֹשַׁב יְקָרוֹ בַּשָּׁמַיִם מִמַּעַל
וּשְׁכִינַת עֻזּוֹ בְּגָבְהֵי מְרוֹמִים.
הוּא אֱלֹהֵינוּ, אֵין עוֹד.
אֱמֶת מַלְכֵּנוּ, אֶפֶס זוּלָתוֹ
כַּכָּתוּב בְּתוֹרָתוֹ
וְיָדַעְתָּ הַיּוֹם וַהֲשֵׁבֹתָ אֶל־לְבָבֶךָ דברים ד
כִּי יהוה הוּא הָאֱלֹהִים בַּשָּׁמַיִם מִמַּעַל וְעַל־הָאָרֶץ מִתָּחַת, אֵין עוֹד:

לְיוֹצֵר בְּרֵאשִׁית *To the Author of creation.* The word *bereshit,* creation, in this context means existence – "the Author of existence." The word יוֹצֵר is written in the present tense – similarly, "שֶׁהוּא נוֹטֶה שָׁמַיִם וְיוֹסֵד אָרֶץ, Who extends the heavens and establishes the earth." We do not refer to a past event of creation, but an ongoing act of creation in which God continually engages. The world does not function autonomously, governed by inner dynamics. He not only created, but continually sustains the world.

וְיָדַעְתָּ הַיּוֹם... כִּי יהוה הוּא הָאֱלֹהִים *You shall know… this day that the Lord is God.* Maimonides (*Hilkhot Yesodei HaTorah* 1:1) asserts the following:

Therefore, we place our hope in You, LORD our God,
that we may soon see the glory of Your power,
when You will remove abominations from the earth,
and idols will be utterly destroyed,
when the world will be perfected under the sovereignty of the Almighty,
when all humanity will call on Your name,
to turn all the earth's wicked toward You.
All the world's inhabitants will realize and know
that to You every knee must bow and every tongue swear loyalty.
Before You, LORD our God, they will kneel and bow down
and give honor to Your glorious name.
They will all accept the yoke of Your kingdom,
and You will reign over them soon and for ever.
For the kingdom is Yours, and to all eternity You will reign in glory,
as it is written in Your Torah: "The LORD will reign for ever and ever." *Ex. 15*
▸ And it is said: "Then the LORD shall be King over all the earth; *Zech. 14*
on that day the LORD shall be One and His name One."

Some add:

Have no fear of sudden terror or of the ruin when it overtakes the wicked. *Prov. 3*
Devise your strategy, but it will be thwarted; *Is. 8*
propose your plan, but it will not stand, for God is with us.
When you grow old, I will still be the same. *Is. 46*
When your hair turns gray, I will still carry you.
I made you, I will bear you, I will carry you, and I will rescue you.

---

bizarre conclusions. Jewish history is not pushed by impelling events in the past but is rather pulled by a divine promise regarding the future, leading toward a glorious destiny. Jewish history is thus not etiological but teleological; events take place via design and purpose rather than cause and effect. The Jewish historical experience is determined not by the point of departure but by the destination. As one example, there is a strong awareness among most Jews that Israel is the Promised Land. The promise is a destiny yet to be fulfilled. Our present-day support for Israel is fueled not by past events, but by anticipation of something beautiful and miraculous which beckons on the horizon, the ideal represented by the conclusion of this verse, "On that day the LORD shall be One and His name One." The eschatological vision of Judaism drives Jewish history.

עַל כֵּן נְקַוֶּה לְּךָ יהוה אֱלֹהֵינוּ, לִרְאוֹת מְהֵרָה בְּתִפְאֶרֶת עֻזֶּךָ
לְהַעֲבִיר גִּלּוּלִים מִן הָאָרֶץ, וְהָאֱלִילִים כָּרוֹת יִכָּרֵתוּן
לְתַקֵּן עוֹלָם בְּמַלְכוּת שַׁדַּי.
וְכָל בְּנֵי בָשָׂר יִקְרְאוּ בִשְׁמֶךָ לְהַפְנוֹת אֵלֶיךָ כָּל רִשְׁעֵי אָרֶץ.
יַכִּירוּ וְיֵדְעוּ כָּל יוֹשְׁבֵי תֵבֵל
כִּי לְךָ תִּכְרַע כָּל בֶּרֶךְ, תִּשָּׁבַע כָּל לָשׁוֹן.
לְפָנֶיךָ יהוה אֱלֹהֵינוּ יִכְרְעוּ וְיִפֹּלוּ, וְלִכְבוֹד שִׁמְךָ יְקָר יִתֵּנוּ
וִיקַבְּלוּ כֻלָּם אֶת עֹל מַלְכוּתֶךָ
וְתִמְלֹךְ עֲלֵיהֶם מְהֵרָה לְעוֹלָם וָעֶד.
כִּי הַמַּלְכוּת שֶׁלְּךָ הִיא וּלְעוֹלְמֵי עַד תִּמְלֹךְ בְּכָבוֹד
כַּכָּתוּב בְּתוֹרָתֶךָ, יהוה יִמְלֹךְ לְעֹלָם וָעֶד: שמות טו
◂ וְנֶאֱמַר, וְהָיָה יהוה לְמֶלֶךְ עַל־כָּל־הָאָרֶץ זכריה יד
בַּיּוֹם הַהוּא יִהְיֶה יהוה אֶחָד וּשְׁמוֹ אֶחָד:

Some add:

אַל־תִּירָא מִפַּחַד פִּתְאֹם וּמִשֹּׁאַת רְשָׁעִים כִּי תָבֹא: משלי ג
עֻצוּ עֵצָה וְתֻפָר, דַּבְּרוּ דָבָר וְלֹא יָקוּם, כִּי עִמָּנוּ אֵל: ישעיה ח
וְעַד־זִקְנָה אֲנִי הוּא, וְעַד־שֵׂיבָה אֲנִי אֶסְבֹּל אֲנִי עָשִׂיתִי וַאֲנִי אֶשָּׂא וַאֲנִי אֶסְבֹּל וַאֲמַלֵּט: ישעיה מו

עַל כֵּן נְקַוֶּה *Therefore, we place our hope.* According to the view expressed here, man will ultimately come to willingly accept God. There is no mention of coercion. We pray that God should sensitize man's conscience so he will finally recognize His absolute sovereignty. We request that God should facilitate man's enlightenment, and express the hope that all of mankind will experience His grandeur. Man will eventually understand and acknowledge God's existence and comply with His will; the idolatrous philosophies and false ideas will be abandoned. This is a vision of universal repentance – all of humanity shall cleanse and redeem itself.

וְהָיָה יהוה לְמֶלֶךְ עַל־כָּל־הָאָרֶץ *Then the Lord shall be King over all the earth.* Universal history is a chronology of cause and effect, a process known as etiology: one event occurs and, as a result, a second event follows. Jewish history, however, cannot be interpreted in an etiological manner without reaching

MOURNER'S KADDISH

The following prayer, said by mourners, requires the presence of a minyan.

Mourner: יִתְגַּדַּל Magnified and sanctified may His great name be,
in the world He created by His will.
May He establish His kingdom
in your lifetime and in your days,
and in the lifetime of all the house of Israel,
swiftly and soon – and say: Amen.

All: May His great name be blessed for ever and all time.

Mourner: Blessed and praised, glorified and exalted,
raised and honored, uplifted and lauded
be the name of the Holy One,
blessed be He, beyond any blessing,
song, praise and consolation
uttered in the world – and say: Amen.

May there be great peace from heaven,
and life for us and all Israel – and say: Amen.

Bow, take three steps back, as if taking leave of the Divine Presence, then bow, first left, then right, then center, while saying:

May He who makes peace in His high places,
make peace for us and all Israel – and say: Amen.

---

and solemnly that we are not giving up, that we are not surrendering, that we will carry on the work of our ancestors as though nothing has happened, that we will not be satisfied with less than the full realization of the ultimate goal – the establishment of God's kingdom, the resurrection of the dead, and eternal life for man. (*Out of the Whirlwind*)

קדיש יתום

The following prayer, said by mourners, requires the presence of a מנין.

אבל: יִתְגַּדַּל וְיִתְקַדַּשׁ שְׁמֵהּ רַבָּא (קהל: אָמֵן)
בְּעָלְמָא דִּי בְרָא כִרְעוּתֵהּ
וְיַמְלִיךְ מַלְכוּתֵהּ
בְּחַיֵּיכוֹן וּבְיוֹמֵיכוֹן וּבְחַיֵּי דְכָל בֵּית יִשְׂרָאֵל
בַּעֲגָלָא וּבִזְמַן קָרִיב, וְאִמְרוּ אָמֵן. (קהל: אָמֵן)

קהל ואבל: יְהֵא שְׁמֵהּ רַבָּא מְבָרַךְ לְעָלַם וּלְעָלְמֵי עָלְמַיָּא.

אבל: יִתְבָּרַךְ וְיִשְׁתַּבַּח וְיִתְפָּאַר
וְיִתְרוֹמַם וְיִתְנַשֵּׂא וְיִתְהַדָּר וְיִתְעַלֶּה וְיִתְהַלָּל
שְׁמֵהּ דְּקֻדְשָׁא בְּרִיךְ הוּא (קהל: בְּרִיךְ הוּא)
לְעֵלָּא מִן כָּל בִּרְכָתָא וְשִׁירָתָא, תֻּשְׁבְּחָתָא וְנֶחֱמָתָא
דַּאֲמִירָן בְּעָלְמָא, וְאִמְרוּ אָמֵן. (קהל: אָמֵן)

יְהֵא שְׁלָמָא רַבָּא מִן שְׁמַיָּא
וְחַיִּים, עָלֵינוּ וְעַל כָּל יִשְׂרָאֵל, וְאִמְרוּ אָמֵן. (קהל: אָמֵן)

Bow, take three steps back, as if taking leave of the Divine Presence, then bow, first left, then right, then center, while saying:

עֹשֶׂה שָׁלוֹם בִּמְרוֹמָיו
הוּא יַעֲשֶׂה שָׁלוֹם עָלֵינוּ וְעַל כָּל יִשְׂרָאֵל, וְאִמְרוּ אָמֵן. (קהל: אָמֵן)

יִתְגַּדַּל וְיִתְקַדַּשׁ שְׁמֵהּ רַבָּא *Magnified and sanctified may His great name be.* When the mourner recites these words, he declares: No matter how powerful death is, notwithstanding the ugly end of man, however terrifying the grave is, however nonsensical and absurd everything appears, no matter how black one's despair is and how nauseating an affair life is, we declare and profess publicly

Ma'ariv for Motza'ei Shabbat

In many congregations, the following two psalms are sung before Ma'ariv at the end of Shabbat.

לְדָוִד Of David. Blessed is the LORD, my Rock, who trains my hands for war, my fingers for battle. He is my Benefactor, my Fortress, my Stronghold and my Refuge, my Shield in whom I trust, He who subdues nations under me. LORD, what is man that You care for him, what are mortals that You think of them? Man is no more than a breath, his days like a fleeting shadow. LORD, part Your heavens and come down; touch the mountains so that they pour forth smoke. Flash forth lightning and scatter them; shoot Your arrows and panic them. Reach out Your hand from on high; deliver me and rescue me from the mighty waters, from the hands of strangers, whose every word is worthless, whose right hands are raised in falsehood. To You, God, I will sing a new song; to You I will play music on a ten-stringed harp. He who gives salvation to kings, who saved His servant David from the cruel sword: may He deliver me and rescue me from the hands of strangers, whose every word is worthless, whose right hands are raised in falsehood. Then our sons will be like saplings, well nurtured in their youth. Our daughters will be like pillars carved for a palace. Our barns will be filled with every kind of provision. Our sheep will increase by thousands, even tens of thousands in our fields. Our oxen will draw heavy loads. There will be no breach in the walls, no going into captivity, no cries of distress in our streets. Happy are the people for whom this is so; happy are the people whose God is the LORD. *Ps. 144*

לַמְנַצֵּחַ For the conductor of music. With stringed instruments. A psalm, a song. May God be gracious to us and bless us. May He make His face shine on us, Selah. Then will Your way be known on earth, Your salvation among all the nations. Let the peoples praise You, God; let all peoples praise You. Let nations rejoice and sing for joy, for You judge the peoples with equity, and guide the nations of the earth, Selah. Let the peoples praise You, God; let all peoples praise You. The earth has yielded its harvest. May God, our God, bless us. God will bless us, and all the ends of the earth will fear Him. *Ps. 67*

The service continues with Ma'ariv on page 2

מעריב למוצאי שבת

In many congregations, the following two psalms are sung before מעריב *on* מוצאי שבת*.*

תהלים קמד
לְדָוִד, בָּרוּךְ יהוה צוּרִי, הַמְלַמֵּד יָדַי לַקְרָב, אֶצְבְּעוֹתַי לַמִּלְחָמָה: חַסְדִּי וּמְצוּדָתִי מִשְׂגַּבִּי וּמְפַלְטִי לִי, מָגִנִּי וּבוֹ חָסִיתִי, הָרוֹדֵד עַמִּי תַחְתָּי: יהוה מָה־אָדָם וַתֵּדָעֵהוּ, בֶּן־אֱנוֹשׁ וַתְּחַשְּׁבֵהוּ: אָדָם לַהֶבֶל דָּמָה, יָמָיו כְּצֵל עוֹבֵר: יהוה הַט־שָׁמֶיךָ וְתֵרֵד, גַּע בֶּהָרִים וְיֶעֱשָׁנוּ: בְּרוֹק בָּרָק וּתְפִיצֵם, שְׁלַח חִצֶּיךָ וּתְהֻמֵּם: שְׁלַח יָדֶיךָ מִמָּרוֹם, פְּצֵנִי וְהַצִּילֵנִי מִמַּיִם רַבִּים, מִיַּד בְּנֵי נֵכָר: אֲשֶׁר פִּיהֶם דִּבֶּר־שָׁוְא, וִימִינָם יְמִין שָׁקֶר: אֱלֹהִים שִׁיר חָדָשׁ אָשִׁירָה לָּךְ, בְּנֵבֶל עָשׂוֹר אֲזַמְּרָה־לָּךְ: הַנּוֹתֵן תְּשׁוּעָה לַמְּלָכִים, הַפּוֹצֶה אֶת־דָּוִד עַבְדּוֹ מֵחֶרֶב רָעָה: פְּצֵנִי וְהַצִּילֵנִי מִיַּד בְּנֵי נֵכָר, אֲשֶׁר פִּיהֶם דִּבֶּר־שָׁוְא, וִימִינָם יְמִין שָׁקֶר: אֲשֶׁר בָּנֵינוּ כִּנְטִעִים, מְגֻדָּלִים בִּנְעוּרֵיהֶם, בְּנוֹתֵינוּ כְזָוִיֹּת, מְחֻטָּבוֹת תַּבְנִית הֵיכָל: מְזָוֵינוּ מְלֵאִים, מְפִיקִים מִזַּן אֶל־זַן, צֹאונֵנוּ מַאֲלִיפוֹת מְרֻבָּבוֹת בְּחוּצוֹתֵינוּ: אַלּוּפֵינוּ מְסֻבָּלִים, אֵין פֶּרֶץ וְאֵין יוֹצֵאת, וְאֵין צְוָחָה בִּרְחֹבֹתֵינוּ: אַשְׁרֵי הָעָם שֶׁכָּכָה לּוֹ, אַשְׁרֵי הָעָם שֶׁיהוה אֱלֹהָיו:

תהלים סז
לַמְנַצֵּחַ בִּנְגִינֹת, מִזְמוֹר שִׁיר: אֱלֹהִים יְחָנֵּנוּ וִיבָרְכֵנוּ, יָאֵר פָּנָיו אִתָּנוּ סֶלָה: לָדַעַת בָּאָרֶץ דַּרְכֶּךָ, בְּכָל־גּוֹיִם יְשׁוּעָתֶךָ: יוֹדְוּךָ עַמִּים אֱלֹהִים, יוֹדְוּךָ עַמִּים כֻּלָּם: יִשְׂמְחוּ וִירַנְּנוּ לְאֻמִּים, כִּי־תִשְׁפֹּט עַמִּים מִישֹׁר, וּלְאֻמִּים בָּאָרֶץ תַּנְחֵם סֶלָה: יוֹדְוּךָ עַמִּים אֱלֹהִים, יוֹדְוּךָ עַמִּים כֻּלָּם: אֶרֶץ נָתְנָה יְבוּלָהּ, יְבָרְכֵנוּ אֱלֹהִים אֱלֹהֵינוּ: יְבָרְכֵנוּ אֱלֹהִים, וְיִירְאוּ אוֹתוֹ כָּל־אַפְסֵי־אָרֶץ:

The service continues with מעריב *on page 3.*

After Shoshanat Yaakov, the congregation continues below:

וִיהִי נֹעַם May the pleasantness of the LORD our God be upon us. *Ps. 90*
Establish for us the work of our hands, O establish the work of our hands.

יֹשֵׁב He who lives in the shelter of the Most High dwells in the *Ps. 91*
shadow of the Almighty. I say of the LORD, my Refuge and Stronghold, my God in whom I trust, that He will save you from the fowler's snare and the deadly pestilence. With His pinions He will cover you, and beneath His wings you will find shelter; His faithfulness is an encircling shield. You need not fear terror by night, nor the arrow that flies by day; not the pestilence that stalks in darkness, nor the plague that ravages at noon. A thousand may fall at your side, ten thousand at your right hand, but it will not come near you. You will only look with your eyes and see the punishment of the wicked. Because you [have said:] "The LORD is my Refuge," taking the Most High as your shelter, no harm will befall you, no plague come near your tent, for He will command His angels about you, to guard you in all your ways. They will lift you in their hands, lest your foot stumble on a stone. You will tread on lions and vipers; you will trample on young lions and snakes. [God says:] "Because he loves Me, I will rescue him; I will protect him, because he acknowledges My name. When he calls on Me, I will answer him; I will be with him in distress, I will deliver him and bring him honor.
▸ With long life I will satisfy him and show him My salvation.
With long life I will satisfy him and show him My salvation.

---

shares in his covenantal existence. Finitude and infinity, temporality and eternity, creature and Creator become involved in the same community. They bind themselves together and participate in a unitive existence. This phrase can be understood only within the perspective of the covenantal community which involves God in the destiny of His fellow members. (*The Lonely Man of Faith*)

After שׁוֹשַׁנַּת יַעֲקֹב*, the congregation continues below:*

תהלים צ **וִיהִי נֹעַם אֲדֹנָי אֱלֹהֵינוּ עָלֵינוּ וּמַעֲשֵׂה יָדֵינוּ כּוֹנְנָה עָלֵינוּ וּמַעֲשֵׂה יָדֵינוּ כּוֹנְנֵהוּ:**

תהלים צא **יֹשֵׁב בְּסֵתֶר עֶלְיוֹן, בְּצֵל שַׁדַּי יִתְלוֹנָן: אֹמַר לַיהוה מַחְסִי וּמְצוּדָתִי, אֱלֹהַי אֶבְטַח־בּוֹ: כִּי הוּא יַצִּילְךָ מִפַּח יָקוּשׁ, מִדֶּבֶר הַוּוֹת: בְּאֶבְרָתוֹ יָסֶךְ לָךְ, וְתַחַת־כְּנָפָיו תֶּחְסֶה, צִנָּה וְסֹחֵרָה אֲמִתּוֹ: לֹא־תִירָא מִפַּחַד לָיְלָה, מֵחֵץ יָעוּף יוֹמָם: מִדֶּבֶר בָּאֹפֶל יַהֲלֹךְ, מִקֶּטֶב יָשׁוּד צָהֳרָיִם: יִפֹּל מִצִּדְּךָ אֶלֶף, וּרְבָבָה מִימִינֶךָ, אֵלֶיךָ לֹא יִגָּשׁ: רַק בְּעֵינֶיךָ תַבִּיט, וְשִׁלֻּמַת רְשָׁעִים תִּרְאֶה: כִּי־אַתָּה יהוה מַחְסִי, עֶלְיוֹן שַׂמְתָּ מְעוֹנֶךָ: לֹא־תְאֻנֶּה אֵלֶיךָ רָעָה, וְנֶגַע לֹא־יִקְרַב בְּאָהֳלֶךָ: כִּי מַלְאָכָיו יְצַוֶּה־לָּךְ, לִשְׁמָרְךָ בְּכָל־דְּרָכֶיךָ: עַל־כַּפַּיִם יִשָּׂאוּנְךָ, פֶּן־תִּגֹּף בָּאֶבֶן רַגְלֶךָ: עַל־שַׁחַל וָפֶתֶן תִּדְרֹךְ, תִּרְמֹס כְּפִיר וְתַנִּין: כִּי בִי חָשַׁק וַאֲפַלְּטֵהוּ, אֲשַׂגְּבֵהוּ כִּי־יָדַע שְׁמִי: יִקְרָאֵנִי וְאֶעֱנֵהוּ, עִמּוֹ אָנֹכִי בְצָרָה, אֲחַלְּצֵהוּ וַאֲכַבְּדֵהוּ:**

◂ אֹרֶךְ יָמִים אַשְׂבִּיעֵהוּ, וְאַרְאֵהוּ בִּישׁוּעָתִי:

אֹרֶךְ יָמִים אַשְׂבִּיעֵהוּ, וְאַרְאֵהוּ בִּישׁוּעָתִי:

עִמּוֹ אָנֹכִי בְצָרָה *I will be with him in distress.* The agony and nightmare of the creation, its loneliness and desolation, are transferred to the bosom of the Infinite and are transformed, as it were, into the mysterious pains of the *Shekhina,* as if God were sharing the separation of the creation and suffering the pain of its exile: "I am with them in their distress." The *Shekhina* itself, as it were, is in need of redemption, and man prays for the redemption of the *Shekhina,* with which he too will be redeemed. (*And From There You Shall Seek*)

God is never outside of the covenantal community. He joins man and

For commentary on Ve'Ata Kadosh, see pages 128–131.

▸ You are the Holy One, enthroned on the praises of Israel. *Ps. 22*
And [the angels] call to one another, saying, "Holy, holy, holy *Is. 6*
is the LORD of hosts; the whole world is filled with His glory."

And they receive permission from one another, saying: *Targum Yonatan Is. 6*
"Holy in the highest heavens, home of His Presence; holy on earth,
the work of His strength; holy for ever and all time is the LORD of hosts;
the whole earth is full of His radiant glory."

▸ Then a wind lifted me up and I heard behind me the sound of a *Ezek. 3*
great noise, saying, "Blessed is the LORD's glory from His place."

Then a wind lifted me up and I heard behind me *Targum Yonatan Ezek. 3*
the sound of a great tempest of those who uttered praise, saying,
"Blessed is the LORD's glory from the place of the home of His Presence."

The LORD shall reign for ever and all time. *Ex. 15*

The LORD's kingdom is established for ever and all time. *Targum Onkelos Ex. 15*

יהוה LORD, God of Abraham, Isaac and Yisrael, our ancestors, may *1 Chr. 29*
You keep this for ever so that it forms the thoughts in Your people's
heart, and directs their heart toward You. He is compassionate. He *Ps. 78*
forgives iniquity and does not destroy. Repeatedly He suppresses
His anger, not rousing His full wrath. For You, my LORD, are good *Ps. 86*
and forgiving, abundantly kind to all who call on You. Your righ- *Ps. 119*
teousness is eternally righteous, and Your Torah is truth. Grant *Micah 7*
truth to Jacob, loving-kindness to Abraham, as You promised our
ancestors in ancient times. Blessed is my LORD for day after day He *Ps. 68*
burdens us [with His blessings]; God is our salvation, Selah! The *Ps. 46*
LORD of hosts is with us; the God of Jacob is our refuge, Selah!
LORD of hosts, happy is the one who trusts in You. LORD, save! *Ps. 84* *Ps. 20*
May the King answer us on the day we call.

בָּרוּךְ Blessed is He, our God, who created us for His glory, separating us from those who go astray; who gave us the Torah of truth, planting within us eternal life. May He open our heart to His Torah, imbuing our heart with the love and awe of Him, that we may do His will and serve Him with a perfect heart, so that we neither toil in vain nor give birth to confusion.

For commentary on וְאַתָּה קָדוֹשׁ*, see pages 128–131.*

▸ וְאַתָּה קָדוֹשׁ יוֹשֵׁב תְּהִלּוֹת יִשְׂרָאֵל: וְקָרָא זֶה אֶל־זֶה וְאָמַר תהלים כב
קָדוֹשׁ, קָדוֹשׁ, קָדוֹשׁ, יהוה צְבָאוֹת, מְלֹא כָל־הָאָרֶץ כְּבוֹדוֹ: ישעיה ו
וּמְקַבְּלִין דֵּין מִן דֵּין וְאָמְרִין, קַדִּישׁ בִּשְׁמֵי מְרוֹמָא עִלָּאָה בֵּית שְׁכִינְתֵהּ תרגום יונתן ישעיה ו
קַדִּישׁ עַל אַרְעָא עוֹבַד גְּבוּרְתֵהּ, קַדִּישׁ לְעָלַם וּלְעָלְמֵי עָלְמַיָּא
יהוה צְבָאוֹת, מַלְיָא כָל אַרְעָא זִיו יְקָרֵהּ.

▸ וַתִּשָּׂאֵנִי רוּחַ, וָאֶשְׁמַע אַחֲרַי קוֹל רַעַשׁ גָּדוֹל יחזקאל ג
בָּרוּךְ כְּבוֹד־יהוה מִמְּקוֹמוֹ:
וּנְטָלַתְנִי רוּחָא, וּשְׁמָעִית בַּתְרַי קָל זִיעַ סַגִּיא, דִּמְשַׁבְּחִין וְאָמְרִין תרגום יונתן יחזקאל ג
בְּרִיךְ יְקָרָא דַיהוה מֵאֲתַר בֵּית שְׁכִינְתֵהּ.

יהוה יִמְלֹךְ לְעֹלָם וָעֶד: שמות טו
יהוה מַלְכוּתֵהּ קָאֵם לְעָלַם וּלְעָלְמֵי עָלְמַיָּא. תרגום אונקלוס שמות טו

יהוה אֱלֹהֵי אַבְרָהָם יִצְחָק וְיִשְׂרָאֵל אֲבֹתֵינוּ, שָׁמְרָה־זֹּאת לְעוֹלָם דברי הימים א׳ כט
לְיֵצֶר מַחְשְׁבוֹת לְבַב עַמֶּךָ, וְהָכֵן לְבָבָם אֵלֶיךָ: וְהוּא רַחוּם יְכַפֵּר תהלים עח
עָוֹן וְלֹא־יַשְׁחִית, וְהִרְבָּה לְהָשִׁיב אַפּוֹ, וְלֹא־יָעִיר כָּל־חֲמָתוֹ:
כִּי־אַתָּה אֲדֹנָי טוֹב וְסַלָּח, וְרַב־חֶסֶד לְכָל־קֹרְאֶיךָ: צִדְקָתְךָ תהלים פו תהלים קיט
צֶדֶק לְעוֹלָם וְתוֹרָתְךָ אֱמֶת: תִּתֵּן אֱמֶת לְיַעֲקֹב, חֶסֶד לְאַבְרָהָם, מיכה ז
אֲשֶׁר־נִשְׁבַּעְתָּ לַאֲבֹתֵינוּ מִימֵי קֶדֶם: בָּרוּךְ אֲדֹנָי יוֹם יוֹם יַעֲמָס־ תהלים סח
לָנוּ, הָאֵל יְשׁוּעָתֵנוּ סֶלָה: יהוה צְבָאוֹת עִמָּנוּ, מִשְׂגָּב לָנוּ אֱלֹהֵי תהלים מו
יַעֲקֹב סֶלָה: יהוה צְבָאוֹת, אַשְׁרֵי אָדָם בֹּטֵחַ בָּךְ: יהוה הוֹשִׁיעָה, תהלים פד תהלים כ
הַמֶּלֶךְ יַעֲנֵנוּ בְיוֹם־קָרְאֵנוּ:

בָּרוּךְ הוּא אֱלֹהֵינוּ שֶׁבְּרָאָנוּ לִכְבוֹדוֹ, וְהִבְדִּילָנוּ מִן הַתּוֹעִים,
וְנָתַן לָנוּ תּוֹרַת אֱמֶת, וְחַיֵּי עוֹלָם נָטַע בְּתוֹכֵנוּ. הוּא יִפְתַּח לִבֵּנוּ
בְּתוֹרָתוֹ, וְיָשֵׂם בְּלִבֵּנוּ אַהֲבָתוֹ וְיִרְאָתוֹ וְלַעֲשׂוֹת רְצוֹנוֹ וּלְעָבְדוֹ
בְּלֵבָב שָׁלֵם, לְמַעַן לֹא נִיגַע לָרִיק וְלֹא נֵלֵד לַבֶּהָלָה.

יְהִי רָצוֹן May it be Your will, O Lord our God and God of our ancestors, that we keep Your laws in this world, and thus be worthy to live, see and inherit goodness and blessing in the Messianic Age and in
the life of the World to Come. So that my soul may sing to You and *Ps. 30*
not be silent. Lord, my God, for ever I will thank You. Blessed is *Jer. 17*
the man who trusts in the Lord, whose trust is in the Lord alone.
Trust in the Lord for evermore, for God, the Lord, is an everlast- *Is. 26*
ing Rock. ▸ Those who know Your name trust in You, for You, Lord, *Ps. 9*
do not forsake those who seek You. The Lord desired, for the sake *Is. 42*
of Israel's merit, to make the Torah great and glorious.

FULL KADDISH

Leader: יִתְגַּדַּל Magnified and sanctified may His great name be,
in the world He created by His will.
May He establish His kingdom in your lifetime
and in your days,
and in the lifetime of all the house of Israel,
swiftly and soon –
and say: Amen.

All: May His great name be blessed for ever and all time.

Leader: Blessed and praised, glorified and exalted,
raised and honored, uplifted and lauded be
the name of the Holy One, blessed be He,
beyond any blessing,
song, praise and consolation uttered in the world –
and say: Amen.

The line beginning with "Titkabel" is omitted.

May there be great peace from heaven,
and life for us and all Israel –
and say: Amen.

Bow, take three steps back, as if taking leave of the Divine Presence, then bow, first left, then right, then center, while saying:

May He who makes peace in His high places,
make peace for us and all Israel –
and say: Amen.

יְהִי רָצוֹן מִלְּפָנֶיךָ יהוה אֱלֹהֵינוּ וֵאלֹהֵי אֲבוֹתֵינוּ, שֶׁנִּשְׁמֹר חֻקֶּיךָ
בָּעוֹלָם הַזֶּה, וְנִזְכֶּה וְנִחְיֶה וְנִרְאֶה וְנִירַשׁ טוֹבָה וּבְרָכָה, לִשְׁנֵי
יְמוֹת הַמָּשִׁיחַ וּלְחַיֵּי הָעוֹלָם הַבָּא. לְמַעַן יְזַמֶּרְךָ כָבוֹד וְלֹא יִדֹּם, תהלים ל
יהוה אֱלֹהַי, לְעוֹלָם אוֹדֶךָּ: בָּרוּךְ הַגֶּבֶר אֲשֶׁר יִבְטַח בַּיהוה, ירמיה יז
וְהָיָה יהוה מִבְטַחוֹ: בִּטְחוּ בַיהוה עֲדֵי־עַד, כִּי בְּיָהּ יהוה צוּר ישעיה כו
עוֹלָמִים: › וְיִבְטְחוּ בְךָ יוֹדְעֵי שְׁמֶךָ, כִּי לֹא־עָזַבְתָּ דֹרְשֶׁיךָ, יהוה: תהלים ט
יהוה חָפֵץ לְמַעַן צִדְקוֹ, יַגְדִּיל תּוֹרָה וְיַאְדִּיר: ישעיה מב

קדיש שלם

ש״ץ: יִתְגַּדַּל וְיִתְקַדַּשׁ שְׁמֵהּ רַבָּא (קהל: אָמֵן)
בְּעָלְמָא דִּי בְרָא כִרְעוּתֵהּ
וְיַמְלִיךְ מַלְכוּתֵהּ
בְּחַיֵּיכוֹן וּבְיוֹמֵיכוֹן וּבְחַיֵּי דְכָל בֵּית יִשְׂרָאֵל
בַּעֲגָלָא וּבִזְמַן קָרִיב, וְאִמְרוּ אָמֵן. (קהל: אָמֵן)

קהל וש״ץ: יְהֵא שְׁמֵהּ רַבָּא מְבָרַךְ לְעָלַם וּלְעָלְמֵי עָלְמַיָּא.

ש״ץ: יִתְבָּרַךְ וְיִשְׁתַּבַּח וְיִתְפָּאַר
וְיִתְרוֹמַם וְיִתְנַשֵּׂא וְיִתְהַדָּר וְיִתְעַלֶּה וְיִתְהַלָּל
שְׁמֵהּ דְּקֻדְשָׁא בְּרִיךְ הוּא (קהל: בְּרִיךְ הוּא)
לְעֵלָּא מִן כָּל בִּרְכָתָא וְשִׁירָתָא, תֻּשְׁבְּחָתָא וְנֶחֱמָתָא
דַּאֲמִירָן בְּעָלְמָא, וְאִמְרוּ אָמֵן. (קהל: אָמֵן)

The line beginning with תִּתְקַבַּל *is omitted.*

יְהֵא שְׁלָמָא רַבָּא מִן שְׁמַיָּא
וְחַיִּים, עָלֵינוּ וְעַל כָּל יִשְׂרָאֵל, וְאִמְרוּ אָמֵן. (קהל: אָמֵן)

Bow, take three steps back, as if taking leave of the Divine Presence, then bow, first left, then right, then center, while saying:

עֹשֶׂה שָׁלוֹם בִּמְרוֹמָיו
הוּא יַעֲשֶׂה שָׁלוֹם עָלֵינוּ וְעַל כָּל יִשְׂרָאֵל
וְאִמְרוּ אָמֵן. (קהל: אָמֵן)

BIBLICAL VERSES OF BLESSING

וְיִתֶּן־לְךָ May God give you dew from heaven and the richness of the earth, and *Gen. 27*
corn and wine in plenty. May peoples serve you and nations bow down to you.
Be lord over your brothers, and may your mother's sons bow down to you.
A curse on those who curse you, but a blessing on those who bless you.

וְאֵל שַׁדַּי May God Almighty bless you; may He make you fruitful and numerous *Gen. 28*
until you become an assembly of peoples. May He give you and your descen-
dants the blessing of Abraham, that you may possess the land where you are
now staying, the land God gave to Abraham. This comes from the God of your *Gen. 49*
father – may He help you – and from the Almighty – may He bless you with
blessings of the heaven above and the blessings of the deep that lies below, the
blessings of breast and womb. The blessings of your father surpass the blessings
of my fathers to the bounds of the endless hills. May they rest on the head of
Joseph, on the brow of the prince among his brothers. He will love you and *Deut. 7*
bless you and increase your numbers. He will bless the fruit of your womb and
the fruit of your land: your corn, your wine and oil, the calves of your herds
and the lambs of your flocks, in the land He swore to your fathers to give you.
You will be blessed more than any other people. None of your men or women
will be childless, nor any of your livestock without young. The LORD will keep
you free from any disease. He will not inflict on you the terrible diseases you
knew in Egypt, but He will inflict them on those who hate you.

הַמַּלְאָךְ May the angel who rescued me from all harm, bless these boys. May *Gen. 48*
they be called by my name and the names of my fathers Abraham and Isaac,
and may they increase greatly on the earth. The LORD your God has increased *Deut. 1*
your numbers so that today you are as many as the stars in the sky. May the
LORD, God of your fathers, increase you a thousand times, and bless you as
He promised you.

בָּרוּךְ You will be blessed in the city, and blessed in the field. You will be blessed *Deut. 28*
when you come in, and blessed when you go out. Your basket and your knead-
ing trough will be blessed. The fruit of your womb will be blessed, and the
crops of your land, and the young of your livestock, the calves of your herds
and the lambs of your flocks. The LORD will send a blessing on your barns,
and on everything you put your hand to. The LORD your God will bless you
in the land He is giving you. The LORD will open for you the heavens, the
storehouse of His bounty, to send rain on your land in season, and to bless all
the work of your hands. You will lend to many nations but will borrow from
none. For the LORD your God will bless you as He has promised: you will lend *Deut. 15*
to many nations but will borrow from none. You will rule over many nations,
but none will rule over you. Happy are you, Israel! Who is like you, a people *Deut. 33*

פסוקי ברכה

וְיִתֶּן־לְךָ הָאֱלֹהִים מִטַּל הַשָּׁמַיִם וּמִשְׁמַנֵּי הָאָרֶץ, וְרֹב דָּגָן וְתִירֹשׁ: יַעַבְדוּךָ בראשית כז
עַמִּים וְיִשְׁתַּחֲוֻ לְךָ לְאֻמִּים, הֱוֵה גְבִיר לְאַחֶיךָ וְיִשְׁתַּחֲווּ לְךָ בְּנֵי אִמֶּךָ,
אֹרְרֶיךָ אָרוּר וּמְבָרְכֶיךָ בָּרוּךְ:

וְאֵל שַׁדַּי יְבָרֵךְ אֹתְךָ וְיַפְרְךָ וְיַרְבֶּךָ, וְהָיִיתָ לִקְהַל עַמִּים: וְיִתֶּן־לְךָ אֶת־ בראשית כח
בִּרְכַּת אַבְרָהָם, לְךָ וּלְזַרְעֲךָ אִתָּךְ, לְרִשְׁתְּךָ אֶת־אֶרֶץ מְגֻרֶיךָ אֲשֶׁר־נָתַן
אֱלֹהִים לְאַבְרָהָם: מֵאֵל אָבִיךָ וְיַעְזְרֶךָּ וְאֵת שַׁדַּי וִיבָרְכֶךָּ, בִּרְכֹת שָׁמַיִם בראשית מט
מֵעָל, בִּרְכֹת תְּהוֹם רֹבֶצֶת תָּחַת, בִּרְכֹת שָׁדַיִם וָרָחַם: בִּרְכֹת אָבִיךָ גָּבְרוּ
עַל־בִּרְכֹת הוֹרַי עַד־תַּאֲוַת גִּבְעֹת עוֹלָם, תִּהְיֶיןָ לְרֹאשׁ יוֹסֵף וּלְקָדְקֹד
נְזִיר אֶחָיו: וַאֲהֵבְךָ וּבֵרַכְךָ וְהִרְבֶּךָ, וּבֵרַךְ פְּרִי־בִטְנְךָ וּפְרִי־אַדְמָתֶךָ, דְּגָנְךָ דברים ז
וְתִירֹשְׁךָ וְיִצְהָרֶךָ, שְׁגַר־אֲלָפֶיךָ וְעַשְׁתְּרֹת צֹאנֶךָ, עַל הָאֲדָמָה אֲשֶׁר־נִשְׁבַּע
לַאֲבֹתֶיךָ לָתֶת לָךְ: בָּרוּךְ תִּהְיֶה מִכָּל־הָעַמִּים, לֹא־יִהְיֶה בְךָ עָקָר וַעֲקָרָה
וּבִבְהֶמְתֶּךָ: וְהֵסִיר יהוה מִמְּךָ כָּל־חֹלִי, וְכָל־מַדְוֵי מִצְרַיִם הָרָעִים אֲשֶׁר
יָדַעְתָּ, לֹא יְשִׂימָם בָּךְ, וּנְתָנָם בְּכָל־שֹׂנְאֶיךָ:

הַמַּלְאָךְ הַגֹּאֵל אֹתִי מִכָּל־רָע יְבָרֵךְ אֶת־הַנְּעָרִים, וְיִקָּרֵא בָהֶם שְׁמִי וְשֵׁם בראשית מח
אֲבֹתַי אַבְרָהָם וְיִצְחָק, וְיִדְגּוּ לָרֹב בְּקֶרֶב הָאָרֶץ: יהוה אֱלֹהֵיכֶם הִרְבָּה דברים א
אֶתְכֶם, וְהִנְּכֶם הַיּוֹם כְּכוֹכְבֵי הַשָּׁמַיִם לָרֹב: יהוה אֱלֹהֵי אֲבוֹתֵכֶם יֹסֵף
עֲלֵיכֶם כָּכֶם אֶלֶף פְּעָמִים, וִיבָרֵךְ אֶתְכֶם כַּאֲשֶׁר דִּבֶּר לָכֶם:

בָּרוּךְ אַתָּה בָּעִיר, וּבָרוּךְ אַתָּה בַּשָּׂדֶה: בָּרוּךְ אַתָּה בְּבֹאֶךָ, וּבָרוּךְ אַתָּה דברים כח
בְּצֵאתֶךָ: בָּרוּךְ טַנְאֲךָ וּמִשְׁאַרְתֶּךָ: בָּרוּךְ פְּרִי־בִטְנְךָ וּפְרִי אַדְמָתְךָ וּפְרִי
בְהֶמְתֶּךָ, שְׁגַר אֲלָפֶיךָ וְעַשְׁתְּרוֹת צֹאנֶךָ: יְצַו יהוה אִתְּךָ אֶת־הַבְּרָכָה
בַּאֲסָמֶיךָ וּבְכֹל מִשְׁלַח יָדֶךָ, וּבֵרַכְךָ בָּאָרֶץ אֲשֶׁר־יהוה אֱלֹהֶיךָ נֹתֵן לָךְ:
יִפְתַּח יהוה לְךָ אֶת־אוֹצָרוֹ הַטּוֹב אֶת־הַשָּׁמַיִם, לָתֵת מְטַר־אַרְצְךָ בְּעִתּוֹ,
וּלְבָרֵךְ אֵת כָּל־מַעֲשֵׂה יָדֶךָ, וְהִלְוִיתָ גּוֹיִם רַבִּים וְאַתָּה לֹא תִלְוֶה: כִּי־יהוה דברים טו
אֱלֹהֶיךָ בֵּרַכְךָ כַּאֲשֶׁר דִּבֶּר־לָךְ, וְהַעֲבַטְתָּ גּוֹיִם רַבִּים וְאַתָּה לֹא תַעֲבֹט,
וּמָשַׁלְתָּ בְּגוֹיִם רַבִּים וּבְךָ לֹא יִמְשֹׁלוּ: אַשְׁרֶיךָ יִשְׂרָאֵל, מִי כָמוֹךָ, עַם דברים לג

saved by the LORD? He is your Shield and Helper and your glorious Sword. Your enemies will cower before you, and you will tread on their high places.

מָחִיתִי I have wiped away your transgressions like a cloud, your sins like the *Is. 44*
morning mist. Return to Me for I have redeemed you. Sing for joy, O heavens, for the LORD has done this; shout aloud, you depths of the earth; burst into song, you mountains, you forests and all your trees, for the LORD has
redeemed Jacob, and will glory in Israel. Our Redeemer, the LORD of hosts is *Is. 47*
His name, the Holy One of Israel.

יִשְׂרָאֵל Israel is saved by the LORD with everlasting salvation. You will never *Is. 45*
be ashamed or disgraced to time everlasting. You will eat your fill and praise *Joel 2*
the name of the LORD your God, who has worked wonders for you. Never again shall My people be shamed. Then you will know that I am in the midst of Israel, that I am the LORD your God, and there is no other. Never again
will My people be shamed. You will go out in joy and be led out in peace. The *Is. 55*
mountains and hills will burst into song before you, and all the trees of the
field will clap their hands. Behold, God is my salvation, I will trust and not *Is. 12*
be afraid. The LORD, the LORD, is my strength and my song. He has become my salvation. With joy you will draw water from the springs of salvation. On that day you will say, "Thank the LORD, proclaim His name, make His deeds known among the nations." Declare that His name is exalted. Sing to the LORD, for He has done glorious things; let this be known throughout the world. Shout aloud and sing for joy, you who dwell in Zion, for great in your midst
is the Holy One of Israel. On that day they will say, "See, this is our God; we *Is. 25*
set our hope in Him and He saved us. This is the LORD in whom we hoped; let us rejoice and be glad in His salvation."

בֵּית Come, house of Jacob: let us walk in the light of the LORD. He will be the *Is. 2* *Is. 32*
sure foundation of your times; a rich store of salvation, wisdom and knowl-
edge – the fear of the LORD is a person's treasure. In everything he did, David *1 Sam. 18*
was successful, for the LORD was with him.

פָּדָה He redeemed my soul in peace from the battle waged against me, for the *Ps. 55*
sake of the many who were with me. The people said to Saul, "Shall Jonathan *1 Sam. 14*
die – he who has brought about this great deliverance in Israel? Heaven forbid! As surely as the LORD lives, not a hair of his head shall fall to the ground, for he did this today with God's help." So the people rescued Jonathan and he did not
die. Those redeemed by the LORD shall return; they will enter Zion singing; *Is. 35*
everlasting joy will crown their heads. Gladness and joy will overtake them, and sorrow and sighing will flee away.

נוֹשַׁע בַּיהוה, מָגֵן עֶזְרֶךָ וַאֲשֶׁר־חֶרֶב גַּאֲוָתֶךָ, וְיִכָּחֲשׁוּ אֹיְבֶיךָ לָךְ, וְאַתָּה
עַל־בָּמוֹתֵימוֹ תִדְרֹךְ:

מָחִיתִי כָעָב פְּשָׁעֶיךָ וְכֶעָנָן חַטֹּאותֶיךָ, שׁוּבָה אֵלַי כִּי גְאַלְתִּיךָ: רָנּוּ שָׁמַיִם ישעיה מד
כִּי־עָשָׂה יהוה, הָרִיעוּ תַּחְתִּיּוֹת אָרֶץ, פִּצְחוּ הָרִים רִנָּה, יַעַר וְכָל־עֵץ בּוֹ,
כִּי־גָאַל יהוה יַעֲקֹב וּבְיִשְׂרָאֵל יִתְפָּאָר: גֹּאֲלֵנוּ, יהוה צְבָאוֹת שְׁמוֹ, קְדוֹשׁ ישעיה מז
יִשְׂרָאֵל:

יִשְׂרָאֵל נוֹשַׁע בַּיהוה תְּשׁוּעַת עוֹלָמִים, לֹא־תֵבֹשׁוּ וְלֹא־תִכָּלְמוּ עַד־עוֹלְמֵי ישעיה מה
עַד: וַאֲכַלְתֶּם אָכוֹל וְשָׂבוֹעַ, וְהִלַּלְתֶּם אֶת־שֵׁם יהוה אֱלֹהֵיכֶם אֲשֶׁר־עָשָׂה יואל ב
עִמָּכֶם לְהַפְלִיא, וְלֹא־יֵבֹשׁוּ עַמִּי לְעוֹלָם: וִידַעְתֶּם כִּי בְקֶרֶב יִשְׂרָאֵל
אָנִי, וַאֲנִי יהוה אֱלֹהֵיכֶם וְאֵין עוֹד, וְלֹא־יֵבֹשׁוּ עַמִּי לְעוֹלָם: כִּי־בְשִׂמְחָה ישעיה נה
תֵצֵאוּ וּבְשָׁלוֹם תּוּבָלוּן, הֶהָרִים וְהַגְּבָעוֹת יִפְצְחוּ לִפְנֵיכֶם רִנָּה, וְכָל־עֲצֵי
הַשָּׂדֶה יִמְחֲאוּ־כָף: הִנֵּה אֵל יְשׁוּעָתִי אֶבְטַח, וְלֹא אֶפְחָד, כִּי־עָזִּי וְזִמְרָת ישעיה יב
יָהּ יהוה, וַיְהִי־לִי לִישׁוּעָה: וּשְׁאַבְתֶּם־מַיִם בְּשָׂשׂוֹן, מִמַּעַיְנֵי הַיְשׁוּעָה:
וַאֲמַרְתֶּם בַּיּוֹם הַהוּא, הוֹדוּ לַיהוה קִרְאוּ בִשְׁמוֹ, הוֹדִיעוּ בָעַמִּים עֲלִילֹתָיו,
הַזְכִּירוּ כִּי נִשְׂגָּב שְׁמוֹ: זַמְּרוּ יהוה כִּי גֵאוּת עָשָׂה, מוּדַעַת זֹאת בְּכָל־
הָאָרֶץ: צַהֲלִי וָרֹנִּי יוֹשֶׁבֶת צִיּוֹן, כִּי־גָדוֹל בְּקִרְבֵּךְ קְדוֹשׁ יִשְׂרָאֵל: וְאָמַר ישעיה כה
בַּיּוֹם הַהוּא, הִנֵּה אֱלֹהֵינוּ זֶה קִוִּינוּ לוֹ וְיוֹשִׁיעֵנוּ, זֶה יהוה קִוִּינוּ לוֹ, נָגִילָה
וְנִשְׂמְחָה בִּישׁוּעָתוֹ:

בֵּית יַעֲקֹב לְכוּ וְנֵלְכָה בְּאוֹר יהוה: וְהָיָה אֱמוּנַת עִתֶּיךָ, חֹסֶן יְשׁוּעֹת חָכְמַת ישעיה ב ישעיה לב
וָדָעַת, יִרְאַת יהוה הִיא אוֹצָרוֹ: וַיְהִי דָוִד לְכָל־דְּרָכָו מַשְׂכִּיל, וַיהוה עִמּוֹ: שמואל א׳ יח

פָּדָה בְשָׁלוֹם נַפְשִׁי מִקְּרָב־לִי, כִּי־בְרַבִּים הָיוּ עִמָּדִי: וַיֹּאמֶר הָעָם אֶל־ תהלים נה שמואל א׳ יד
שָׁאוּל, הֲיוֹנָתָן יָמוּת אֲשֶׁר עָשָׂה הַיְשׁוּעָה הַגְּדוֹלָה הַזֹּאת בְּיִשְׂרָאֵל,
חָלִילָה, חַי־יהוה אִם־יִפֹּל מִשַּׂעֲרַת רֹאשׁוֹ אַרְצָה, כִּי־עִם־אֱלֹהִים עָשָׂה
הַיּוֹם הַזֶּה, וַיִּפְדּוּ הָעָם אֶת־יוֹנָתָן וְלֹא־מֵת: וּפְדוּיֵי יהוה יְשֻׁבוּן וּבָאוּ צִיּוֹן ישעיה לה
בְּרִנָּה, וְשִׂמְחַת עוֹלָם עַל־רֹאשָׁם, שָׂשׂוֹן וְשִׂמְחָה יַשִּׂיגוּ, וְנָסוּ יָגוֹן וַאֲנָחָה:

הָפַכְתָּ You have turned my sorrow into dancing. You have removed my sackcloth *Ps. 30*
and clothed me with joy. The LORD your God refused to listen to Balaam; in- *Deut. 23*
stead the LORD your God turned the curse into a blessing, for the LORD your
God loves you. Then maidens will dance and be glad; so too will young men and *Jer. 31*
old together; I will turn their mourning into gladness; I will give them comfort
and joy instead of sorrow.

בּוֹרֵא I create the speech of lips: Peace, peace to those far and near, says the LORD, *Is. 57*
and I will heal them. Then the spirit came upon Amasai, chief of the captains, *1 Chr. 12*
and he said: "We are yours, David! We are with you, son of Jesse! Peace, peace to
you, and peace to those who help you; for your God will help you." Then David
received them and made them leaders of his troop. And you shall say: "To life! *1 Sam. 25*
Peace be to you, peace to your household, and peace to all that is yours!" The *Ps. 29*
LORD will give strength to His people; the LORD will bless His people with peace.

אָמַר Rabbi Yoḥanan said: Wherever you find the greatness of the Holy One, *Megilla 31a*
blessed be He, there you find His humility. This is written in the Torah, repeated
in the Prophets, and stated a third time in the Writings. It is written in the
Torah: "For the LORD your God is God of gods and LORD of lords, the great, *Deut. 10*
mighty and awe-inspiring God, who shows no favoritism and accepts no bribe."
Immediately afterwards it is written, "He upholds the cause of the orphan and
widow, and loves the stranger, giving him food and clothing." It is repeated in the
Prophets, as it says: "So says the High and Exalted One, who lives for ever and *Is. 57*
whose name is Holy: I live in a high and holy place, but also with the contrite
and lowly in spirit, to revive the spirit of the lowly, and to revive the heart of the
contrite." It is stated a third time in the Writings: "Sing to God, make music for *Ps. 68*
His name, extol Him who rides the clouds – the LORD is His name – and exult
before Him." Immediately afterwards it is written: "Father of the orphans and
Justice of widows, is God in His holy habitation."

יְהִי May the LORD our God be with us, as He was with our ancestors. May He *1 Kings 8*
never abandon us or forsake us. You who cleave to the LORD your God are all *Deut. 4*
alive this day. For the LORD will comfort Zion, He will comfort all her ruins; *Is. 51*
He will make her wilderness like Eden, and her desert like a garden of the LORD.
Joy and gladness will be found there, thanksgiving and the sound of singing. It *Is. 42*
pleased the LORD for the sake of [Israel's] righteousness to make the Torah
great and glorious.

שִׁיר הַמַּעֲלוֹת A song of ascents. Happy are all who fear the LORD, who walk in His *Ps. 128*
ways. When you eat the fruit of your labor, happy and fortunate are you. Your
wife shall be like a fruitful vine within your house; your sons like olive saplings
around your table. So shall the man who fears the LORD be blessed. May the
LORD bless you from Zion; may you see the good of Jerusalem all the days of
your life; and may you live to see your children's children. Peace be on Israel!

הָפַכְתָּ מִסְפְּדִי לְמָחוֹל לִי, פִּתַּחְתָּ שַׂקִּי, וַתְּאַזְּרֵנִי שִׂמְחָה: וְלֹא־אָבָה יהוה תהלים ל דברים כג
אֱלֹהֶיךָ לִשְׁמֹעַ אֶל־בִּלְעָם, וַיַּהֲפֹךְ יהוה אֱלֹהֶיךָ לְּךָ אֶת־הַקְּלָלָה לִבְרָכָה,
כִּי אֲהֵבְךָ יהוה אֱלֹהֶיךָ: אָז תִּשְׂמַח בְּתוּלָה בְּמָחוֹל, וּבַחֻרִים וּזְקֵנִים יַחְדָּו, ירמיה לא
וְהָפַכְתִּי אֶבְלָם לְשָׂשׂוֹן, וְנִחַמְתִּים, וְשִׂמַּחְתִּים מִיגוֹנָם:

בּוֹרֵא נִיב שְׂפָתָיִם, שָׁלוֹם שָׁלוֹם לָרָחוֹק וְלַקָּרוֹב אָמַר יהוה, וּרְפָאתִיו: וְרוּחַ ישעיה נז דברי הימים א׳ יב
לָבְשָׁה אֶת־עֲמָשַׂי רֹאשׁ הַשָּׁלִישִׁים, לְךָ דָוִיד וְעִמְּךָ בֶן־יִשַׁי, שָׁלוֹם שָׁלוֹם
לְךָ וְשָׁלוֹם לְעֹזְרֶךָ, כִּי עֲזָרְךָ אֱלֹהֶיךָ, וַיְקַבְּלֵם דָּוִיד וַיִּתְּנֵם בְּרָאשֵׁי הַגְּדוּד:
וַאֲמַרְתֶּם כֹּה לֶחָי, וְאַתָּה שָׁלוֹם וּבֵיתְךָ שָׁלוֹם וְכֹל אֲשֶׁר־לְךָ שָׁלוֹם: יהוה שמואל א׳ כה תהלים כט
עֹז לְעַמּוֹ יִתֵּן, יהוה יְבָרֵךְ אֶת־עַמּוֹ בַשָּׁלוֹם:

אָמַר רַבִּי יוֹחָנָן: בְּכָל מָקוֹם שֶׁאַתָּה מוֹצֵא גְּדֻלָּתוֹ שֶׁל הַקָּדוֹשׁ בָּרוּךְ מגילה לא.
הוּא, שָׁם אַתָּה מוֹצֵא עַנְוְתָנוּתוֹ. דָּבָר זֶה כָּתוּב בַּתּוֹרָה, וְשָׁנוּי בַּנְּבִיאִים,
וּמְשֻׁלָּשׁ בַּכְּתוּבִים. כָּתוּב בַּתּוֹרָה: כִּי יהוה אֱלֹהֵיכֶם הוּא אֱלֹהֵי הָאֱלֹהִים דברים י
וַאֲדֹנֵי הָאֲדֹנִים, הָאֵל הַגָּדֹל הַגִּבֹּר וְהַנּוֹרָא, אֲשֶׁר לֹא־יִשָּׂא פָנִים וְלֹא יִקַּח
שֹׁחַד: וּכְתִיב בַּתְרֵהּ: עֹשֶׂה מִשְׁפַּט יָתוֹם וְאַלְמָנָה, וְאֹהֵב גֵּר לָתֶת לוֹ לֶחֶם
וְשִׂמְלָה: שָׁנוּי בַּנְּבִיאִים, דִּכְתִיב: כִּי כֹה אָמַר רָם וְנִשָּׂא שֹׁכֵן עַד וְקָדוֹשׁ ישעיה נז
שְׁמוֹ, מָרוֹם וְקָדוֹשׁ אֶשְׁכּוֹן, וְאֶת־דַּכָּא וּשְׁפַל־רוּחַ, לְהַחֲיוֹת רוּחַ שְׁפָלִים
וּלְהַחֲיוֹת לֵב נִדְכָּאִים: מְשֻׁלָּשׁ בַּכְּתוּבִים, דִּכְתִיב: שִׁירוּ לֵאלֹהִים, זַמְּרוּ תהלים סח
שְׁמוֹ, סֹלּוּ לָרֹכֵב בָּעֲרָבוֹת בְּיָהּ שְׁמוֹ, וְעִלְזוּ לְפָנָיו: וּכְתִיב בַּתְרֵהּ: אֲבִי
יְתוֹמִים וְדַיַּן אַלְמָנוֹת, אֱלֹהִים בִּמְעוֹן קָדְשׁוֹ:

יְהִי יהוה אֱלֹהֵינוּ עִמָּנוּ כַּאֲשֶׁר הָיָה עִם־אֲבֹתֵינוּ, אַל־יַעַזְבֵנוּ וְאַל־יִטְּשֵׁנוּ: מלכים א׳ ח
וְאַתֶּם הַדְּבֵקִים בַּיהוה אֱלֹהֵיכֶם, חַיִּים כֻּלְּכֶם הַיּוֹם: כִּי־נִחַם יהוה צִיּוֹן, נִחַם דברים ד ישעיה נא
כָּל־חָרְבֹתֶיהָ, וַיָּשֶׂם מִדְבָּרָהּ כְּעֵדֶן וְעַרְבָתָהּ כְּגַן־יהוה, שָׂשׂוֹן וְשִׂמְחָה יִמָּצֵא
בָהּ, תּוֹדָה וְקוֹל זִמְרָה: יהוה חָפֵץ לְמַעַן צִדְקוֹ, יַגְדִּיל תּוֹרָה וְיַאְדִּיר: ישעיה מב

שִׁיר הַמַּעֲלוֹת, אַשְׁרֵי כָּל־יְרֵא יהוה, הַהֹלֵךְ בִּדְרָכָיו: יְגִיעַ כַּפֶּיךָ כִּי תֹאכֵל, תהלים קכח
אַשְׁרֶיךָ וְטוֹב לָךְ: אֶשְׁתְּךָ כְּגֶפֶן פֹּרִיָּה בְּיַרְכְּתֵי בֵיתֶךָ, בָּנֶיךָ כִּשְׁתִלֵי זֵיתִים,
סָבִיב לְשֻׁלְחָנֶךָ: הִנֵּה כִי־כֵן יְבֹרַךְ גָּבֶר יְרֵא יהוה: יְבָרֶכְךָ יהוה מִצִּיּוֹן, וּרְאֵה
בְּטוּב יְרוּשָׁלָםִ, כֹּל יְמֵי חַיֶּיךָ: וּרְאֵה־בָנִים לְבָנֶיךָ, שָׁלוֹם עַל־יִשְׂרָאֵל:

HAVDALA

The Leader takes the cup of wine in the right hand and says:

הִנֵּה Behold, God is my salvation. I will trust and not be afraid. *Is. 12*
The LORD, the LORD, is my strength and my song.
He has become my salvation.
With joy you will draw water from the springs of salvation.
Salvation is the LORD's; on Your people is Your blessing, Selah. *Ps. 3*
The LORD of hosts is with us, the God of Jacob is our stronghold, Selah. *Ps. 46*
LORD of hosts: happy is the one who trusts in You. *Ps. 84*
LORD, save! May the King answer us on the day we call. *Ps. 20*
For the Jews there was light and gladness, joy and honor – so may it be for us. *Esther 8*
I will lift the cup of salvation and call on the name of the LORD. *Ps. 116*

When making Havdala for others, add:
Please pay attention, my masters.
Blessed are You, LORD our God, King of the Universe,
who creates the fruit of the vine.

Hold the spice box and say:

Blessed are You, LORD our God, King of the Universe,
who creates the various spices.

Smell the spices and put the spice box down.
Lift the hands toward the flame of the Havdala candle and say:

Blessed are You, LORD our God, King of the Universe,
who creates the lights of fire.

Holding the cup of wine again in the right hand, say:

בָּרוּךְ Blessed are You, LORD our God, King of the Universe, who distinguishes between sacred and secular, between light and darkness, between Israel and the nations, between the seventh day and the six days of work. Blessed are You, LORD, who distinguishes between sacred and secular.

---

previous night; why then did God not inspire Adam to create fire until the second night? The answer is that God did not grant Adam inspiration on the first night because it was Shabbat, on which God rested from creation. Only once Shabbat was completed did God grant man the inspiration required for him to continue the work of creation, and this is what we commemorate when we recite the blessing over fire in Havdala on Motza'ei Shabbat.

סדר הבדלה

The שליח ציבור *takes the cup of wine in the right hand and says:*

הִנֵּה אֵל יְשׁוּעָתִי אֶבְטַח, וְלֹא אֶפְחָד ישעיה יב
כִּי־עָזִּי וְזִמְרָת יָהּ יהוה, וַיְהִי־לִי לִישׁוּעָה:
וּשְׁאַבְתֶּם־מַיִם בְּשָׂשׂוֹן, מִמַּעַיְנֵי הַיְשׁוּעָה:
לַיהוה הַיְשׁוּעָה, עַל־עַמְּךָ בִרְכָתֶךָ סֶּלָה: תהלים ג
יהוה צְבָאוֹת עִמָּנוּ, מִשְׂגָּב לָנוּ אֱלֹהֵי יַעֲקֹב סֶלָה: תהלים מו
יהוה צְבָאוֹת, אַשְׁרֵי אָדָם בֹּטֵחַ בָּךְ: תהלים פד
יהוה הוֹשִׁיעָה, הַמֶּלֶךְ יַעֲנֵנוּ בְיוֹם־קָרְאֵנוּ: תהלים כ
לַיְּהוּדִים הָיְתָה אוֹרָה וְשִׂמְחָה וְשָׂשֹׂן וִיקָר: כֵּן תִּהְיֶה לָּנוּ. אסתר ח
כּוֹס־יְשׁוּעוֹת אֶשָּׂא, וּבְשֵׁם יהוה אֶקְרָא: תהלים קטז

When making הבדלה *for others, add:*

סַבְרִי מָרָנָן

בָּרוּךְ אַתָּה יהוה אֱלֹהֵינוּ מֶלֶךְ הָעוֹלָם, בּוֹרֵא פְּרִי הַגָּפֶן.

Hold the spice box and say:

בָּרוּךְ אַתָּה יהוה אֱלֹהֵינוּ מֶלֶךְ הָעוֹלָם, בּוֹרֵא מִינֵי בְשָׂמִים.

Smell the spices and put the spice box down.
Lift the hands toward the flame of the הבדלה *candle and say:*

בָּרוּךְ אַתָּה יהוה אֱלֹהֵינוּ מֶלֶךְ הָעוֹלָם, בּוֹרֵא מְאוֹרֵי הָאֵשׁ.

Holding the cup of wine again in the right hand, say:

בָּרוּךְ אַתָּה יהוה אֱלֹהֵינוּ מֶלֶךְ הָעוֹלָם, הַמַּבְדִּיל בֵּין קֹדֶשׁ לְחוֹל, בֵּין אוֹר לְחֹשֶׁךְ, בֵּין יִשְׂרָאֵל לָעַמִּים, בֵּין יוֹם הַשְּׁבִיעִי לְשֵׁשֶׁת יְמֵי הַמַּעֲשֶׂה.
בָּרוּךְ אַתָּה יהוה, הַמַּבְדִּיל בֵּין קֹדֶשׁ לְחוֹל.

בּוֹרֵא מְאוֹרֵי הָאֵשׁ *Who creates the lights of fire.* The Gemara (*Pesaḥim* 54a) notes: "We do not recite a blessing over light except at the termination of the Sabbath, since it was then created for the first time." The Gemara explains: "At the termination of the Sabbath, the Holy One Blessed be He inspired Adam with knowledge of a kind similar to divine [knowledge], and he procured two stones and rubbed them on each other, and fire issued from them." Seemingly, the creation of fire on Motza'ei Shabbat is merely coincidental. In fact, however, the first night on which Adam was enveloped in darkness was the

VE'ATA KADOSH: HALLEL OF THE HIDDEN GOD*

On Purim, the Megilla is read both at night and in the morning. While there is unanimity among rabbinic authorities as to the requirement to recite the *sheheheyanu* blessing prior to the recitation of the Megilla on the night of Purim, there is some disagreement regarding the need to repeat the *berakha* when rereading the Megilla on Purim morning. According to Maimonides (*Hilkhot Megilla* 1:3), *sheheḥeyanu* is not recited in the morning since it was already said the previous evening. Ri, on the other hand, maintains that since the primary reading is the daytime reading, there is indeed a requirement to repeat the *berakha* (Tosafot, *Megilla* 4a s.v. *ḥayav*).

On the surface, Ri's opinion seems difficult to understand. True, the reading of the Megilla during the day was instituted by the prophets while the reading of the previous evening was established only later by *Ḥazal*. Yet the question remains: if the mitzva performance is identical, why the need for a second *sheheḥeyanu*?

In a well-known passage (*Megilla* 14a), the Gemara raises the question as to why there is no Hallel recited on Purim. One of the reasons provided by the Gemara is that the Megilla reading itself comprises Hallel. According to this opinion, two distinct mitzvot are simultaneously fulfilled through the reading of the Megilla: the mitzva of Megilla itself as well as the mitzva of Hallel. Based on this, we can explain the repetition of the *sheheḥeyanu* blessing. With the exception of Pesaḥ night, the obligation to recite Hallel is exclusively discharged during the day. As a result, the *sheheḥeyanu* recited in the evening is a prelude to the mitzva of reading the Megilla itself, while the second *berakha* during the day is made as a prelude to a different mitzva: the fulfillment of Hallel implicit in the morning Megilla recitation.

One might now ask why this "Hallel" of Purim morning requires a *sheheḥeyanu* at all, since at no other time during the year is *sheheḥeyanu* recited as a prelude to Hallel. The answer is that the Hallel of Purim is

* This *derasha* by the Rav, originally presented in Yiddish in 1956, was translated by Dr. Arnold Lustiger.

unique since it is the only time one can fulfill the mitzva of Hallel without actually reciting the specific chapters in Psalms that comprise Hallel. We recite *sheheḥeyanu* in the morning not because of the mitzva of Hallel *per se*, but because of the unique form that Hallel assumes on Purim morning.

The supposition that the mitzva of Hallel is fulfilled through the reading of the Megilla itself begs for explanation. Every other fulfillment of Hallel, whether on Rosh Ḥodesh, Ḥanukka, or Yom Tov, is fulfilled simply through reading the chapters of Psalms which comprise Hallel. Why on Purim alone is the mitzva of Hallel fulfilled through reading the holiday narrative? Furthermore, at the Seder table on Pesaḥ night, after discussing the miracle of the Exodus from Egypt at great length we recite Hallel. Why don't we similarly maintain that retelling the story of the Exodus at the Seder constitutes a fulfillment of Hallel?

To address this question, we must first explore the nature of Hallel itself in light of a Talmudic passage: "R. Yosi said, Let my lot be among those who recite Hallel every day. But did not the master say, whoever recites Hallel every day is a blasphemer? Regarding what [did R. Yosi make his statement]? *Pesukei DeZimra*" (*Shabbat* 118b).

The arrangement of those chapters of Psalms that we commonly refer to as Hallel is known in the Talmud as *Hallel HaMitzri*, the Egyptian Hallel. The theme of this Hallel is the miraculous. "When Israel left Egypt… the sea saw and fled, the Jordan flowed backwards, the mountains skipped like rams… He transformed the rock to a pond of water…" These are the occasions when the Creator breaches the processes of nature and temporarily suspends the laws of the physical world, the world of "day and night shall not cease" (Gen. 8:22). The appellation *Hallel HaMitzri* is used because the primary theme of this Hallel is the supernatural event that God performed on behalf of His people on the night of the Exodus. On that night, He intervened with nature – the rules of physics, of action and reaction, cause and effect, were suspended. On the night of Pesaḥ, we recount His wonders and miracles – God obstructed the processes of nature to liberate His people from slavery.

However, as the Gemara implies, there is another type of Hallel, the Hallel of *Pesukei DeZimra*. The theme of *Pesukei DeZimra* is not the miraculous but rather the mundane forces of nature: "He created heaven and earth, the sea and everything in it… He brings forth His snow like wool,

◂ who can

who can stand before His cold…the skies above praise Him…the sun and moon praise Him, the stars of light praise Him." The chapters starting with Ashrei and concluding with Psalm 150 are a type of Hallel in which God reveals Himself through the powerful forces of nature. Is there truly any greater miracle than the sun rising in the morning?

If one recites *Hallel HaMitzri* every day, he is considered blasphemous because one should not require the daily invocation of supernatural miracles to appreciate His greatness. Recitation of *Hallel HaMitzri* daily would suggest that our praise of God is predicated exclusively on His performance of such wonders.

When does God intervene in nature and perform such miracles? He does so when He has no choice, when He, so to speak, can no longer accomplish His objectives through natural means. If God had not miraculously intervened in Egypt when He did, the Jewish people would have assimilated entirely, and the chosen people would have disappeared.

Yet, as is evident from the following Midrash, such miraculous intervention is far from His preferred course of action (*Shemot Rabba* 15):

> [The Exodus from Egypt] is analogous to a *Kohen* whose *teruma* falls into a graveyard. He says, "What can I do? To defile myself is impossible, and to abandon the *teruma* is impossible! It is better for me to defile myself once, return, and purify myself so that I not lose my *teruma*." So were our forefathers the *teruma* of the Holy One, Blessed be He, as it says: "Israel is holy to the Lord, the first of His grain" (Jer. 2:3). The Holy One, Blessed be He said, "How can I redeem them? To abandon them is impossible! It is preferable for Me to descend and save them," as it says (Ex. 3:8): "And I will descend to save them from the hands of Egypt."

Holiness in Judaism can be broadly defined as maintaining separation. When God intervenes supernaturally, His holiness is diminished because His separateness is diminished. Since the redemption from Egypt required God's supernatural intervention, His involvement constituted a "descent," as it were, in His holiness, in His separateness. For this reason, God labels the Exodus from Egypt as a descent.

God directs the complex cosmic drama; the light that speeds through the universe, the flying nebulae, all act in accord with His decree. The organic and biological world is a greater manifestation of His will than all the plagues visited upon Egypt! Is there anything extraordinary in God being able to overrun Egypt with frogs? His ability to drown the Egyptian army is trivial compared to His manifestation through nature.

Thus, R. Yosi says, "Let my lot be among those who recite Hallel [i.e., *Pesukei DeZimra*] every day." When one truly appreciates that the most magnificent manifestation of God on earth is His revelation through nature, he recites *Pesukei DeZimra*, reflecting the profound sense of awe that is experienced upon witnessing natural phenomena.

When His nation passed through the Red Sea and exclaimed, "This is my God and I will glorify Him," they were able to point to God leading them to freedom (Rashi, Ex. 15:2). Yet, had the Children of Israel been on a higher spiritual level, God would have taken them out of Egypt through natural means, without resorting to overt miracles. If the Jews had been on a more elevated spiritual plane, He would not have had to violate the natural process to save them. He did so in Egypt only because time was of the essence. Israel was on the brink of total assimilation. Had He not intervened through overt miracles, there would have been no nation left to save.

The miracle of Purim is fundamentally different from all other miracles that are commemorated in the Jewish calendar because it is not a revealed miracle. It is a "natural" miracle. There is no incident in the Megilla that one might consider as anything but a natural occurrence. As elaborated by *Ḥazal* (*Megilla* 15b), the natural miracle of Purim is the theme of Psalm 22, which begins:

> For the leader; upon *Ayelet HaShaḥar* [literally, the morning star; interpreted as a reference to Esther]... My God, my God, why have You forsaken me... O my God, I call by day but You answer not, and at night and there is no surcease for me.

When Esther entered the inner chamber to approach the king and plead on behalf of her people, she was fully aware of the serious implication of her action, as evidenced by her message to Mordekhai (4:11): "There is only one law for any man or woman who comes before the king, into the inner courtyard, without being called: to be killed."

◂ *Ḥazal*

Ḥazal say that upon first seeing the queen, King Ahasuerus withheld his scepter. His first inclination was to put her to death for brazenly entering the inner chamber uninvited. Esther had hoped that her hesitant approach to the king would herald a supernatural event that would lead to the salvation of the Jews, in the same way that God had performed open miracles on behalf of His people in the past. She was therefore bitterly disappointed when Ahasuerus did not immediately extend his scepter. At that point, Esther thought that all was lost, her efforts to save the Jewish people were in vain. In despair, she exclaimed: "My God, my God, why have You forsaken me?"

When the capricious king changed his mind and held out his scepter, Esther knew that the deliverance of the Jews would take place. However, she also understood that this rescue was to be different from the other salvations in Jewish history. This time the Jews would be saved through natural means.

Psalm 22 therefore continues with this verse: וְאַתָּה קָדוֹשׁ יוֹשֵׁב תְּהִלּוֹת יִשְׂרָאֵל, *You are the Holy One, enthroned on the praises of Israel.* As explained earlier, holiness denotes separateness. When God redeems Israel through natural means, He is *kadosh,* hidden, separate from man, concealed behind a cloud. When King Ahasuerus finally extended his scepter, Esther realized that although God would answer her prayers, He would still remain *kadosh,* separate. He would provide salvation by performing a "natural" miracle. As a result of this belated realization, Esther exclaimed: *You are the Holy One, enthroned on the praises of Israel.* And when God orchestrates salvation from afar, maintaining the separateness of a *kadosh,* He acts in accordance with the praises that Jews recite daily: the praises of *Pesukei DeZimra* rather than those of *Hallel HaMitzri.*

In the Purim drama, God directed a sequence of events that when considered separately do not appear extraordinary. He set in motion a series of seemingly mundane and plausible incidents so the salvation had the appearance of emerging naturally.

Esther herself is called *Ayelet HaShaḥar* in the Gemara (*Yoma* 29a). *Ayelet HaShaḥar* refers to the rise of the morning star at the very beginning of dawn. The inception of dawn is very subtle. When one looks towards the east at the earliest moment of dawn, the slow brightening of the sky is not even perceptible. At the very moment that the Purim salvation was incubating, one could only see an evil, politically astute Haman getting drunk with a king whom he easily manipulated. The darkness, the despair of this long night seemed so overpowering that one might have mistakenly concluded that there was no guiding hand behind those events.

In appreciation of this aspect of Purim, after the Megilla readings of both evening and morning we recite the portion of *U'Va LeTziyon* starting with וְאַתָּה קָדוֹשׁ יוֹשֵׁב תְּהִלּוֹת יִשְׂרָאֵל. וְקָרָא זֶה אֶל זֶה וְאָמַר קָדוֹשׁ קָדוֹשׁ קָדוֹשׁ יְהוָה צְבָאוֹת מְלֹא כָל הָאָרֶץ כְּבוֹדוֹ, *You are the Holy One, enthroned on the praises of Israel. And [the angels] call to one another, saying, "Holy, holy, holy is the Lord of hosts, the whole world is filled with His glory."*

The appellation "Lord of hosts" connotes that He is the Master of the host of seemingly inconsequential events on earth. As the prayer continues: קַדִּישׁ בִּשְׁמֵי מְרוֹמָא עִלָּאָה בֵּית שְׁכִינְתֵּהּ, *Holy in the highest heavens, home of His presence*. Initially, it seems that He only controls the celestial sphere, that He is entirely removed from the events taking place on earth. Only after we step back and view these natural events in perspective can we appreciate their sequence and thus perceive His providence: קַדִּישׁ עַל אַרְעָא עוֹבַד גְּבוּרְתֵּהּ, *holy on earth, the work of His strength*.

Although we cannot see His guiding hand, what happens on earth is far from random; it is "the work of His strength." After we gain this appreciation we affirm: קַדִּישׁ לְעָלַם וּלְעָלְמֵי עָלְמַיָּא, *holy for ever and all time*.

Upon narrating the story of the Exodus on Pesaḥ, we do not recite the prayer of *Ve'Ata Kadosh*. As we spill the wine and enumerate the ten plagues, the revelation of God's presence is evident. On Pesaḥ, we do not need to declare our faith that He is "holy on earth, the work of His strength," since at the moment of the splitting of the sea we could see Him clearly. "By signs, and by wonders, and by war, and by a mighty hand… according to all that the Lord your God did for you in Egypt before your eyes" (Deut. 4:34).

In contrast, when we read the Megilla, we relive the black night when a drunken king and his evil advisor tried to seal the fate of the Jews. Yet, as it states in the Megilla, "On that night," when the situation was dark and bleak, "the sleep of the king was disturbed" (Es. 6:1). The night did not give way to the morning light quickly, yet events were orchestrated in a way that very slowly led to salvation. This process happened naturally,

◂ culminating in,

culminating in, "Thus was Haman hung up, on the very post he had prepared for Mordekhai; and the king's fury subsided" (Es. 7:10).

The Gemara (*Megilla* 19a) comments: "The Megilla is called a letter [*iggeret*] and it is called a book [*sefer*]." The word sefer in ancient Hebrew refers exclusively to words written on parchment. As such, it suggests a permanent record. For example, "Take these documents [*sefarim*] and place them in an earthenware vessel so they will endure for many years" (Jer. 32:14). "'He shall write for himself a copy of this law in a book' – in a book and not on paper" (*Sifrei*, Deut. 160). Ink on parchment is durable. An *iggeret*, on the other hand, is written on paper, the message is temporary. One reads a letter and soon discards it.

Megillat Esther is unique because it is designated as both an *iggeret* and a *sefer*. Superficially, the events that are recounted in the Megilla would not seem to have any lasting significance. The narrative at first seems to be a mildly interesting tale of political intrigue, an *iggeret* that one reads and soon discards, like a newspaper. On the other hand, the Megilla is also a *sefer*, a profound book that recounts a very significant and momentous event in Jewish history. As a *sefer*, millions of people read it on Purim and will continue to do so.

The *sefer* aspect of the Megilla narrative is reflected in halakha. Commenting on the phrase in the Megilla, "words of peace and truth" (Es. 9:30), the Gemara derives that the Megilla requires etched lines, "like the truth of Torah" (*Megilla* 16b). Rabbenu Tam (Tosafot, *Gittin* 6b) explains that the "truth of Torah" refers to *Shema Yisrael*. Indeed, this story is as basic and fundamental to our religion as the cardinal declaration of faith itself. Jews recited *Shema Yisrael* as they prepared to sacrifice their lives for the sanctification of God's name, during moments in our history when the night of exile was at its darkest. Rabbi Akiva could perceive God's presence as his body was being perforated with combs of iron and the word *eḥad* issued from his dying lips. By celebrating the holiday of Purim, we demonstrate our belief in Divine Providence during a dark, tragic night. The Gemara rereads the verse: "On that night," when no one thought that God would intervene, when the situation seemed hopeless, "the sleep of the King of the Universe was disturbed" (*Megilla* 15b). The night imperceptibly gave way to dawn, to salvation. We proclaim *Ve'Ata*

Kadosh despite the superficial perception of God's absence: "My God, my God, why have You forsaken me?"

A dispute is recorded in the Mishna and the subsequent Gemara regarding where in the Book of Esther the Megilla reading on Purim should commence (*Megilla* 19a). The halakha follows the opinion which maintains that we must read the Megilla in its entirety. But why do we even bother to read the beginning of the Megilla, with its depiction of a drunken king and his petulant wife? Why are we obligated to recite the dual blessing of *al mikra Megilla* and *sheheḥeyanu* before hearing such trivial details?

The answer is that in the Megilla narrative, no detail is trivial. If we did not know about Vashti's fall, we would not understand the significance of the flow of these events. What did the conflict of Vashti and Ahasuerus have to do with them? Only later did they recognize that the process of salvation began the moment Ahasuerus became intoxicated at his royal feast. Were it not for Vashti's fall from the king's graces and Esther's subsequent rise to the throne, Haman would have been triumphant. Megillat Esther is a *sefer* because every detail must be taken into account to appreciate how the saga reaches it denouement.

Purim (lots) is the name of the holiday, not the singular *pur*, because there have been many attempts to destroy us in exile. Yet, while God has saved us every time we faced annihilation in the diaspora, He also remained hidden, *kadosh*.

In Egypt, the miracles were so numerous that Israel did not have to act to defeat the Egyptians: "Stand fast and see the salvation of the LORD… The LORD shall do battle for you, and you shall remain silent" (Ex. 14:13-14). In contrast, the battle against Amalek was never fought through overt miracles. The battle had to be fought conventionally: "And Moses said unto Joshua: 'Choose us out men, and go out, fight with Amalek'" (Ex. 17:9). Why this difference in the method of salvation?

Pharaoh's persecution of the Israelites was due to simple economic considerations. The persecution was a means of maintaining a pool of cheap labor to serve his kingdom's needs. In contrast, Amalek's battle was not against Jews *per se*, it was against the God of Israel Himself. Amalek fights God through His people. Amalek's antagonism towards the Jewish people is rooted in the fact that Mordekhai did not bow nor prostrate himself before Haman. And Haman knew that if Mordekhai did not bow, the simple shoemaker would not bow either. Mordekhai lived differently, he ate differently, his children were different. When Haman characterized the Jews to Ahasuerus, he himself emphasized this uniqueness: "There is one people … whose laws are different from those of all the other peoples" (Es. 3:8). Haman did not hate the Jews *per se*. Had they worshiped idols, he could have tolerated them. Haman hated the Jewish religion, the Jews' uniqueness, their determination to cling to their faith and uphold the Torah. When the battle is against the Jews, as in Egypt, God Himself fights on their behalf. But when the battle is waged against God, the Jews must do the fighting, without any overt supernatural intervention. His people must take the initiative and lead the battle, while God remains *kadosh*, subtly controlling events.

The Gemara (*Megilla* 7a) recounts that when Esther requested that the Megilla be canonized, the Rabbis initially hesitated until they found a scriptural basis for canonization: כְּתֹב זֹאת זִכָּרוֹן בַּסֵּפֶר וְשִׂים בְּאָזְנֵי יְהוֹשֻׁעַ כִּי מָחֹה אֶמְחֶה אֶת זֵכֶר עֲמָלֵק מִתַּחַת הַשָּׁמָיִם, *Write this for a memorial in the book, and rehearse it in the ears of Joshua: for I will utterly blot out the remembrance of Amalek from under heaven* (Ex. 17:14). The Book of Esther was canonized because the message of Purim must constantly be reinforced in our own battle with Amalek. There are moments in this struggle when we seem to face imminent defeat – when, like Esther, we ask God why He has forsaken us. Yet, towards the end of the night when it is darkest, at the moment of deepest despair, we await the rise of the morning star and proclaim: וְאַתָּה קָדוֹשׁ יוֹשֵׁב תְּהִלּוֹת יִשְׂרָאֵל.

רשימות

RESHIMOT

PARASHAT SHEKALIM: THE MITZVA OF *MAḤATZIT HASHEKEL*

Regarding the mitzva of *maḥatzit hashekel*, the half-shekel donated annually to the Temple which was used to purchase the communal offerings, the question arises: is the mitzva of *maḥatzit hashekel* a means for the individual to acquire a portion of the communal offerings that will be offered in the course of the year, or, is the obligation of the individual simply to give the *maḥatzit hashekel* to the Beit HaMikdash, and not a means to acquire a portion in the communal offerings?

This question seems to be the subject of a debate among the *Rishonim*. Rashi (*Ketubot* 108a) refers to the *maḥatzit hashekel* which one is "obligated to give each year for the communal offerings." Rashi's comment implies that the *maḥatzit hashekel* is a means of acquiring a portion of the communal offerings. This is consistent with Rashi's commentary on Exodus (30:15), and is the implication of Naḥmanides' comments (Ex. 30:12) as well as the explanation of the mitzva offered by *Sefer HaḤinukh* (mitzva 105).

For Maimonides, however, it seems that the mitzva of *maḥatzit hashekel* consists of the act of giving the *maḥatzit hashekel* to the Beit HaMikdash. In the first chapter of *Hilkhot Shekalim*, Maimonides states that there is a mitzva to give a *maḥatzit hashekel*, but only in chapter 4 does he state what is done with the funds. This implies that the mitzva consists entirely of the act of giving; once the people have fulfilled their obligations to give the *maḥatzit hashekel*, the administrators of the Beit HaMikdash used them to purchase the *korbanot*. The purchase of the *korbanot* pertains to the disbursement of the funds, and such disbursement is not inherently connected to the mitzva of giving the *maḥatzit hashekel*.

Maimonides (*Hilkhot Shekalim* 1:1) also states that one must "sell the clothes on his back to acquire a *maḥatzit hashekel*." Generally, monetary debts can be discharged with currency or other objects of value. The fact that only a specific form of currency can be used for *maḥatzit hashekel* implies that the mitzva is the act of giving a specific coin as opposed to payment of a debt. Furthermore, one cannot give the *maḥatzit hashekel*

◂ in multiple

in multiple installments; rather, the entire amount must be given at one time. This too indicates that the mitzva is the act of giving, and not merely the acquisition of a share in the communal offerings.

PARASHAT ZAKHOR AND THE READING OF THE MEGILLA

The Torah (Deut. 25:17) commands us to remember what Amalek did to us as we left Egypt but does not specify how to do this. Naḥmanides (Deut., *ad loc.*) quotes the *Sifrei*: "'Remember what Amalek did to you' – with your mouth [i.e., verbally]." Naḥmanides continues: "I do not know what this verbal remembrance is, and whether it means that we should read the *parasha* of Amalek publicly. This would then be a source in the Torah for [the enactment of the Mishna] 'On the second week [of Adar], *Zakhor*' (*Megilla* 29a), and a support in the Torah for the reading of the Megilla." Naḥmanides' concluding words require explanation: What is the support from this verse for the mitzva to read the Megilla? Even if there exists an obligation to remember Amalek's actions verbally, reading the passage of *Zakhor* alone should suffice. Where do we see any implication about reading the Megilla?

Naḥmanides explicitly states that one fulfills the obligation of remembering Amalek's actions verbally by reading *Parashat Zakhor*. It seems that Naḥmanides maintains that if one failed to read *Parashat Zakhor*, the Biblical obligation to remember Amalek's actions may still be discharged by reading the Megilla. Reading the Megilla constitutes an act of remembering Amalek's actions. It would then emerge that by fulfilling the prophetic command to read from the Megilla, one also fulfills the Torah obligation to remember Amalek. This is what Naḥmanides means that this interpretation of the *Sifrei* is "a support in the Torah for the reading of the Megilla."

The Talmud Yerushalmi (*Megilla* 1:5) records that "Eighty-five elders, among them thirty some prophets, were troubled by this matter. They said, '...Moses informed us that no prophet would innovate anything for you, and Mordekhai and Esther are trying to innovate something for us!' They did not move from their place, arguing about the matter, until the Holy One, Blessed be He, lit up their eyes and they found it [an allusion to the Megilla] written in the Torah, Prophets, and Writings." The Yerushalmi cites the verse, "Write this as a remembrance in a book" (Ex. 17:14) as the source in the Torah for the Megilla. Naḥmanides (Deut. 4:2) understands the Yerushalmi as referring to reading the Megilla (cf. Ran, commentary on Rif, *Megilla* 1b). According to Naḥmanides, the source in the Torah for the enactment of reading the Megilla is the commandment to remember Amalek's actions.

However, the position of Naḥmanides seems to stand in contrast to the ruling of *Shulḥan Arukh* (*Oraḥ Ḥayim* 685:7) that people in villages lacking a quorum must go someplace that has a quorum for the reading of *Zakhor* in order to hear the Biblically-mandated Torah reading. According to Naḥmanides, it would seem they could fulfill their obligation to remember Amalek's actions by reading the Megilla. Also, it is inherently difficult to understand how one may fulfill the obligation to remember Amalek's actions verbally by reading the Megilla when it contains no mention of Amalek's actions as we left Egypt.

Nevertheless, the idea that the Megilla and *Parashat Zakhor* are connected can be found in many places, in addition to the above comment of Naḥmanides. The Gemara (*Megilla* 30a) says that when Purim falls on Shabbat, we read *Zakhor* the week prior so that the reading precedes the doing. From this passage, the idea emerges that celebrating Purim is a form of eradicating the memory of Amalek, which must come after the remembrance of Amalek's actions through the reading of *Parashat Zakhor*.

Based on this, we can understand why on Purim morning we read from the Torah first, and afterward from the Megilla. On any other holiday on which we read from one of the Megillot, such as when we read Ruth on Shavuot, we first read from the Megilla and afterward from the Torah. But on Purim, the Torah reading precedes the Megilla because the Torah reading constitutes remembrance of Amalek, and the Megilla reading constitutes eradicating the memory of Amalek.

TA'ANIT ESTHER ACCORDING TO MAIMONIDES

Maimonides (*Hilkhot Ta'aniyot* 5:5) writes:

> ונהגו כל ישראל בזמנים אלו להתענות. ובי"ג באדר זכר לתענית שהתענו בימי המן שנאמר דברי הצומות וזעקתם.
>
> And all of Israel customarily fast at these times [mentioned in Zech. (8:19), i.e., the 17th of Tammuz, the 9th of Av, the 3rd of Tishrei, and the 10th of Tevet]; and on the thirteenth of Adar, in commemoration of the fast that they fasted in the time of Haman, as the verse states, "their fast days and entreaties" (Es. 9:31).

According to this version of the text, Maimonides equates the obligation of Ta'anit Esther with the other fast days. This view is in concurrence with Rabbenu Tam (cited by Rosh, *Megilla* 1:1) that Ta'anit Esther originates in the Megilla itself, and is not a later institution. However, unlike Rabbenu Tam who considers Ta'anit Esther to be a commemoration of the fasting that took place on the thirteenth of Adar when the Jews battled against their enemies, Maimonides maintains that Ta'anit Esther commemorates the fast which the people fasted "in the time of Haman" – since Haman was executed in Nisan eleven months prior to the battle of Adar, this reference must necessarily refer to the fast which Esther observed prior to entering Ahasuerus' chamber.

However, this interpretation of Maimonides' words, predicated on the printed version of the text, presents a number of difficulties. In his commentary on the Mishna (*Rosh HaShana* 18b), Maimonides maintains that the obligation to fast after the destruction of the Temple is not a matter of custom, but an obligation. If so, the phrase ונהגו כל ישראל בזמנים אלו להתענות is incorrect, since fasting on these days is obligatory and not customary. Second, why does Maimonides write "בזמנים אלו, in these times," and not "בימים אלו, on these days"? Third, the construction of the sentence is perplexing. Maimonides should have written, ונהגו כל ישראל להתענות בזמנים אלו, with the verb preceding the object, and not ונהגו כל ישראל בזמנים אלו להתענות.

Rav Zalman of Volozhin suggested a minor emendation which is corroborated by manuscripts of the *Mishneh Torah* and resolves these problems. According to Rav Zalman, the letter *vav* in the word ובי"ג should be omitted, so that the text reads: "ונהגו כל ישראל בזמנים אלו להתענות בי"ג באדר, all of Israel customarily fasts in our times on the thirteenth of Adar." In this version, the words בזמנים אלו refer not to the other fast days, but to our current times – Maimonides records that Ta'anit Esther is a post-Talmudic fast, and he distinguishes between Ta'anit Esther which is customary, and the other fast days which are obligatory.

But if Maimonides maintains that Ta'anit Esther is a custom which was introduced in the time of the Geonim, and not a decree which dates back to the Megilla itself, why does he invoke the verse in the Megilla, דברי הצומות וזעקתם, as the source for Ta'anit Esther?

The Megilla (Es. 9:30–31) states:

> וַיִּשְׁלַח סְפָרִים אֶל כָּל הַיְּהוּדִים...לְקַיֵּם אֵת יְמֵי הַפֻּרִים הָאֵלֶּה בִּזְמַנֵּיהֶם כַּאֲשֶׁר קִיַּם עֲלֵיהֶם מָרְדֳּכַי הַיְּהוּדִי וְאֶסְתֵּר הַמַּלְכָּה וְכַאֲשֶׁר קִיְּמוּ עַל נַפְשָׁם וְעַל זַרְעָם דִּבְרֵי הַצּוֹמוֹת וְזַעֲקָתָם.
>
> The scrolls were to confirm these days of Purim in their times, just as Mordekhai the Jew and Esther the queen had fixed them; and, indeed, as they had all fixed their fast days and entreaties, for themselves and for their children.

We know that Esther debated with the Rabbis whether it was possible to establish Purim as a holiday. They felt that it was a violation of *bal tosif*, the prohibition against adding new mitzvot to the Torah. Esther responded that there was a precedent, in that the Rabbis and prophets had previously established the four fast days following the destruction of the First Temple. Thus, she felt that it was also justified to establish rabbinically mandated holidays. The foregoing verse should thus be interpreted as follows: the days were established as holidays, in the same manner in which the fast days, i.e., the four fasts, were previously established by the prophets, immediately following the destruction of the First Temple, seventy years prior to the miracle of Purim.

This is the interpretation provided by ibn Ezra on this verse. If Maimonides agreed with this interpretation, then his reference to the verse דברי הצומות וזעקתם as the origin for Ta'anit Esther is misplaced, since that passage refers to the four fasts of Zechariah and not to Ta'anit Esther. How then did Maimonides interpret this verse?

There is another possible interpretation suggested by the cantillation notes on this verse. The words דברי הצומות וזעקתם follow an *etnaḥta,* which divides the first portion of the verse from the second. Following ibn Ezra's interpretation, there should be no pause before these words, as וכאשר קימו על נפשם ועל זרעם דברי הצומות וזעקתם forms one thought unit: they accepted to celebrate Purim just as they had previously accepted the fast days.

Apparently, the author of the cantillation notes interpreted the verse as follows: Esther made three requests of the Sages. First, she requested that the holiday of Purim be established permanently. This is described in Esther 9:20-27. Second, she requested that the Megilla be incorporated into the canon of Scripture. This is described in verse 29. In verse 31, Esther makes a final request to affirm the holiday.

This final affirmation of the holiday was required inasmuch as Purim had changed its character from a *mitzva derabbanan* to one of *divrei kabbala* as a result of the incorporation of the Megilla into the canon of Scripture. Thus, the words of the request, לקיים את ימי הפורים האלה בזמניהם כאשר קים עליהם מרדכי היהודי ואסתר המלכה וכאשר קימו על נפשם ועל זרעם, refer to the reacceptance of the holiday which they had previously accepted. These words refer solely to the change in the identity of the holiday to one of *divrei kabbala.*

If this is the case, then the words דברי הצומות וזעקתם can be understood as a separate clause to mean that in conjunction with the new affirmation of the holiday, they also accepted the fast days, i.e., Ta'anit Esther. Interestingly, *Masekhet Sofrim* (17:4) records that originally Ta'anit Esther was instituted as a three-day fast which corresponds to the fast of Esther herself. This explains why the verse refers to "צומות, fast days," in the plural. This is entirely consistent with the explanation implied by the cantillation notes that the Jews accepted both the holiday of Purim and the fasts of Purim.

According to the printed version of the *Mishneh Torah,* Maimonides could agree with this interpretation implied by the cantillation notes. Ta'anit Esther would then have its roots in the Megilla. However, according to Rav Zalman of Volozhin's emendation, Maimonides maintains that Ta'anit Esther is merely customary. If so, we are left with the original difficulty regarding Maimonides' interpretation of the words דברי הצומות וזעקתם.

The solution to this problem is based on the Gemara which derives the obligation to read the Megilla both at night and during the day from the verse (Ps. 22:3), "O my God, I call by day but You answer not, and at night and there is no surcease for me" (*Megilla* 4a). The Gemara interprets this verse as relating to the Megilla because the Megilla commemorates not only our salvation, but also our distress. Thus, the words דברי הצומות וזעקתם mean that the Megilla itself contains a commemoration of our distress. Maimonides invokes these words in relation to the custom of Ta'anit Esther not because he understands these words as a reference to Ta'anit Esther but because it is this aspect of Purim which the custom of Ta'anit Esther reflects; it commemorates the anxiety and distress experienced by the protagonists at the time of the first Purim. The justification for introducing the custom of Ta'anit Esther is that the Megilla itself contains both motifs of *ze'aka*, crying out, and *hoda'a*, thanksgiving.

TA'ANIT ESTHER IN THE MESSIANIC ERA

In *Hilkhot Ta'aniyot* (5:19), Maimonides writes that "all of these fasts [mentioned in Zechariah (8:19), i.e., the 17th of Tammuz, the 9th of Av, the 3rd of Tishrei, and the 10th of Tevet] will be nullified in the Messianic era." Does this statement apply to Ta'anit Esther as well? The possibility exists that the observance of Ta'anit Esther is attached to the celebration of Purim, and just as Purim will be relevant even in the Messianic era (as Maimonides establishes in *Hilkhot Megilla* 2:18), this fast day should be retained as well.

The view that Ta'anit Esther is an independent fast day is reflected in the opinion of the Geonim (*Otzar HaGeonim, Megilla* no. 35) which maintains that in a leap year, although Purim is observed only in the second Adar, Ta'anit Esther is observed in both months of Adar. This implies that Ta'anit Esther exists independently from Purim and therefore would most likely be voided as a fast day in the Messianic era along with the other fast days that will be nullified. However, this opinion is not accepted as halakha, and thus the question remains.

◂ In addition

In addition to the holidays that we observe today, *Megillat Ta'anit* enumerates other joyous days on which fasting was prohibited. Prior to the annulment of these holidays (see *Rosh HaShana* 18b-19a), it was prohibited to fast on the day that preceded or succeeded the holiday. Pursuant to this ruling, Ran (*Ta'anit* 7a in Rif pagination) discusses why fasting on the day before Purim is permitted. He cites Ravad, who justifies Ta'anit Esther on account of it being itself a commemoration of the miracle, and because it is alluded to in the verse "The scrolls were to confirm these days of Purim in their times... as they had all fixed their fast days and entreaties, for themselves and for their children" (Esther 9:31) – in other words, just as they accepted the holiday, so did they accept the fast day. This emphasizes a fundamental link between Purim and Ta'anit Esther – Ta'anit Esther is tied to the publicizing of the miracle as well. There is therefore no issue in having Ta'anit Esther immediately precede or succeed Purim, as the fast day is not a contradiction to the joy of Purim. According to this view, it would seem that Ta'anit Esther will endure in the Messianic era because it forms a part of the Purim commemoration, just as it could coexist with the prohibition against fasting on the day before a holiday.

Maimonides (*Hilkhot Ta'aniyot* 5:5) maintains like Ravad that the verse "as they had all fixed their fast days and entreaties" is the source for Ta'anit Esther, and thus it would seem he would maintain that Ta'anit Esther will remain intact forever. However, ibn Ezra (Esther 9:31) identifies the fast days in this verse as the four fast days mentioned in Zechariah (8:19) – what the verse means, according to ibn Ezra, is that the Jews accepted to celebrate Purim just as they had accepted to fast on these days of mourning. According to this approach, the verse is not a source for the link between Ta'anit Esther and Purim.

Whether Ta'anit Esther is tied to the obligations of Purim may have another implication as well. Rema (*Oraḥ Ḥayim* 686:2) states that Ta'anit Esther is not fully obligatory and therefore we are more lenient than other fasts in allowing a person who is not feeling well to break the fast. Rashi, in a responsum (cited in *Beit Yosef, Oraḥ Ḥayim* 686) is also lenient with regard to Ta'anit Esther. *Hagahot Maimoniyot* (*Hilkhot Ta'aniyot* 2), however, suggests that it may be an obligatory fast. Seemingly, if Ta'anit Esther is a component of the mitzva of Purim, then it should have the stringencies of an obligatory fast.

◂ The unique

The unique spirit of Ta'anit Esther manifests itself in another halakha as well. Maimonides (*Hilkhot Ta'aniyot* 5:5) writes that if any of the four fast days fall out on Shabbat, we delay the observance of the fast day until Sunday. This is based on a principle established in *Masekhet Megilla* (5a) that we don't advance the commemoration of a calamity. If the 13th of Adar falls out on Shabbat, however, Ta'anit Esther is moved up to Thursday. Seemingly, the explanation for this distinction is that Ta'anit Esther, unlike the other fast days, is not a day of calamity, but tied to the joy of Purim (cf. *Maggid Mishneh*, who gives a different explanation).

THE STATUS OF MEGILLAT ESTHER

The Gemara (*Megilla* 7a) cites a dispute among the Sages about whether Megillat Esther has the status of Holy Scripture such that it causes ritual impurity to one's hands (see *Shabbat* 14a). R. Yehoshua maintains that Megillat Esther does not cause ritual impurity, and R. Elazar HaModa'i disagrees. Shmuel rules in accordance with R. Yehoshua. The Gemara then asks, "Does this mean that Shmuel holds that Megillat Esther was not composed with divine inspiration? But did not Shmuel say, Megillat Esther was composed with divine inspiration?" The Gemara answers its question: "It was composed [with divine inspiration] to be read, but not to be written." Tosafot (s.v. *ne'emra*) ask, if the Megilla was not composed to be written, why must one read the Megilla from a written scroll (*Megilla* 10a)? Tosafot answer that the writing of the Megilla is only a rabbinic requirement, but not based on divine inspiration.

However, the Gemara can be explained in another way as well. When we use the term "*Sefer Torah*," we refer to two distinct concepts and laws: 1) its sanctity as a *Sefer Torah*; and 2) an object which has the status of a written Torah scroll. In many instances, we encounter a written Torah scroll which does not possess the particular sanctity of a *Sefer Torah*. There are a number of laws which depend upon the sanctity of the *Sefer Torah* and not upon the object of the *Sefer Torah*, and on the other hand, there are many laws which depend not on the sanctity of the *Sefer Torah*, but on its status as written Torah. For example, the mitzva to write a *Sefer Torah* is fulfilled only with something that possesses the sanctity of a *Sefer Torah*. Likewise, with regard to reading the Torah in public and taking an

◂ oath upon

oath upon a holy object, we require the sanctity of a *Sefer Torah*. However, with regard to the law that one may not recite written matters by heart, it is not the sanctity of the *Sefer Torah* but its status as written Torah which permits recitation and study of the text. The distinction between oral and written is not identical to the distinction between that which possesses sanctity and that which does not; the relevant distinction here is writing which confers the status of "written Torah" and writing which does not confer that status.

To give a straightforward example: a *Sefer Torah* which is missing one letter lacks the sanctity of a *Sefer Torah* entirely. One does not fulfill with it the mitzva of writing a *Sefer Torah*, one cannot read it in the synagogue, nor can one take an oath upon it. Even the tip of a *yod* impedes the sanctity of a *Sefer Torah*. However, with regard to whether one is allowed to read and study from this scroll in reference to the law that one may not study written matters by heart, we do not require a complete *Sefer Torah*, and the status of written Torah descends upon fragments as well. There are different gradations for how much must be written with regard to different laws, but all agree that one does not require a complete *Sefer Torah* in order to teach students.

In truth, the Torah contains two separate discussions of this issue. In *Parashat Ki Tisa* (Ex. 34:27), it states: "And God said to Moses, Write for yourself these words." At that point Moses had not yet received the entire Torah; thus, this establishes a distinct halakha of writing a part of the Torah, as the Gemara explains (*Gittin* 60a). In *Parashat Vayelekh* (Deut. 31:24), however, we find the law of writing the entire Torah: "And it came to pass, when Moses had made an end of writing the words of this Torah in a book, until they were finished." These verses refer to the writing of the entire Torah, "until they were finished," in order to read it in the assembly (*Hakhel*) and to place it alongside the Ark of the Covenant, as the verses state (*ibid.*, verses 10-11), "And Moses commanded them saying, At the end of seven years at the time of the sabbatical year…you shall read this Torah," and as it states (*ibid.*, verses 25-26), "And Moses commanded the Levites who carried the ark of God's covenant saying, Take this book of the Torah and place it beside the ark of the covenant of the LORD your God."

These two *parshiyot*, which at first glance contradict one another, are tied to the two laws which we have already mentioned. *Parashat Ki*

Tisa addresses the status of written Torah, and in *Parashat Vayelekh*, we discover the law of the sanctity of the Torah, which requires a complete Torah specifically.

A parallel to this double law exists with regard to Megillat Esther as well. We must distinguish between the sanctity of Scripture which attaches itself to the Megilla, as it does for all twenty-four books of the Bible, and the status of Megillat Esther as a unique entity in the written Torah. These two concepts are not dependent upon one another. The Megilla may possess the unique status of Megillat Esther, as written Torah, without the sanctity of Scripture. This is what the Gemara means that although Shmuel maintains that Megillat Esther does not ritually defile – i.e., it is not part of the Scriptural canon with regard to its sanctity, upon which ritual defilement depends – nevertheless, Shmuel agrees that it is part of the written Torah, and it has a unique character which is a reflection of divinely inspired writing.

Even according to Shmuel, one who studies the Megilla fulfills the obligation of Torah study, and it lacks not even a modicum in relation to other books of the Bible. One who erases or destroys a Megilla violates the prohibition of "You shall not do so unto the Lord your God" (Deut. 12:4). With respect to these things, it is identical to other books of the Bible. It is distinct only with regard to one detail, that of ritual defilement. The words of the Gemara, "It was composed to be read, but not to be written," mean: It was composed to be written as part of the written Torah and for the purpose of the fulfillment of reading the Megilla, but it was not composed to be written as part of Scripture and to partake of that sanctity. It has the status of Torah but not the status of Scriptural sanctity. This resolves the question of Tosafot – why can one not read the Megilla by heart? The answer is that even on a Biblical level, the Megilla has the status of written Torah, and one must read from such a Megilla.

In truth, the Gemara (*Megilla* 19a) addresses the dual character of the Megilla, recording in the name of Rav that the Megilla is called both an "epistle" and a "book" – "it is called a book to teach us that if it is sewn with linen threads it is invalid, and it is called an epistle to teach us that sewing with even three sinews is sufficient." In other words, it has the status of an epistle as an independent entity of Megillat Esther, even if it does not possess the sanctity of Scripture, and it is called a book with regard to all the laws of the sanctity of Scripture.

◂ THE PARADOX

THE PARADOX OF PURIM: A RABBINIC HOLIDAY RECORDED IN TANAKH

There is a basic difference, halakhically, between Ḥanukka and Purim. Purim is mentioned in the Torah, a term which encompasses all twenty-four books of Scripture. There is a Megilla devoted to Purim, and it is provided with sanctity like any other book of Scripture. For instance, one who destroys or burns a Megillat Esther violates the injunction of "You shall not do so unto the LORD your God" (Deut. 12:4). As far as the general category of *kedusha* which has been assigned to Scripture is concerned, Megillat Esther does not differ from any other part of the Bible. It too was written with divine inspiration. Yet, although the mitzvot of Purim are all enumerated in Megillat Esther, these mitzvot are only rabbinic in nature.

This leads to a strange paradox. The Torah details mitzvot which are to be traced to rabbinic legislation. The rabbinic festival of Purim is mentioned in the Torah. As a corpus, as a book, Megillat Esther does not differ from Genesis, or from any other book of Scripture. The sanctity is uniform, universal. The *kedusha* permeates every word of Megillat Esther just as it penetrates and infiltrates every letter of *Shema Yisrael*. But, paradoxically, the mitzvot that are mentioned in the Megilla are only rabbinically mandated. The document is *de'oraita*, Biblical, but the mitzvot themselves, their validity, obligatory character, and binding force, are only rabbinic.

Another mitzva which shares this paradox is that of the four fast days mentioned in Zechariah (8:19). This means that the character of the days as obligatory fast days is recorded in the Prophets, in God's word. Yet, the obligation to observe those fast days is only rabbinic in nature. Interestingly, the fast days are also recorded in Megillat Esther which states (Es. 9:31):

> *To confirm these days of Purim in their times, just as Mordekhai the Jew and Esther the queen had fixed them; and, indeed, as they had all fixed their fast days and entreaties.*

This paradox is not explainable. It is very peculiar that a *mitzva derabbanan* is documented in the Torah. The conclusion which can be drawn from this is that, fundamentally, there is little distinction between a *mitzva de'oraita* and *mitzva derabbanan*. As to the reward and as to the punishment in the world to come, there is very little difference between the two. A *mitzva derabbanan* is just as important and has as much redemptive qualities as a *mitzva de'oraita*. Both are equally capable of elevating the Jew to great heights. Because *mitzvot derabbanan* are documented in the Torah, we can infer that the validity, the obligatory character, the normative character of a *mitzva derabbanan* differs very little from that of a *mitzva de'oraita*. It cannot be explained, but it is a fact.

Maimonides seems to concur with this characterization. He writes (*Hilkhot Megilla* 1:1):

> *Reading the Megilla on the appropriate day is a rabbinic ordinance, and it is well-known that it was instituted by the prophets.*

The second clause, "and it is well-known that it was instituted by the prophets," *prima facie*, appears to be unnecessary. Maimonides' style is generally very terse. Of course, it is true that the mitzva of reading the Megilla was introduced by the *Anshei Knesset HaGedola*, which was comprised of many prophets. Why, however, is it necessary for Maimonides to add that this was legislated by prophets?

Interestingly, when Maimonides discusses the mitzvot of *kevod ve'oneg Shabbat*, which are mentioned in Isaiah (58:13), he writes: "Four principles have been formulated with reference to Shabbat, two of which are mandated by the Torah, and two of which are rabbinic in origin, but were explicated by the prophets" (*Hilkhot Shabbat* 30:1). Likewise, when discussing the four fast days, Maimonides writes (*Hilkhot Ta'aniyot* 5:5): "These four fast days were explicated by the prophets." What additional message does Maimonides intend to convey with these words?

It seems that this group of mitzvot which have been documented in Scripture are treated by Maimonides as a separate entity. Though these mitzvot cannot be classified as *mitzvot de'oraita*, they are nevertheless mentioned and described by the prophets. Maimonides wishes to underscore that even though these mitzvot are rabbinically mandated, the book which deals with them, which narrates the events which lead up to them, which describes the mitzvot, formulates their obligations and defines their precepts, is part of *Torah Shebikhtav*. Maimonides likewise stresses the fact that the document of Purim is part of the *Torah Shebikhtav* even though it was first introduced by *Anshei Knesset HaGedola*.

A parallel

A parallel phenomenon exists in Maimonides' use of the term *divrei sofrim*. In general, Maimonides uses the term "*divrei sofrim*" to denote rabbinic imperatives. But there are exceptions, in which the term *divrei sofrim* is used to connote a *de'oraita* law. These exceptions are with respect to *kiddushei kesef* (*Hilkhot Ishut* 1:2) and impurities for which the *nazir* must shave his hair (*Hilkhot Tumat Met* 5:2), which he describes as *midivrei sofrim*, even though both of those halakhot are *de'oraita*. He does so since those two halakhot could never have been derived from *peshuto shel mikra*, the plain sense of the Torah. Rather, a tradition was required in order to establish these halakhot. However, these cases are the exception to the rule. Generally, Maimonides employs the term *midivrei sofrim* to denote a rule which is rabbinically mandated.

Whether the Megilla is actually part of Scripture is the subject of a controversy among the Sages of the Mishna (*Megilla* 7a). Some maintain that the Megilla is not part of Scripture. They therefore rule that Megillat Esther is not subject to the same laws of ritual defilement as are the other scrolls of Tanakh. We have accepted the opinion that Esther is an integral part of Scripture.

The Gemara (*ibid.*) relates that Esther was confronted with two issues. The first was the issue of establishing Purim as a permanent holiday. The *Anshei Knesset HaGedola* were in doubt whether to impose it as a holiday or not. The *Anshei Knesset HaGedola* acceded to that request and Purim was established as a holiday. Esther then insisted that Megillat Esther be declared as part of Scripture since it was written with divine inspiration.

The Megilla describes the dialogue between Esther and the Sages (Es. 9:30-31):

> *And they sent out scrolls to all the Jews, across one hundred and twenty-seven provinces, all of Ahasuerus' realm – words of peace and truth. The scrolls were to confirm these days of Purim in their times, just as Mordekhai the Jew and Esther the queen had fixed them; and, indeed, as they had all fixed their fast days and entreaties.*

Esther demanded that Purim be made equal in importance and significance to that of the four fast days. What is the link between the fast days and Purim? Esther apparently asked the *Anshei Knesset HaGedola* to incorporate and integrate Megillat Esther within Tanakh. The *Anshei*

Knesset HaGedola declined, because they reasoned that if Megillat Esther would be incorporated within Tanakh, the holiday of Purim would, *ipso facto*, become a *de'oraita* institution. How is it possible, they asked, for a *mitzva derabbanan* to be mentioned, to be described and to be recorded in a book whose sanctity equals that of *Shema Yisrael*? They felt that this would be an internal contradiction. Moreover, they felt that this would be a violation of the prohibition against adding to the Torah (Deut. 4:2).

Esther responded that a similar precedent is found with respect to the four fast days. Though the fast days are a rabbinic institution, they are mentioned in Zechariah. Thus, she argued that this paradox has already been accepted. An institution which is only rabbinic is described, recorded and reported in Tanakh. Accordingly, Purim should be made the equal of the fast days.

The verse continues:

וּמַאֲמַר אֶסְתֵּר קִיַּם דִּבְרֵי הַפֻּרִים הָאֵלֶּה וְנִכְתָּב בַּסֵּפֶר.

> *And so, Esther's word confirmed this practice of Purim; and it was written down in the scroll.*

The word קִיַּם used in this verse does not mean that Esther implemented the observance of the holiday of Purim. She did much more than that. The word קִיַּם means that Esther authenticated the holiday of Purim, insofar as the scroll was incorporated among the books of Tanakh. As Rashi comments: "Esther requested that the Rabbis incorporate this book together with the other *Ketuvim*; this is what the phrase וְנִכְתָּב בַּסֵּפֶר denotes."

The Megilla is called Megillat Esther and not Megillat Mordekhai. Why? Mordekhai played the same role as Esther. If not for Mordekhai, Esther would never have appeared before Ahasuerus, would never have pleaded before Ahasuerus and would never have rescued her people. Mordekhai's sense of responsibility and commitment to his people saved the community from being exterminated. Why then is it called Megillat Esther and not Megillat Mordekhai? Apparently, it was Esther who persisted in arguing that this "letter of Purim" be incorporated among the books of Tanakh. The verse relates (Es. 9:29):

> *And Esther, daughter of Aviḥayil, the queen, together with Mordekhai the Jew, wrote with all their authority, for this second letter of Purim to be confirmed.*

◂ Apparently

Apparently, Mordekhai appeared before the *Sanhedrin*, advanced the request that the *iggeret*, letter, be integrated as part of Tanakh, and was turned down. Esther was the one who devised the argument that an identical precedent had already been established with respect to the four fast days. Esther's reasoning was accepted by the *Sanhedrin* and the "letter of Purim" was incorporated as a book of Tanakh, וְנִכְתָּב בַּסֵּפֶר.

THE NATURE OF THE MITZVA OF MEGILLA READING

In discussing the laws of *Keriat HaTorah* and its *berakhot*, *Masekhet Sofrim* (14:3) dictates that "One must make a *berakha* of *al mikra megilla* when reading from the Song of Songs, Ruth, Lamentations, and Esther." Implicit in this statement is that the root of the obligation to make a *berakha* is identical for each of these Megillot, and therefore the *berakha* itself is the same for them. More specifically for our purposes, it should be noted that the reading of Megillat Esther is being equated with the reading of *Ketuvim* in general.

This inference may be used to understand a puzzling omission in the Gemara. The Gemara in two places (*Shabbat* 23a; *Sukka* 46a) discusses how we can recite a *berakha*, including the word "*vetzivanu*, He commanded us," on the Ḥanukka lights, when the mitzva is rabbinically enacted. But nowhere does the Gemara discuss the basis for the *berakha* over the Megilla reading, although this obligation is only rabbinic in nature as well.

According to *Masekhet Sofrim*, however, just as the *berakha* of *al mikra megilla* is recited when reading the other four scrolls, although there is no mitzva to do so, so too the *berakha* is recited on reading Megillat Esther. In other words, the *berakha* is recited not on the rabbinic mitzva of reading the Megilla but rather as a *berakha* on the corpus of Torah (in this case, *Ketuvim*). In a similar vein, Rav Ḥayim Soloveitchik explained the view of *Shulḥan Arukh* that women are to recite *Birkot HaTorah* each day, although the *Shulḥan Arukh* maintains that women may not recite *berakhot* on mitzvot for which they are not obligated – the explanation, according to Rav Ḥayim, is that these blessings are not recited on the mitzva of Torah study but on the corpus of the Torah itself.

◂ This principle

This principle that the mitzva to read Megillat Esther is subsumed under the category of reading *Ketuvim* may be further established from the ruling of the Yerushalmi (*Megilla* 3:4) that the Megilla may not be read on Shabbat because of the prohibition against reading from *Ketuvim* on Shabbat. If the requirement to read the Megilla would be an independent mitzva specific to Megillat Esther, then it would not be included in the prohibition to read from *Ketuvim* as it has effectively been removed from that category. From the Yerushalmi's reason, it is clear that the Megilla is read not as an independent entity but is considered part of the general category of reading *Ketuvim*.

Ḥiddushei HaRan (*Megilla* 5a) lends support to the premise that reading the Megilla is included under the category of reading Scripture. Ran writes that according to the opinion which requires a quorum of ten men in order to read the Megilla, it is nevertheless not listed in the Mishna among the other mitzvot which require a quorum because it is included in reading from the Torah and Nevi'im, which are mentioned in the Mishna.

The Gemara (*Megilla* 18a) states that a foreigner who hears the Megilla in Hebrew fulfills his obligation, even though he does not understand the words, as there is a mitzva of "reading and publicizing the miracle (*pirsumei nisa*)." It would seem that there are two components to the mitzva: reading from Scripture, and publicizing the miracle. With this principle, we can explain the two separate blessings made before reading the Megilla: *al mikra megilla*, as discussed above, is for the reading of Scripture, and *she'asah nissim* is a *berakha* for the *pirsumei nisa* component.

Based on this, we can understand another difficult Gemara. The Gemara (*Megilla* 19a-b) states that one may not read the Megilla from a scroll containing the rest of *Ketuvim*; the Gemara qualifies that this ruling applies only to a public reading. This requires explanation – why should this be invalid in public but not in private? The answer, it would seem, is that since such a scroll may be used in public for the purpose of reading *Ketuvim*, there is no element of *pirsumei nisa* when such a scroll is used for the Megilla; in private, however, any reading from a scroll constitutes *pirsumei nisa*.

Tosafot (*Megilla* 5a) discuss whether one who reads the Megilla in private must recite a blessing before its reading or not. At first glance, this

◂ doubt

doubt is difficult to understand – why would one entertain the possibility that fulfilling the mitzva in private does not require a *berakha*? However, according to the previously established principle, we can understand the doubt of Tosafot. Since in private one lacks the element of reading *Ketuvim* in public, it is conceivable that one would not recite the blessing, because the blessing was instituted for reading *Ketuvim* in public, as per *Masekhet Sofrim*. Tosafot decide the issue in favor of making a blessing even when reading alone; yet we may explain that this is because even private reading of the Megilla constitutes a fulfillment of the reading of *Ketuvim*.

With this principle we can also explain the view of the *Ba'al Halakhot Gedolot* (quoted in Tosafot, *Megilla* 4a) who maintains that women are obligated only in hearing the Megilla read, but are not obligated to read it. According to *Turei Even* (*Megilla, ibid.*) women are only obligated in the rabbinic mitzva of Megilla, because they were part of the miracles, but not in the mitzva on the level of prophetic enactment, *divrei kabbala*. We may now explain that a woman's obligation consists only of the *pirsumei nisa* element (as women were included in the miracle), but not the element of reading *Ketuvim*. The element of reading *Ketuvim* stems from the obligation of Talmud Torah from which women are exempt, and therefore they are exempt from this aspect of the mitzva. This understanding is supported by R. Moses of Coucy (*Semag, Hilkhot Megilla*) who writes that women cannot read the Megilla for men, "as reading the Megilla is like *Keriat HaTorah* and therefore she cannot help him discharge his obligation."

A similar explanation can be given for why women customarily did not listen to the reading of *Parashat Zakhor*. *Sefer HaḤinukh* (mitzva 603) writes that women are not obligated in this mitzva because they are exempt from waging war, and this mitzva is for the purpose of waging war against Amalek. However, *Minḥat Ḥinukh* raises two objections to this theory: First, how can one base the laws of a mitzva on the speculative theory that the mitzva of remembering Amalek is for the purpose of eradicating Amalek? Second, the Mishna (*Sota* 44b) explicitly obligates women in obligatory wars, of which the war against Amalek is a prime example. However, there may be another reason to exempt women from the mitzva of remembering Amalek. Ravad, in his commentary on *Sifra* (*Beḥukotai* 1:3), comments that the obligation of remembering Amalek

◂ requires

requires studying the laws of Megilla. If so, the mitzva of remembering Amalek is categorized as Talmud Torah, from which women are exempt.

Finally, if reading the Megilla constitutes Talmud Torah, then the Gemara's statement (*Megilla* 3a), "מבטלין תלמוד תורה לשמוע מקרא מגילה, One must interrupt the study of Torah in order to hear the reading of the Megilla," is difficult to understand. Doesn't reading the Megilla also constitute Talmud Torah? How then can reading the Megilla be considered interrupting Talmud Torah? The answer is that Talmud Torah is not a uniform mitzva; it is a question of degree. There is a difference between reading verses without understanding and analyzing a Talmudic *sugya*. Both performances constitute Talmud Torah, but there is a hierarchy which establishes levels of Talmud Torah. This is the sense in which reading the Megilla can be seen as an interruption of Talmud Torah.

CANTILLATION OF THE MEGILLA

Sha'arei Teshuva (*Oraḥ Ḥayim* 690:1), citing *Beit Yehuda*, records that "there are places in which it is the custom to read [Megillat Esther] without the cantillation; but this should not be done." My father, Rav Moshe Soloveitchik, used to say that in fact there is no need to be meticulous with the cantillation of the Megilla, in accordance with the custom quoted in *Beit Yehuda*. [Cf. *Mishna Berura* (691:25) who likens the reading of the Megilla to the reading of the Torah for which we are careful to cantillate properly.]

The reason for my father's opinion is as follows. The Gemara (*Nedarim* 37b; *Megilla* 3a) derives the halakha of reading with cantillation from a verse in Nehemiah (8:8), with the following *derasha*: "'And they read in the book, the Torah of God' – this is the Scriptural text; 'distinctly' – this is the translation; 'and they gave the sense' – these are the divisions of the text into separate verses; 'and they caused them to understand the reading' – these are the cantillation notes."

From this *derasha* it is evident that the halakha of reading with the cantillation notes has nothing to do with the requirements of the actual reading obligation, as is the case with the requirement to properly read the words. Rather, the obligation of reading the verses with their cantillation notes stems from the element of Torah study encompassed in the

◂ reading

reading of the Torah; this requires the proper exposition of the Torah, which is accomplished by reading the verses with their cantillation notes.

This is clear as well from the fact that the Gemara implies that the cantillation is a part of the Oral Torah, despite the fact that it is the cantillation of the written word. This indicates that the cantillation is required as an elucidation of the written word, an idea compelled by the verse: "and they caused them to understand the reading," which is a requirement of Torah study. Just as the translation of the Torah, derived from this verse, is certainly a component of the Oral Torah (as the Targum was given to Moses at Sinai), so too is the cantillation an element of the Oral Torah, which explains the written word.

It may therefore be concluded that only with regard to *Keriat HaTorah*, which is an obligation of communal Torah study, is the cantillation required. However, the reading of Megillat Esther, which has no component of Torah study, does not necessitate the use of the cantillation, considering that the cantillation is only required as a form of the Oral Torah, and as an elucidation of the written word, and the reading of the Megilla does not constitute Torah study which would require explanation.

The fact that the reading of Megillat Esther does not constitute communal Torah study is implied by the Gemara (*Megilla* 3a) which states: "We interrupt Torah study for the reading of the Megilla," indicating that the Megilla itself is not a fulfillment of Torah study.

According to this reasoning, that the reading of the Megilla is an obligation unrelated to Torah study, and considering that the reading of the Targum is necessary as an elucidation of the reading only where the study of the text is required, it should follow that there is no need to translate the Megilla reading. However, the Gemara (*Megilla* 21b) states: "With regard to Hallel and the Megilla, even ten people may read and ten people may translate." Rashi emends the text by removing the words "and ten people may translate," explaining that there is no Targum for the *Ketuvim*. However, Tosafot argue with Rashi, and maintain the text. This would be problematic, since as explained, there should be no need for the Targum with regard to Megillat Esther. The answer presents itself, however, that the need for reading the Targum of Megillat Esther doesn't stem from the same obligation as that of Torah reading, which is of the nature of Torah study, rather it is an independent halakha related to the

◂ concept of

concept of *pirsumei nisa*, or publicizing the miracle. (The question can then be asked though, why *pirsumei nisa* would not require the cantillation as well, according to this reasoning.)

Naḥmanides in his comments on the Gemara (*Megilla* 19a) which states that "the Megilla is referred to as a book and it is referred to as a letter," explains that with regard to issues extraneous to the Megilla scroll itself, such as how the Megilla is read, its laws are like those of a letter and not a book, which is why one may read the Megilla while sitting or standing, unlike the reading of the Torah which must be done while standing. Naḥmanides concludes by saying that one may interrupt the reading of the Megilla in the middle of a verse, since with regard to its reading it has the status of a letter. This means that although the verses of the Torah may not be broken up due to the rule that "any verse that Moses did not divide, we may not divide," the Megilla is different, since it is read like a letter. Based on this we can conclude that there is no need for cantillation when reading the Megilla.

Ritva articulates this idea explicitly: "My teacher says that with regard to issues that are inherent [to the physical text of the Megilla], such as scoring and ink, it has the status of a book. However, with regard to something extraneous, it has the status of a letter, to be read both standing and sitting. Therefore, it is the custom to read it without the cantillation, and without the division of verses."

However, in truth, the reasoning of Ritva and Naḥmanides is different than that expressed by my father. According to my father, cantillation is not required when reading Megillat Esther because it does not have the status of Torah learning, and cantillation is a requirement which relates to Torah study. According to Ritva and Naḥmanides, however, the requirement of cantillation depends on whether it is read as a book or as a letter. Moreover, it would appear from their words that cantillation is inherent to the laws of reading, and is always required when reading Scripture, unless it is read as a letter. This would seem to contradict the opinion of my father about why cantillation is not required for the Megilla.

READING THE MEGILLA ON BEHALF OF ANOTHER

Maimonides (*Hilkhot Megilla* 1:2) writes: "Whether one reads for himself or hears the Megilla from another, he fulfills his obligation." Maimonides seems to equate one who reads the Megilla on his own to one who hears it from another, implying that one can fulfill his obligation through hearing the Megilla alone even on a *lekhatḥila* (ideal) level. This would seem to be based on the principle of *shome'a ke'oneh* – that one who hears is like one who recites – and therefore we treat the listener like one who actually reads himself.

Yet Tosafot (*Berakhot* 21b s.v. *ad* and *Sukka* 38b s.v. *shema*) write that when it comes to Kaddish and Kedusha, it is preferable that one actually respond and not simply listen because recital is considered *hiddur mitzva*, a preferable way to perform the mitzva. This would seem to contradict the view of Maimonides who holds that listening is the same as reading without reservation.

In reality, however, there is no dispute. Tosafot are only referring to the recitation of Kedusha in which there is a reading followed by a response, for this constitutes a *davar shebikedusha*, as is the case with regard to Hallel and the Song of the Sea (see *Sota* 30b). It is only in these areas where Tosafot claim that it is preferable for one to actually recite the words. [In fact, *Shibbolei HaLeket* (*siman* 20) holds that the concept of *shome'a ke'oneh* is inapplicable with regard to Kedusha.] With regard to the Megilla, however, where there is only an element of recital and not one of response, there is no difference whether one recites it himself or hears it from another and fulfills his obligation through *shome'a ke'oneh*. One could differentiate further by noting that regarding Kedusha, there is an ideal of reciting it in a clear and pleasant voice which one can fulfill only by reciting it himself. Megilla has no such ideal and thus one can fulfill the mitzva even *lekhatḥila* by listening.

We find a surprising view regarding reading the Megilla on behalf of others in *Shulḥan Arukh* (*Oraḥ Ḥayim* 689:8), who writes that in a place lacking a *minyan* of ten adult men, those capable of reading the Megilla for themselves must read it individually. *Magen Avraham* (689:10) explains that according to this view, the laws regarding the reading of the Megilla are similar to those of prayer, in which the leader can exempt only those who are unable to pray on their own.

◂ We can

We can explain the reasoning of *Magen Avraham* in two ways. First, Rav Naḥman (*Megilla* 14a) states that reading the Megilla on Purim takes the place of Hallel. If so, just as with regard to Hallel one can exempt only those who are unable to recite it on their own (*Magen Avraham* 422:5), the same is true for reading the Megilla as well.

Alternatively, reading the Megilla, in addition to its fulfillment as reading of Scripture, is also a fulfillment of prayer, and it therefore follows the rules of prayer. Rashi (*Megilla* 4a) explains that the reason we read the Megilla both at night and during the day is in commemoration of the miracle that occurred, imitating the way that Mordekhai, Esther and the rest of the Jews prayed during their time of sorrow throughout the day and night. This repetition can be further understood by viewing the reading in light of prayer, where *Ḥazal* teach that if one is not answered following his first prayer he should repeat the prayer. Our prayer through reading the Megilla serves as a request addressed to God to remember the way in which He redeemed the Jews through the miracle of Purim, asking that He in turn redeem us as well.

WOMEN'S OBLIGATION IN MEGILLA ACCORDING TO *HALAKHOT GEDOLOT* AND *MIDRASH HANE'ELAM*

Magen Avraham (689:6) cites an enigmatic view of the *Midrash HaNe'elam* on Ruth according to which a woman should not read the Megilla for herself, but should instead hear a man's reading. This view requires explanation. Why shouldn't a woman read the Megilla to discharge her own obligation? The opinion of *Halakhot Gedolot*, cited by *Shulḥan Arukh* (*Oraḥ Ḥayim* 689:2), is that women cannot read the Megilla on behalf of men. Ostensibly, this view maintains that while men are obligated to read the Megilla, women are obligated only to listen (see Tosafot, *Megilla* 4a s.v. *nashim*). If so, there is no reason that a woman should not read the Megilla to fulfill her own obligation. However, the *Hagahot Maimoniyot* (*Hilkhot Megilla* 1) cites a passage in the Yerushalmi which presents another possible explanation for the opinion of the *Halakhot Gedolot*. The Yerushalmi (*Megilla* 2:5) states, "Bar Kapara said: One must read [the Megilla] before women and children, since they too were in a state of crisis. Rabbi Yehoshua ben

◂ Levi followed

Levi followed this ruling – he would gather his children and household and read it before them."

According to the Yerushalmi, women are obligated in the Megilla as members of the household but do not have an individual obligation. Thus, when the *Halakhot Gedolot* states that women are obligated to hear the Megilla, this is because women are obligated only as part of a communal entity. This also explains the view of *Magen Avraham* that women should not read the Megilla for themselves but rather should hear a man's reading: According to this view, the structure of the enactment is that women should hear the Megilla being read as part of the community, but they do not have an independent obligation themselves.

THE MINIMUM TEXT OF THE MEGILLA READING

The Mishna (*Megilla* 19a) states: "From where does one read the Megilla and thereby fulfill his obligation? Rabbi Meir says: All of it. Rabbi Judah says: From 'Now there was a Jewish man…' (2:5). Rabbi Yosi says: From 'Some time after this [King Ahasuerus ennobled Haman]…' (3:1)." The Gemara concludes that the law follows Rabbi Meir. Maimonides, however, uses a peculiar expression in codifying this law, writing "it is a mitzva to read all of it" (*Hilkhot Megilla* 1:3). This implies that while one should preferably read the Megilla in its entirety, it is not mandatory to do so. Thus, one who reads only a portion of the Megilla has fulfilled some aspect of the obligation. Maimonides may distinguish between the fulfillment of Hallel inherent in the Megilla reading, and the technical act of reading the Megilla itself. Although the latter requires the reading of the entire text (as is the case with regard to other obligatory texts, such as the reading of *Megillat Sota* and the *Parashat Bikkurim*), the fulfillment of Hallel does not require reading the entire text. Nevertheless, this explanation remains difficult.

There is a parallel to this phenomenon in another mitzva, namely *Keriat Shema*. Here too, reading a portion of the text suffices for the discharge of certain facets of the mitzva. This is true even if the recitation of all three chapters of *Keriat Shema* is Biblically mandated. The Gemara states (*Berakhot* 17a) that members of the funeral procession are exempt from reciting *Shema*. If after returning from the burial, there is time to recite only one chapter or one verse it should nevertheless be recited. We can infer from this that although one is required to recite all three chapters, there is a level of fulfillment achieved by reading even a portion of *Shema*. This principle may apply to Megilla as well, except that with regard to Megilla the minimum portion which must be read is delineated by the Mishna as containing either *tokfo shel Haman,* the story of Haman, or *tokfo shel Mordekhai,* the story of Mordekhai.

THE NATURE OF *MATANOT LA'EVYONIM*

With regard to the mitzva of *matanot la'evyonim,* which obligates each individual to give gifts to at least two poor people on Purim, one can raise the following question: Is this part of the general mitzva of *tzedaka,* or is it a separate obligation which is part of the joy of Purim, like the mitzvot of *mishloaḥ manot* and *seudat Purim*? A possible ramification of this question is whether the funds that one distributes on Purim count toward fulfilling the concept of *ma'aser kesafim,* tithing for charity. If *matanot la'evyonim* is part of the general mitzva of *tzedaka,* then the Purim funds should count toward *ma'aser kesafim.* But if *matanot la'evyonim* is a distinct Purim obligation, it stands to reason that the money used for this mitzva does not count toward *ma'aser kesafim* (see *Magen Avraham* 694:1 citing Maharil).

In fact, it seems that this question is the subject of a dispute among the commentators. The Targum (Es. 9:22) translates *matanot la'evyonim* as "money for charity," clearly relating to this mitzva as one of *tzedaka.* My grandfather, R. Ḥayim Soloveitchik, also considered this obligation to be a subset of the general mitzva of *tzedaka.* However, Maimonides' view (*Hilkhot Megilla* 2:17), that it is better to increase *matanot la'evyonim* than *mishloaḥ manot,* "for there is no greater and grander joy than to gladden the hearts of the poor, the orphans, the widows, and the converts," implies that this is part of the mitzva of rejoicing on Purim, and not the general mitzva of *tzedaka.*

Regarding the general obligation of *tzedaka,* we must sometimes determine the eligibility of the recipient (see *Bava Batra* 9a); with regard to Purim, however, the Yerushalmi (*Megilla* 1:4) states that "whoever extends his hand to receive – we give him." It would seem from this discrepancy between the halakhot of *matanot la'evyonim* and of ordinary *tzedaka* that the mitzva of *matanot la'evyonim* is an independent mitzva relating to the joy of Purim. [Naḥmanides and Ritva (*Bava Metzia* 78b) write explicitly that the reason for the discrepancy regarding *matanot la'evyonim* is that the mitzva of *matanot la'evyonim* is not merely charity but is also based on the joy of Purim. See also Tosafot (*Bava Metzia ibid.*) who ask why one cannot divert *matanot la'evyonim* funds for another charitable purpose when regarding other charity funds this is permitted. This question implies that *matanot la'evyonim* is an instance of charity; otherwise, we have no reason to assume the rules of charity apply to *matanot la'evyonim. Tosafot HaRosh* resolve the question by positing that the Purim funds are different from other charity funds because of the mitzva of Purim joy. – *Ed.*]

THE PROHIBITION OF *MELAKHA* ON PURIM

According to the Gemara (*Megilla* 5b), Mordekhai originally thought to prohibit *melakha* (labor) on Purim, but the Jewish people did not accept this prohibition – we see this from the fact that initially (Es. 9:19), Purim is referred to as "*yom tov*," but subsequently (Es. 9:22) only as a day of "*mishteh vesimḥa*" (feast and rejoicing) without the words "*yom tov*." To understand the nature of the prohibition of *melakha* which Mordekhai wished to institute, it is instructive to examine some additional cases in which there is a limitation on *melakha*. Performance of *melakha* while drawing the water for preparation of the *Para Aduma* ashes invalidates the ashes. Ravad (*Hilkhot Para Aduma* 7:3) explains that in this case, performing *melakha* is disqualifying not in its own right but because the labor constitutes *hese'aḥ hada'at* (distraction), and the distraction invalidates the ashes. Similarly, Mordekhai's initial proposal to prohibit *melakha* on Purim was not a prohibition of *melakha per se*, as is the case on other holidays, but a prohibition which emanates from the obligation of *simḥa* on Purim – *melakha* would have been prohibited only because it would detract from the joy of the day. This explanation for the prohibition of *melakha* relates as well to the prohibition of *melakha* on *Ḥol HaMoed*. Ritva (*Moed Katan* 13a, in the name of R. Yedidya) explains that unlike the prohibition of *melakha* on Yom Tov proper, the prohibition on *Ḥol HaMoed* is a result of the obligation of *simḥat Yom Tov*. Likewise, that the

◂ prohibition

prohibition for a mourner to perform *melakha* during the seven days of mourning is because performing *melakha* constitutes *hese'aḥ hada'at* from the feeling of mourning.

AVELUT AND *SIMḤA* ON PURIM

There is a dispute between *Shulḥan Arukh* and Rema (*Oraḥ Ḥayim* 696:4) whether a mourner who is in the midst of the seven days of mourning practices *avelut* on Purim. According to *Shulḥan Arukh,* the mourning practices continue, while Rema maintains that Purim is not a day of mourning, but unlike Yom Tov, it does not cancel the remaining days of mourning either. At first glance, both views are difficult to understand. Purim is a day of joy, and Yom Tov cancels *avelut* because of the mitzva of joy (*Moed Katan* 14b). If so it would seem that on Purim there should be no mourning practices, and the *avelut* should be canceled as well.

In fact, however, there is a basic distinction between Yom Tov and Purim. On Yom Tov, the mitzva of joy stems from the inherent *kedushat hayom,* sanctity of the day; and it is the fact that the day itself is one of joy which cancels the *avelut.* Since the mourning period is viewed as a unit, once the day of Yom Tov interrupts the *avelut,* it cancels the remainder as well. On Purim, however, the mitzva of joy is not part of the character of the day itself, because Purim does not possess *kedushat hayom.* The dispute between *Shulḥan Arukh* and Rema, therefore, is whether the mitzva of joy alone is enough to suspend the rules of *avelut* for that day, but all agree that the *avelut* is not canceled altogether.

In addition, on Yom Tov, the mitzva of joy is based on being in the presence of God, *lifnei Hashem,* as the Torah states, "and you shall rejoice before the LORD your God" (Deut. 16:11). This aspect of joy cancels the *avelut,* as seen in the following halakha. The Gemara (*Moed Katan* 14b) states that the *Kohen Gadol* does not observe *avelut,* because every day for the Kohen Gadol has the same status that Yom Tov has for everyone else. How are we to understand this equation between the daily life of the Kohen Gadol and Yom Tov for everyone else? In codifying this halakha, Maimonides (*Hilkhot Bi'at Mikdash* 1:10) adds the explanation, "for he is always in the Temple." In other words, because the *Kohen Gadol* is to be found in the Temple, the place of God's presence, his every day has the status of a Yom Tov, in which we are all in God's presence. The fact that Yom Tov cancels *avelut* is not based on the mitzva of joy alone – after all, the *Kohen Gadol* does not have a constant mitzva to rejoice – but on the joy that stems from being in the presence of God.

In truth, the two distinctions between Yom Tov and Purim are one and the same. Yom Tov possesses *kedushat hayom,* transforming the day into one which takes place in the presence of God. Purim, on the other hand, does not possess *kedushat hayom* and therefore the day does not share this transformative character.*

This distinction between Yom Tov and Purim is also manifest in the way the joy of each expresses itself. Regarding Purim, "Rava said: One is obligated to become inebriated until he cannot distinguish between 'Cursed be Haman' and 'Blessed be Mordekhai'" (*Megilla* 7b). Maimonides (*Hilkhot Megilla* 2:15) codifies this as well. However, on Yom Tov, we have never come across a law or a norm that would require a person to become drunk. To the contrary, Maimonides emphasizes that we should not get drunk:

> When one eats and drinks and rejoices on the festivals, he must not overindulge in wine, in frivolity, or in light-headedness ... For drunkenness and frivolity are not *simḥa,* but rather licentiousness and folly, and we were not commanded as to licentiousness and folly but rather as to the *simḥa* in the service of Creator of all (*Hilkhot Yom Tov* 6:20).

Also, as far as the *simḥa* of Yom Tov is concerned, our Sages introduced the concept of "*ḥetzyo laShem veḥetzyo lakhem,* half of the day is dedicated to God and half of the day is dedicated to you" (*Pesaḥim* 68b). Half of the festival is dedicated to serious worship, to service, to intellectual pursuits, to Torah. The *simḥa* expresses itself in an intellectual gesture – in Torah

* When asked whether *avelut* applies on Purim, the Rav responded that for Ashkenazim who follow the rulings of Rema, he would instruct them not to sit *shiva* on Purim, or even on Shushan Purim, as Rema rules. However, it should be noted that after the Rav's wife passed away on Ta'anit Esther in 1967, the Rav sat *shiva* on Purim as well, in accordance with the view of *Shulḥan Arukh. – Ed.*

study. On Yom Tov, the feeling of joy and the awareness of the unseen presence of the Almighty are identical. Man experiences His companionship, and then there is joy, in the sense of self-fulfillment. By contrast, on Purim, it is a superficial mood – not an inner experience – that is evoked, because on Purim there is apparently no concept of *lifnei Hashem*, of rejoicing in the presence of God.

READING THE MEGILLA IN SHUSHAN AND IN WALLED CITIES

Naḥmanides (*Megilla* 2a) asks why we find a distinction between residents of cities which had a wall at the time of Joshua, who read the Megilla on the fifteenth of Adar, and residents of ordinary cities, who read on the fourteenth, a concept which has no parallel in any other mitzva. He offers the following theory to explain this anomaly. The original Purim was celebrated on different days by the people in Shushan and the other cities, as the Megilla itself states (Es. 9:17-18): "Meanwhile, the rest of the Jews in the king's provinces … on the fourteenth they rested, and made it a day of feasting and happiness. And the Jews who were in Shushan came together both on the thirteenth and on the fourteenth, and rested on the fifteenth, and made that a day of feasting and happiness."

Naḥmanides explains that the original Purim festival was observed by the people immediately after the battle. They celebrated spontaneously without any formal rabbinic decree. However, the people in the walled cities believed that they had not been exposed to danger, since they thought that they had the ability to defend themselves. On the other hand, those who did not live in walled cities were very vulnerable, and so they celebrated their rescue on the first Purim on the fourteenth day of Adar. The people in Shushan celebrated their rescue, in that year, on the fifteenth day of Adar, since they engaged in combat for an additional day.

Accordingly, the next verse immediately continues (Es. 9:19): "Thus it came about that provincial Jews, living in unwalled towns, make the fourteenth day of the month of Adar a day of happiness, of feasting and festivity, and of sending one another good things to eat." The verse clearly states that in the years following the miracle, only the residents of the unwalled cities began a tradition of observing the Purim holiday; the

◂ residents

residents of the walled cities are not mentioned since they did not feel the need to celebrate Purim at all. Later on, the Rabbis and Mordekhai accepted the people's practice, and instituted a holiday based upon the rationale of the residents of the unwalled cities.

Unlike the holiday of Ḥanukka, which was imposed by the Rabbis initially upon the occurrence of the miracles, Purim originated with the spontaneous practice of the people (*minhag*), and was subsequently ratified as a holiday by legislation of Mordekhai and the *Anshei Knesset HaGedola*. They stipulated that the holiday be celebrated formally in the same manner as the initial Purim was celebrated. Thus, the residents of unwalled cities were to celebrate Purim on the fourteenth, as they had on the original Purim, while the residents of Shushan celebrated it on the fifteenth day. However, with regard to the residents of the walled cities, who had not participated in the celebration of the original Purim, and who, unlike the residents of the unwalled cities did not have an established practice which could simply be ratified, the Rabbis were compelled to establish a special date for their holiday. The Rabbis felt that it was necessary to penalize and rebuke the residents of the walled cities for wrongfully concluding that they had not been exposed to any danger. Thus, the Rabbis imposed the holiday for those people on the day after the one celebrated by the residents of the unwalled cities. Coincidentally, this is also the day celebrated by the residents of Shushan.

This is Naḥmanides' theory, and it has halakhic ramifications as well. According to Naḥmanides, the celebration on the fourteenth is a prerequisite (*matir*) for the celebration of the walled cities on the fifteenth. This can be deduced from the Gemara (*Megilla* 19a) which states that "if a resident of an unwalled city travels to a walled city and anticipates returning to his hometown, he should read [the Megilla] as in his hometown [i.e., on the fourteenth]." Rashi explains that if at daybreak on the fourteenth one is in a city which reads on the fourteenth, he must read with them, and if at daybreak on the fifteenth he is in a city which reads on the fifteenth he reads with them.

Ravad, however, disagrees with Rashi's interpretation. Ravad rules that the determining factor is always the traveler's location on the fourteenth of Adar. Thus, one who visits a walled city on the fourteenth must now read the Megilla on the fifteenth, since on the fourteenth he was present in a walled city. This is true even if he plans on departing from the walled city prior to the morning of the fifteenth. Conversely, a resident of a walled city who is in an unwalled city on the fourteenth must read the Megilla on the fourteenth, since his presence on the fourteenth deems him a member of the unwalled city.

Why, according to Ravad, is the status of the traveler always dependent on where he will be on the morning of the fourteenth? The conclusion to be drawn from the position of Ravad is that the fourteenth is the obligating factor (*meḥayev*) which both obligates members of the unwalled cities to read on this day, and simultaneously obligates residents of the walled cities to read on the fifteenth. The fifteenth is only the time for the performance of the mitzva, but the obligating factor is the daybreak of the fourteenth. The fact that the fourteenth day serves as the obligating day serves as a rebuke to the residents of the walled cities for refusing to collaborate with their brethren and for being so confident that they were secure from attack.

In sum, according to Naḥmanides, for the residents of Shushan, the obligating factor is the fifteenth, while for the residents of the walled cities the obligating factor is the fourteenth, even though the celebration is deferred until the fifteenth.

This theory of Naḥmanides explains beautifully why the Megilla pointedly fails to mention the practice of the residents of the walled cities.

Maimonides, however, has an entirely different interpretation for the institution of the fifteenth as the day of celebration for Shushan and the walled cities. In *Hilkhot Megilla* (1:5), Maimonides writes:

> Shushan, the capital city, even though it was not walled in the times of Joshua, reads on the fifteenth, since the miracle occurred there, as it says (Es. 9:18), "[And the Jews who were in Shushan came together both on the thirteenth and on the fourteenth,] and rested on the fifteenth." And why did they make the matter dependent on the days of Joshua? In order to allocate respect to the Land of Israel which was in a state of destruction at that time: in order that [residents of those cities] should read as do the residents of Shushan, and be considered as if these were walled cities. Even though they were then in a state of destruction, since

◂ they were

> they were walled in the times of Joshua, they read on the fifteenth; and through this there is a commemoration of the Land of Israel in this miracle.

What do Maimonides' words, "since the miracle occurred there," convey? According to Maimonides, Shushan was singled out for a separate day of celebration because the people of Shushan participated more actively in the miracle. The populace of Shushan cooperated with Esther in fasting for three days, and the entire city mourned Haman's decree and rejoiced at his defeat. This is the meaning of the phrase, "since the miracle occurred there" – since the people of Shushan participated in the miracle to a greater extent than anyone else, they were accorded a separate day of celebration as a mark of distinction. This stands in contrast with Naḥmanides' view that Shushan celebrates on the fifteenth to commemorate the date of its residents' spontaneous celebration.

Maimonides then asks, why is it that the residents of the walled cities share in the distinction accorded to Shushan? He answers that the Rabbis wished to honor the walled cities in the Land of Israel which were in ruins at that time. The residents of those desolate cities were treated as if they were the residents of Shushan, and had participated in the miracle to the same extent as the residents of Shushan. This is unrelated to the sanctity of walled cities, *kedushat arei ḥoma,* which may or may not inhere in those cities; in fact, Maimonides rules (*Hilkhot Megilla* 1:4) that even walled cities outside of the Land of Israel, which have no sanctity at all, celebrate on the fifteenth. The emphasis was placed on the desolation of the cities within Israel, and the motivation of the Rabbis was to comfort them by according them a special mark of distinction.

According to Maimonides, the obligating factor of the walled cities is the fifteenth of Adar, and not the fourteenth, as maintained by Ravad and Naḥmanides. Maimonides and Naḥmanides further disagree about whether the observance of the walled cities on the fifteenth is a mark of distinction or a penalty. Maimonides considers it to be an honor accorded to the cities of Israel, which nevertheless extends to all cities which share these characteristics, while Naḥmanides maintains that the walled cities coincidentally share the date of the fifteenth with Shushan, but fundamentally observe a deferred celebration of the fourteenth.

WHY *AL HANISSIM* IS NOT INCLUDED IN THE *BERAKHA ME'EIN SHALOSH*

The Talmud (*Shabbat* 24a) discusses whether *Al HaNissim* should be recited in *Birkat HaMazon*, ultimately concluding that it should be recited, in the second blessing. Tosafot (*ibid.*) explain that there is no question that *Al HaNissim* is recited during the Amida prayer, because the Amida is generally recited publicly in the synagogue, and therefore it presents a greater opportunity for *pirsumei nisa*, publicizing of the miracle, than *Birkat HaMazon*, which one generally recites privately at home.

Notwithstanding the explanation offered by Tosafot, the difference between *Al HaNissim* in prayer and in *Birkat HaMazon* can be explained in an additional way. When a person recites the Amida, he is meant to thank God for all of the blessings in his life, "for Your miracles which are with us every day; and for Your wonders and favors at all times, evening, morning and midday." Thus, it is obvious that in the Amida we must give thanks to God for the miracles of Ḥanukka and Purim. The thanksgiving of *Birkat HaMazon*, though, is focused on specific themes; thus the Talmud debates whether the miracles of Ḥanukka and Purim are extraneous to *Birkat HaMazon* and need not be mentioned.

While the Talmud concludes that we do recite *Al HaNissim* in *Birkat HaMazon*, nevertheless, reciting *Al HaNissim* in *Birkat HaMazon* is fundamentally different from the insertion of *Retzei* and *Ya'aleh VeYavo* into *Birkat HaMazon*. The recitations of *Retzei* and *Ya'aleh VeYavo* are based upon the principle enunciated by the Gemara (*Berakhot* 40a): "'Blessed be the LORD day by day' (Ps. 68:20) – offer Him blessings according to the day." This obligation of *hazkarat me'ein hame'ora* (mentioning the day's sanctity) is not relevant to Ḥanukka or Purim, because it applies only to days which possess *kedushat hayom*. Rather, we recite *Al HaNissim* because of the obligation of *pirsumei nisa*, publicizing the miracle. *Retzei* and *Ya'aleh VeYavo*, as fulfillments of the concept of *hazkarat me'ein hame'ora*, are defined as insertions, but are not integrated into the basic text of the *Birkat HaMazon*. However, *Al HaNissim*, when recited, becomes incorporated into the thanksgiving section of *Birkat HaMazon*. In the second blessing, we thank God for the Land of Israel, the Torah, the *brit*, as well as for the miracles of Purim and Ḥanukka on their respective days.

This is the reason we include references to Shabbat and Yom Tov in the *berakha me'ein shalosh,* but make no reference to Ḥanukka and Purim in this *berakha.* On Shabbat and Yom Tov, there is an obligation of *hazkarat me'ein hame'ora,* and that applies equally when one recites the *berakha me'ein shalosh.* However, there is no independent obligation to recite *Al HaNissim,* but rather, as we explained, it is one element of the thanksgiving blessing. The *berakha me'ein shalosh* is by definition an abbreviation of *Birkat HaMazon,* and just as it omits specific references to *brit and* Torah which appear in the blessing of *Nodeh Lekha,* it likewise omits specific reference to Ḥanukka and Purim.